RELATIVISM

Relativism

Cognitive and Moral

Edited with Introductions by

Jack W. Meiland and Michael Krausz

UNIVERSITY OF NOTRE DAME PRESS
NOTRE DAME   LONDON

Library of Congress Cataloging in Publication Data

Main entry under title:

Relativism, cognitive and moral.

   Bibliography: p.
   Contents: The fabrication of facts / Nelson
Goodman — Subjective, objective, and conceptual
relativisms / Maurice Mandelbaum — On the very
idea of a conceptual scheme / Donald Davidson —
[etc.]
   1. Relativity—Addresses, essays, lectures.
2. Ethical relativism—Addresses, essays, lectures.
I. Krausz, Michael. II. Meiland, Jack W.
BD221.R44   121   81-19834
ISBN 0-268-01611-9
ISBN 0-268-01612-7 (pbk)

Contents

Preface

Relativism in its various forms has been important in Western thought for well over one hundred years. This book collects some of the best work done on the topic during the decade 1970-1980, which it intends to make more conveniently available to philosophers and students already interested in the topic and to provide an introduction for those new to the subject. Inevitably, some topics (for example, historical relativism) are not treated at all and some excellent articles had to be omitted, but we hope that our choices have resulted in a useful and reasonably representative volume.

The general introduction attempts to acquaint the newcomer, very briefly and in the simplest terms possible, with the nature of cognitive and moral relativism, the range of issues which these raise, the reasons why these issues are important, the history of these questions, and some directions which argument about them has taken. Undergraduates with little background in philosophy are particularly advised to read the general introduction before proceeding to the individual papers.

Each paper has been provided with a short introduction outlining some of the issues discussed and arguments deployed. In many cases we have also tried to indicate possible lines of criticism in order to encourage dialogue between the paper and the reader and to exhibit the ongoing nature of the debate. At the end of the book a bibliography of recent work on cognitive and moral relativism has been attached to assist those who wish to pursue these questions further.

All of the articles but one have been previously published; the paper by Chris Swoyer was written especially for this volume.

The index was compiled by James Munz.

Contributors

DONALD DAVIDSON is professor of philosophy at the University of California at Berkeley. He has taught at Stanford, Princeton, Rockefeller, and the University of Chicago, and is the author of many philosophical articles, particularly in the theory of action and the philosophy of language. During 1973-74 he was president of the Eastern Division of the American Philosophical Association.

GERALD DOPPELT taught at the University of Pennsylvania and at Berkeley before moving to the University of California at San Diego, where he is now associate professor of philosophy. He has published extensively in the philosophy of science and in epistemology and is currently working on a book on the theory of democratic socialism.

PHILIPPA FOOT is senior research fellow at Somerville College, Oxford, and professor of philosophy at UCLA. She has been a visiting professor at Cornell, MIT, Berkeley, and Princeton, and is the author of many articles in ethics and related areas.

NELSON GOODMAN is professor emeritus of philosophy at Harvard University. He has also taught at the University of Pennsylvania and at Brandeis. In 1967 he was president of the Eastern Division of the American Philosophical Association. He is the author of *The Structure of Appearance; Fact, Fiction, and Forecast;* and *Languages of Art.*

GILBERT HARMAN has been professor of philosophy at Princeton University since 1971. He has been awarded fellowships by the American Council of Learned Societies and the Guggenheim Foundation and is the author of *Thought* and *The Nature of Morality.*

GEOFFREY HARRISON is lecturer in philosophy at the University of Reading.

MICHAEL KRAUSZ is associate professor of philosophy at Bryn Mawr College. The author of many articles in epistemology, philosophy of history, and aesthetics, he is also editor of *Critical Essays on the Philosophy of R.G. Collingwood* and coeditor of *The Concept of Creativity in Science and Art.* Krausz has served as visiting professor at Swarthmore, Haverford, Georgetown, The Hebrew University of Jerusalem, and the American University in Cairo.

DAVID LYONS has taught at Cornell University since 1964, where he is now professor of philosophy and law. He has received fellowships from the Guggenheim Foundation, the Society for the Humanities, and the National Endowment for the Humanities. Among his works are *Forms and Limits of Utilitarianism* and *In the Interest of the Governed.*

MAURICE MANDELBAUM taught for many years at Swarthmore College, Dartmouth College, and at Johns Hopkins University, where he was Andrew W. Mellon Professor of Philosophy from 1967 to 1978. At present he is adjunct professor of philosophy at Dartmouth. He has been a president of the American Philosophical Association and was chairman of its Board of Governors from 1968 to 1974. His works include *The Problem of Historical Knowledge; Philosophy, Science, and Sense Perception;* and *History, Man, and Reason.*

JACK W. MEILAND is professor of philosophy at the University of Michigan. He is the author of *Scepticism and Historical Knowledge, The Nature of Intention,* and *Talking about Particulars,* and has published numerous articles on relativism, the ethics of belief, and the theory of interpretation.

CHRIS SWOYER obtained his Ph.D. at the University of Minnesota in 1976 and is assistant professor of philosophy at the University of Oklahoma. He has papers published or forthcoming in leading philosophical journals and has just completed a book on cognitive relativism.

BERNARD WILLIAMS has been provost of King's College, Cambridge, since 1979. He was professor of philosophy, Bedford College, London, and Knightsbridge Professor of Philosophy at Cambridge. Among his works are *Morality; Problems of the Self; A Critique of Utilitarianism;* and *Descartes: The Project of Pure Inquiry.*

Introduction

Relativism begins with the observation of diversity. We observe that in our own society different people have different beliefs. Some Americans believe in the death penalty for certain types of crimes, while other Americans condemn the death penalty on moral grounds. Some believe premarital sex to be immoral, while others do not. For some abortion is murder, while for others it is a morally acceptable form of birth control. And we find similar diversity when we look at other societies and other historical periods. Some societies have employed slaves routinely, whereas we find slavery morally intolerable. In some societies old people have been killed when they reached a certain age, a practice which we morally abhor.

A typical reaction to such diversity is to employ the notion of "progress" and to distinguish between what is "backward" on the one hand and what is "advanced" or "modern" on the other. Thus, moral and social beliefs and practices which differ from our own are often regarded by us as "unenlightened," while ours are "civilized" and "enlightened." We often regard our own views as the end product of a process of evolution in thought and culture which began with the cruel and inhuman practices of primitive peoples. These primitive views were gradually replaced by more correct views which recognize the sacredness of life, the value of the individual, and the duty of society to serve the individual. This way of interpreting the diversity of moral and social practices leads to the conclusion that our own views are better and closer to the truth than those views which conflict with ours.

But this conclusion should surely make us suspicious of the entire line of reasoning which leads to it. Isn't this conclusion just what one would expect us to reach? And wouldn't we expect those who differ with us to reach similar conclusions about *their own* beliefs and practices? Such interpretations and conclusions may merely reflect the preexisting prejudices and biases of a person (or a society) in favor of his or her (or its) own beliefs and practices. What is clearly needed here is an objective criterion

1

acceptable to everyone: the application of this objective criterion would reveal the true or correct moral beliefs. But is such a criterion available? Any criterion which we might put forward would itself presumably reflect only our own prejudices about the nature of objectivity and moral acceptability. So are we stymied in our search for a way to decide which moral views are correct? The view that all moral positions should be considered equally correct since there is no criterion for picking out the single correct moral code or set of general moral principles is one important form of moral relativism.

Similar arguments can be given about empirical beliefs. Different societies adhere to different empirical beliefs. Ancient peoples had a much different view of the stars and planets, for example, than we now have. Some native tribes believe that trees contain spirits or that disease is the work of evil beings. It is tempting, in a manner precisely parallel to the moral case, to say that those who disagree with us are unenlightened, ignorant of the truth, and at an early stage in the continuous line of progress of thought which leads ultimately to our own superior understanding of the world. Yet we must again ask, According to whose criterion is our understanding of the world superior? It may seem that any criterion which we put forward is likely only to reveal our own biases, our own view about what constitutes knowledge, what counts as a good basis for accepting a belief as true, what counts as legitimate and convincing evidence, and what counts as "the facts."

These observations and views about diversity and the seeming lack of objective and universally valid methods for deciding upon the truth do not yet amount to relativism. Relativism is a characteristic reaction to these observations, but it is not the only possible postition. It is possible and not unusual for a person to react to these observations by throwing up one's hands and claiming that it is just impossible to know the truth about either matters of fact or matters of value. This type of reaction is skepticism. The skeptic holds either that there is no truth or that the truth cannot be known by human beings. Relativism is very often taken to be either identical to, or else a form of or a pathway to, skepticism. And it is easy to understand why skepticism and relativism are so often confused with one another in this way. Relativism, like skepticism, gives up the pursuit of a single truth which is the same for everyone—which is objective, absolute, and knowable. But relativism, unlike skepticism, does not conclude that there is no such thing as truth or that truth is not knowable. Instead, the relativist maintains that truth may be and often is different for each society or each methodological approach or even each individual. That disease is the work of evil spirits may be true for one society but not for another society. Because both relativism and skepticism agree in denying the possibility of knowing absolute, objective, universal truth, they seem much alike. But in fact their differences are even more profound than their similarities.

But what justifies the relativist in taking the line that there are many truths rather than joining the skeptic in denying the possibility of knowing truth? The relativist observes that the absence of criteria for ascertaining a single objective truth does not mean that there are no criteria of truth at all. Instead, societies, methodologies, and individuals have their own criteria of truth. The skeptic focuses on the unknowability of absolute truth and assumes that absolute truth is the only possible variety of truth. The relativist points out that, nevertheless, people still make judgments about rightness and truth. People still do distinguish between what is right and what is wrong, between what is true and what is false. It seems arrogant and unjustified to say that people are wrong in making such judgments when the reason for saying that they are wrong rests on an ideal, called "absolute truth," which is extremely vague and difficult to describe and which in any case seems to be unattainable by human beings. Perhaps some minimal sense can be made of the notion of absolute truth—a truth which corresponds to the way things "really" are—by appealing to the idea of God: absolute truth would be the truth that God knows. But beyond this the notion is difficult to understand. Philosophers have tried to explain the notion of truth, for example, by saying that true statements are those which correspond to the facts. But this attempt to give content to the notion of absolute truth has run into notorious difficulties and does not seem to have advanced our understanding of the notion. Nelson Goodman's paper and its introduction which follow contain more on this. The relativist sees the skeptic as setting up an impossible goal and then as damning the truth that we can and do have because this other sort of truth is impossible. It is as if an explorer, on a fruitless quest for a mythical treasure, tossed aside or ignored the very real (though perhaps lesser) treasures which he encounters along the way. The relativist finds this attitude unreasonable.

Truth is attainable and valuable and therefore must be recognized and sought, even if it is not the absolute truth desired by the skeptic. The relativist believes that each individual or each society should find its own truth and live by that truth. In a similar way, each individual or each society can find out what moral beliefs and practices are right for it and live accordingly. What is true or right *for* a society or an individual is said to be true or right *relative* to that society or that individual. It is knowledge or moral action *for* that society. Thus, we have relativism about knowledge which we will call "cognitive relativism," and relativism about morality which is commonly called "moral relativism" or "ethical relativism."

To say that some belief or practice is true or right for a society or an individual is to say more than simply that that society or that individual holds that belief or practices that practice. If all that was meant by saying a belief is true for Jones is that Jones holds that belief, then every belief that Jones holds would be true for Jones. But the relativist rejects this notion of relative truth; he or she takes the notion of relative truth more seriously than this. "Relative truth" is a form of truth; the expression 'relative truth' is not a name for something bearing little relation to our ordinary conception of truth. And just as our ordinary conception of truth allows a person to hold beliefs which are false, so too the notion of relative truth must allow an individual to hold beliefs which are false *for him* or *her*. If it were not possible for a person to hold beliefs which were false for him or her, then the notion of relative truth would be superfluous; for then to say that a belief is true for Jones would only be a roundabout way of saying that it was one of Jones' beliefs. And we do not need a new way of saying *that*. Precisely what is being said when a belief is said to be true *for* (or relative to) Jones, and precisely what is being said when a moral practice is said to be right *for* (or relative to) this or that society, is one of the principal questions about relativism and is explicitly discussed in many of the selections included in this volume.

Relativistic attitudes are very widespread and extremely influential in contemporary culture, both in intellectual circles and in popular thought and action about moral and social problems. This is why relativism is one of the chief intellectual and social issues of our time and why careful examination and discussion of relativistic doctrines and arguments, such as found in this volume, are urgently needed. The pervasive influence of relativism in modern life has very often been emphasized by people who strongly deplore this influence. For example, the distinguished theologian Paul Tillich noted his "uneasiness about the victory of relativism in all realms of thought and life today" and continues:

> When we look around us, this seems to be a total victory. There is the great spectacle of scientific relativism, observable not only in the preliminary character of every scientific statement but also in the *model* aspect of scientific constructs... if you ask which model or concept is closest to reality, you may receive the answer: none is; what we have here is "game"....
>
> There is the growth of ethical relativism in theory and in practice....
>
> Finally, there is a great and increasing relativism in the most sacred and perhaps most problematic of all realms, that of religion. It is visible today in the encounter of religions all over the world and in the secularist criticism of religion.[1]

Here is the noted philosopher Sir Karl Popper expressing similar sentiments:

> One of the most disturbing features of intellectual life at the present time is the way in which irrationalism is so widely advocated, and irrationalist doctrines taken for granted. In my view one of the main components of modern irrationalism is relativism (the doctrine that truth is relative to our intellectual background or framework: that it may change from one framework to another), and in particular, the doctrine of the impossibility of mutual understanding between different cultures, generations, or historical periods.[2]

Examples of such attitudes are abundant.

It is not difficult to see what these thinkers believe to be so disturbing about relativism. If there is no single absolute truth to be discovered, then it seems to follow that there is no worthwhile goal for inquiry to pursue—or, to put this in another way, there is no point to intellectual work. If we cannot aim at a single universal truth, what is there to aim at? What is there to be discovered and known? If there is no objective truth which is the same for everyone, how can we ever show that other people who differ with us are wrong in their beliefs? It would only be by discovering that old beliefs are wrong and that new beliefs are correct that progress in knowledge can be made. By ruling out the possiblity of objective truth, the cognitive relativist has ruled out the possibility of progress in knowledge. The situation is just as bad with respect to action as it is with respect to thought. The moral relativist tells us that there are no objective, overriding principles which everyone should use in deciding what to do. This seems to result in moral anarchy. Individuals are free to do whatever is "right for them," a condition resulting in the disintegration of the moral and social order as each person follows his or her own moral star. Any social cohesiveness would have to come from the use of power and force rather than from a moral authority that is universally acknowledged.

Many current moral changes from past or traditional practices—the spread of abortion, the alleged breakdown of the family, the rise of self-interest as a motive, and the increasing refusal to subordinate one's own good to that of the community—all these and more are sometimes attributed to the spread of relativistic attitudes which prevent one from condemining the beliefs and practices of others. After all, if my moral beliefs are right only for me, how can I legitimately use them as a basis on which to criticize and urge the rejection of other beliefs? While conservatives and traditionalists often blame liberalizing changes in society on the spread of relativistic attitudes, liberals sometimes blame the maintenance of the social status quo on relativism too: one can argue from relativistic premises to the conclusion that people should not interfere with the practices of ethnic and minority groups and thus justify avoiding any attempt to bring them into the mainstream of modern society. The introduction to Geoffrey Harrison's article in this volume provides more on this topic. Thus, even though relativism is quite a different position from skepticism, it is regarded by many people who represent very different intellectual, moral, and social points of view as having equally radical and disastrous consequences.

Of course, the opponents of relativism do not simply deplore its existence and influence. Opponents also raise important objections to relativism. For example, it is very frequently objected that cognitive relativism is self-contradictory or self-defeating. For, it is said, if *all* beliefs and claims are at most only relatively true, then relativism itself, being a belief or claim, can be only relatively true and hence itself suffers all the disadvantages connected with being relatively true. Such a criticism is put forward in this volume by Maurice Mandelbaum. Again, opponents often object that the notion of "relative truth" is intolerably vague and without content. If to say that a statement is relatively true for Jones is not to say merely that Jones believes that statement, then what does it mean? Swoyer's essay wrestles with this question. The reader will find these and other strong objections, and some replies, throughout the volume.

Although relativism is now exceedingly important, it has not always been so. Relativism did make a significant appearance early in the history of Western thought. Several of the Sophists—teachers and philosophers who lived in Greece during the fifth century B.C.—seem to have espoused relativistic doctrines of one type or another. Protagoras, in particular, is best known for his dictum "Man is the measure of all things," which expresses the relativity of all perception to the individual. Some interpreters have also taken this dictum to express the relativity of all judgments to the individual as well. Plato, a confirmed absolutist, found it necessary to take issue with Protagoras' relativism in his Socratic dialogue the *Theaetetus.* The exact interpretation of Protagoras' dictum is a matter of continuing dispute, but he may have been the first cognitive relativist in Western intellectual history. On the moral side some of the Sophists emphasized the role of convention over that of nature, holding that there was no natural morality and that all morality rests on man-made rules which vary from one group of people to another and none of which are superior in some objective way to the others.

But although relativism of a sort did emerge early in Western thought, it did not become strongly influential until the nineteenth century, beginning with the thought of Herder and Kant. Herder reacted against the

Enlightenment idea of a single, universal human nature and of an inevitable development of all societies through the same series of fixed stages ending in an ideal state. He emphasized the differences among societies and held that each society was to be understood in terms of its own values, beliefs, and ideals by entering into its own mode of thought and experience rather than by adopting some standpoint which transcends all societies and allows them to be measured by a single standard. Thus, Herder was a precursor of the moral and cultural relativism which was such a prominent part of anthropology in the first part of the twentieth century and which is still very much with us. We are not to judge other societies in terms of our own; for example, we are not to see them as struggling to become replicas of our own society. Other societies have their own values and ideals—including their own moral codes—which are just as valid as ours and which we are in no position to condemn in some absolute sense. Their moral notions are to be regarded as right for them. Moreover, we are not entitled to interfere with those societies just because we happen to disapprove of their practices. Cultural relativists believe that such attempts and other influences threaten to destroy aspects of those other societies which make them as unique and valuable as our own. Thus, cultural relativism is the position which begins with value relativism—the view that each set of values, including moral values, is as valid as each other set—and draws the conclusion that no society has a right to attempt to change or otherwise interfere with any other society.

The most paradoxical stage in the modern development of cognitive relativism was the influence of Immanuel Kant. Kant gives every indication of being himself an absolutist of the strictest sort. And yet his guiding idea—that the mind plays a large role in organizing sensory data by imposing concepts or categories on these data and thus determining the form taken by our experience of the world—led to the rise of cognitive relativism in its most characteristic modern form. While rejecting certain parts of Kant's philosophy, those who came after Kant retained the view that the mind provides basic concepts with which experience is organized and interpreted. And they added the all-important and equally revolutionary idea that these concepts may change over time (as in Hegel's thought) or that different individuals and peoples may employ different sets of concepts for this purpose.[3]

These beginnings led to the idea that there are alternative sets of concepts (usually called "conceptual schemes"), each of which provides a quite different but equally valid way of interpreting experience. In its contemporary form this view holds that we are able to choose among alternative conceptual schemes rather than being forced by nature or culture to employ a particular one. This position is so pervasive in our intellectual life that it is a major element in the thinking of philosophers who are in other respects radically different from one another. For example, the neopositivist Rudolf Carnap speaks of "linguistic frameworks"; the neo-Kantian C.I. Lewis speaks of "networks of categories"; and the later Wittgenstein talks about "forms of life."[4] But they are all talking about conceptual schemes in a broader or narrower sense of that expression. And, perhaps even more strikingly, philosophers of the most diverse views will use the same type of grounds—pragmatic grounds—to justify the choice of a particular conceptual scheme.

In one of its most common modern forms cognitive relativism holds that truth and knowledge are relative, not to individual persons or even whole societies, but instead to factors variously called conceptual schemes, conceptual frameworks, linguistic frameworks, forms of life, modes of discourse, systems of thought, Weltanschauungen, disciplinary matrices, paradigms, constellations of absolute presuppositions, points of view, perspectives, or worlds. What counts as truth and knowledge is thought to depend on which conceptual scheme or point of view is being employed rather than being determinable in a way which transcends all schemes or points of view. This form of cognitive relativism allows an individual to have beliefs which are not true, thus handling a puzzle noted earlier in this introduction: a person may have a belief which is not licensed as true by the conceptual scheme being employed by that person. Since modern cognitive relativism relies so heavily on the notion of alternative conceptual schemes, it is not surprising to find antirelativists (such as Donald Davidson in this volume) attacking the viability of the idea of a conceptual scheme. Such attacks are not only attacks on relativism but in fact attacks on one of the cornerstones of modern thought.

In this modern form cognitive relativism bears a striking structural resemblance to moral relativism. In both cognitive relativism and moral relativism, evaluation is relative to a set of abstract principles or concepts. Modern cognitive relativism tells us that a statement is true only relative to a particular conceptual scheme. Modern moral relativism tells us that an action in morally right only relative to a particular moral code or set of moral principles. Because of this structural similarity, both varieties of relativism pose the same basic question to us: How is the use of a particular set of principles or concepts to be justified? There seems to be no higher standard to which to appeal in order to provide such a justification. Thus, truth and moral rightness appear to be relative to sets of principles or concepts rather than single and absolute. Moreover, because of this structural similarity, cognitive and moral relativism have been subjected to roughly similar forms of attack—for example, charges of self-refutation (amply exemplified for both kinds of relativism in this volume). Critics find cognitive relativists charging that all doctrines are relative, while allegedly maintaining their own doctrine of relativism in an absolute way. Critics find moral relativists maintaining the relativity of morals, while at the same time morally condemning in an absolute way any outside interference in other societies.

Relativists have replied to these charges both by directly defending current forms of relativism and by developing new forms (the latter strategy being exemplified in this volume by Doppelt, Williams, and Harman). And so the dispute continues. The selections in this volume were chosen to illustrate the range, depth, and importance of relativistic doctrines, the many fundamental issues which they raise, the problems which burden them, and the defenses with which they can be provided. These selections constitute some of the best and most interesting work done on relativism during the last decade. If they lead readers to think more deeply and fully about the issues of relativism, the purpose of this volume will have been achieved.

NOTES

1. Paul Tillich, *My Search for Absolutes* (New York: Simon and Shuster, 1964), pp. 64–65.
2. Karl Popper, "The Myth of the Framework," in *The Abdication of Philosophy: Philosophy and the Public Good,* ed. Eugene Freeman (LaSalle, Illinois: Open Court, 1976), p. 25.
3. Patrick Gardiner gives an excellent and detailed survey of these historical developments in his essay "German Philosophy and the Rise of Relativism," *The Monist* 64 (1981): 138–54.
4. Rudolf Carnap, "Empiricism, Semantics and Ontology," in *Meaning and Necessity* (Chicago: University of Chicago Press, 1956); C.I. Lewis, *Mind and the World Order* (New York: Dover, 1956); Ludwig Wittgenstein, *Philosophical Investigations* (New York: Macmillan, 1953).

Cognitive Relativism

INTRODUCTION TO

The Fabrication of Facts

Nelson Goodman calls his position in *Ways of Worldmaking* "a radical relativism."[1] He points to "the vast variety" of versions of the world—that is, descriptions of the world given by the various sciences and depictions of the world in the works of artists and writers. Most people would acknowledge the existence of this vast variety but would insist that not all these versions can be right. These people would say that only one complete version can be right and that other versions either are part of this right version or else are simply wrong. Goodman, on the other hand, asserts that many versions of the world can be right at the same time even where these right versions cannot be reconciled with one another (109).

Those who believe that only one version of the world is right typically believe that the right version is the one which corresponds to the world. Thus, these people believe that there is a world which is separate and distinct from any description or depiction of it. In chapter one of *Ways of Worldmaking* Goodman rejects this idea. He says that we "cannot test a version by comparing it with a world undescribed, undepicted, unperceived ... all we learn about the world is contained in right versions of it ... for many purposes right world-descriptions and world-depictions and world-perceptions, the ways-the-world-is, or just versions, can be treated as our worlds" (3–4). Goodman's point here is that we have no access to "the world" as an undescribed or unperceived entity, and therefore we cannot compare our descriptions of the world with the world itself. We have access to the world only through some description or depiction of it. Other philosophers have made this same point by saying that we have no way of apprehending and knowing about the world other than through the use of concepts, and that consequently we can know the world only as conceptualized in one way or another. Therefore, when we compare a description of the world to the world itself, we are comparing our description with the world as conceptualized—which is to say, as already

13

described. We are comparing our description of the world only to another description (conceptualization) of the world. The most that can be established in this way is a relationship between the two descriptions, not a relationship between our description and the world-as-it-is-in-itself. Thus, the notion of "the world," the world-in-itself, is of no use in inquiry. "The world" cannot help us pick out the one right world-version since we have no access to "the world." "The world" performs no function and is an empty idea. It is "a world well lost" (4). If "the world" drops out of our theorizing, we are left only with descriptions and depictions—with versions. Each version is a world for us. Versions are the only worlds with which we can have any relationship. Versions "can be treated as our worlds."

Goodman realizes that if all of the various world-versions could be reduced to one version, that one version might then have a strong claim to be regarded as the single right version. But he points out that reduction "in any reasonably strict sense is rare, almost always partial, and seldom if ever unique." Besides, "how do you go about reducing Constable's or James Joyce's world-view to physics?" (5). So we are left with many worlds. "The world of the Eskimo who has not grasped the comprehensive concept of snow differs not only from the world of the Samoan but also from the world of the New Englander who has not grasped the Eskimo's distinctions." (8-9). Goodman goes on to describe many ways of worldmaking, beginning from "worlds already on hand" and using such techniques as composition, weighting, and ordering.

This position leads to a notion of relative truth. We cannot test a version for truth by comparing it to some standard such as "the world," as we have seen. Nor do observational data fix or determine the truth. Observational data are "multifaceted and irregular" and must be arranged into patterns using freely adopted principles such as simplicity and scope which are not themselves dictated by any facts or observations. The use of different guiding principles will result in different patterns and hence in different truths. Each way of worldmaking and each resulting version will employ or contain its own guiding principles for the construction of truths. There will thus be no single standard for evaluating statements as to their truth or falsity. What is true depends on, and hence is relative to, the guiding principles employed and certain beliefs adhered to : "a version is taken to be true when it offends no unyielding beliefs and none of its own precepts. Among beliefs unyielding at a given time may be long-lived reflections of laws of logic, short-lived reflections of recent observations, and other convictions and prejudices ingrained with varying degrees of firmness. Among precepts, for example, may be choices among alternative frames of reference, weightings, and derivational bases." (17). Goodman additionally holds that not only truth but also reality is relative. Many world-versions are available, and which version is taken to represent reality will depend on one's purposes or habits (20).

In "The Fabrication of Facts" (chapter six of *Ways of Worldmaking*), included in this volume, Goodman pursues these themes by examining the notion of observation further. By discussing the case of apparent motion he shows that there is no single answer to the question "What do I see?" The case is this: "a spot against a contrasting background is exposed very briefly, followed after an interval of from 10 to 45 milliseconds by exposure of a like spot a short distance away. With a shorter time-interval at the same distance, we see two spots as flashed simultaneously; with a longer interval, we see the two spots flashed successively; but within the specified time-interval, we see one spot moving from the first position to the second." (72). Yet, within the specified time-interval some observers report that there are two flashes, not one moving light. Goodman speculates that these people do experience the moving light but take it to be a sign of two distinct flashes, which in fact it is. Both types of reports—"I see a moving light" and "I see two distinct flashes"—are true. We want to say, perhaps, that two different senses of the word 'see' are involved. But that is Goodman's point. Both a physical description ("I see two distinct flashes") and a phenomenal description ("I see a moving light") can be given of what is seen, and each description is as valid as the other. There is no privileged description of what is seen and hence no single unique set of perceptual facts. Thus, perception cannot serve to differentiate right versions from wrong versions. This is not to say that a thinker cannot take "correspondence with the facts" as the criterion of the truth or acceptability of a world-version. However, what counts as "the facts" (including the perceptual facts) *and* what counts as "correspondence with the facts" can vary from version to version. There is no absolutely valid correspondence with the facts that will pick out a version as the single right version.

Goodman's discussion of pre-Socratic philosophy in this selection illustrates the point that different theoreticians employ different principles and precepts in their worldmaking and that there is no basis on which to say that some or one of these principles is right and all the others wrong. For example, philosophers whose aim is reduction of the manifold variety of phenomena to a smaller set of phenomena or to one or more underlying substances will differ, as the pre-Socrates did, on what counts as a satisfactory or worthwhile reduction. Among theoreticians generally there will also be differences as to whether reduction of any kind is to be pursued or whether some other intellectual goal is more appropriate or more satisfying.

Objections to Goodman's position have, naturally, been raised. Israel Scheffler, whose thoughtful criticisms of Thomas Kuhn's allegedly relativist theory of science are discussed later in this volume by Gerald Doppelt, has also criticized Goodman's relativism.[2] Scheffler emphasizes the distinction between objects and our knowledge of them and proceeds to argue as follows: In his discussion of the case of apparent motion Goodman seems to say that objects are created by our cognitive activities: that our principles and precepts, our "unyielding beliefs," the vocabulary we choose to use for our descriptive activities—all of these determine the character and ontological status of objects. Yet, Scheffler argues, from the proposition that we have no access to objects aside from our knowledge of them, it does not follow that objects are created by us. In evaluating this type of criticism we must remember that Goodman never says that there are no such things as objects-in-themselves apart from all our descriptions and perceptions. Instead, he merely regards the notion of an object-in-itself as "empty." As he puts it, "We do better to focus on versions rather than worlds." (96). Goodman is recommending a strategy for theorizing, not asserting that there are no objects-in-themselves. Satisfactory theorizing requires that we make no use of "empty" concepts such as this, and this puts us on the road to relativism. Scheffler might point out that Goodman's principles of theorizing—for instance, his ideas about what renders a notion "empty"—are not obligatory and that one can theorize just as well using other principles. But Goodman can agree with this. Goodman can say that this only shows that his relativism is itself only a version of the world, while pointing out that by the same token his absolutist critics, choosing other cognitive principles, also arrive only at (other) versions of the world too. Thus, Goodman's relativism is reinforced by these considerations.

One major duty of a relativist is to tell us what the purpose of inquiry is. For the absolutist the purpose of inquiry is knowledge—knowledge of "the world." But for Goodman, since "the world" is not accessible to us, no such knowledge is possible. This is one source of the repugnance which many people feel toward cognitive relativism. It seems to them that if relativism is accepted, then inquiry becomes pointless since there is no knowledge to inquire after. However, the relativist can reply to this charge in at least two ways. First, the relativist can accept the position that the purpose of inquiry is the acquisition of knowledge and then point out that inquirers can still acquire knowledge about versions. Second, the relativist can instead substitute a different purpose of inquiry—by saying that inquiry aims (or should aim) at understanding rather than at knowledge. Although Goodman says very little about this topic in *Ways of World-making,* he clearly chooses this second alternative: "Such growth in knowledge is not by formation or fixation of belief but by the advancement of understanding." (22). In order to make this reply cogent, the relativist must begin by elucidating this important but little-understood notion of understanding.

NOTES

1. Nelson Goodman, *Ways of Worldmaking* (Indianapolis: Hackett, 1978), p. 94. All page references in this introduction are to this volume.

2. Israel Scheffler, "The Wonderful Words of Goodman," *Synthese* 45 (1980).

The Fabrication of Facts*

Nelson Goodman

1. Actuality and Artifice

My title, "The Fabrication of Facts," has the virtue not only of indicating pretty clearly what I am going to discuss but also of irritating those fundamentalists who know very well that facts are found not made, that facts constitute the one and only real world, and that knowledge consists of believing the facts. These articles of faith so firmly possess most of us, they so bind and blind us, that "fabrication of fact" has a paradoxical sound. "Fabrication" has become a synonym for "falsehood" or "fiction" as contrasted with "truth" or "fact." Of course, we must distinguish falsehood and fiction from truth and fact; but we cannot, I am sure, do it on the ground that fiction is fabricated and fact found.

Look back a moment at the case of so-called apparent motion. The experimental results I have summarized are not universal; they are merely typical. Not only do different observers perceive motion differently, but some cannot see apparent motion at all. Those who are thus unable to see what they know is not there are classed as naive realists by Kolers, who reports a disproportionately high percentage of them among engineers and physicians.[1]

Yet if an observer reports that he sees two distinct flashes, even at distances and intervals so short that most observers see one moving spot, perhaps he means that he sees the two as we might say we see a swarm of molecules when we look at a chair, or as we do say we see a round table top even when we look at it from a oblique angle. Since an observer can become

*Reprinted with permission of Nelson Goodman from *Ways of Worldmaking* (1978), Hackett Publishing Company, Inc.

adept at distinguishing apparent from real motion, he may take the appearance of motion as a sign that there are two flashes, as we take the oval appearance of the table top as a sign that it is round; and in both cases the signs may be or become so transparent that we look through them to physical events and objects. When the observer visually determines that what is before him is what we agree is before him, we can hardly charge him with an error in visual perception. Shall we say, rather, that he misunderstands the instruction, which is presumably just to tell what he sees? Then how, without prejudicing the outcome, can we so reframe that instruction as to prevent such a 'misunderstanding'? Asking him to make no use of prior experience and to avoid all conceptualization will obviously leave him speechless; for to talk at all he must use words.

The best we can do is to specify the sort of terms, the vocabulary, he is to use, telling him to describe what he sees in perceptual or phenomenal rather than physical terms. Whether or not this yields different responses, it casts an entirely different light on what is happening. That the instruments to be used in fashioning the facts must be specified makes pointless any identification of the physical with the real and of the perceptual with the merely apparent. The perceptual is no more a rather distorted version of the physical facts than the physical is a highly artificial version of the perceptual facts. If we are tempted to say that 'both are versions of the same facts', this must no more be taken to imply that there are independent facts of which both are versions than likeness of meaning between two terms implies that there are some entities called meanings. "Fact" like "meaning" is a syncategorematic term; for facts, after all, are obviously factitious.

The point is classically illustrated, again, by variant versions of physical motion. Did the sun set a while ago or did the earth rise? Does the sun go around the earth or the earth go around the sun? Nowadays, we nonchalantly deal with what was once a life-and-death issue by saying that the answer depends on the framework. But here again, if we say that the geocentric and heliocentric systems are different versions of 'the same facts', we must ask not what these facts are but rather how such phrases as "versions of the same facts" or "descriptions of the same world" are to be understood. This varies from case to case; here, the geocentric and the heliocentric versions, while speaking of the same particular objects—the sun, moon, and planets—attribute very different motions to these objects. Still, we may say the two versions deal with the same facts if we mean by this that they not only speak of the same objects but are also routinely translatable each into the other. As meanings vanish in favor of certain relationships among terms, so facts vanish in favor of certain relationships among versions. In the present case, the relationship is comparatively obvious; sometimes it is much more elusive. For instance, the physical and perceptual versions of motion we were talking about do not evidently deal with all the same objects, and the relationship if any that constitutes license for saying that the two versions describe the same facts or the same world is no ready intertranslatability.

The physical and perceptual world-versions mentioned are but two of the vast variety in the several sciences, in the arts, in perception, and in daily discourse. Worlds are made by making such versions with words, numerals, pictures, sounds, or other symbols of any kind in any medium; and the comparative study of these versions and visions and of their making is what I call a critique of worldmaking. I began such a study in Chapter 1, and I shall now have to summarize and clarify some points in that chapter very briefly before going on to the further problems that are the main concern of the present chapter.

2. MEANS AND MATTER

What I have said so far plainly points to a radical relativism; but severe restraints are imposed. Willingness to accept countless alternative true or right world-versions does not mean that everything goes, that tall stories are as good as short ones, that truths are no longer distinguished from falsehoods, but only that truth must be otherwise conceived than as correspondence with a ready-made world. Though we make worlds by making versions, we no more make a world by putting symbols together at random than a carpenter makes a chair by putting pieces of wood together at random. The multiple worlds I countenance are just the actual worlds made by and answering to true or right versions. Worlds possible or impossible supposedly answering to false versions have no place in my philosophy.

Just what worlds are to be recognized as actual is quite another question. Although some aspects of a philosophical position have a bearing, even what seem severely restrictive views may recognize countless versions as equally right. For example, I am sometimes asked how my relativism can be reconciled with my nominalism. The answer is easy. Although a nominalistic system speaks only of individuals, banning all talk of classes, it may take anything whatever as an individual; that is, the nominalistic prohibition is against the profiligate propagation of entities out of any chosen basis of individuals, but leaves the choice of that basis quite free. Nominalism of itself thus authorizes an abundance of alternative versions based on physical particles or phenomenal elements or ordinary things or whatever else one is willing to take as individuals.[2] Nothing here prevents any given nominalist from preferring on other grounds some among the systems thus recognized as legitimate. In contrast, the typical physicalism, for example, while prodigal in the platonistic instruments it supplies for endless generation of entities, admits of only one correct (even if yet unidentified) basis.

Thus while the physicalist's doctrine "no difference without a physical difference" and the nominalist's doctrine "no difference without a difference of individuals" sound alike, they differ notably in this respect.[3]

All the same, in this general discussion of worldmaking I do not impose nominalistic restrictions, for I want to allow for some difference of opinion as to what actual worlds there are.[4] That falls far short of countenancing merely possible worlds. The platonist and I may disagree about what makes an actual world while we agree in rejecting all else. We may disagree in what we take to be true while we agree that nothing answers to what we take to be false.

To speak of worlds as made by versions often offends both by its implicit pluralism and by its sabotage of what I have called 'something stolid underneath'. Let me offer what comfort I can. While I stress the multiplicity of right world-versions, I by no means insist that there are many worlds—or indeed any; for as I have already suggested, the question whether two versions are of the same world has as many good answers as there are good interpretations of the words "versions of the same world." The monist can always contend that two versions need only be right to be accounted versions of the same world. The pluralist can always reply by asking what the world is like apart form all versions. Perhaps the best answer is that given by Professor Woody Allen when he writes:[5]

> Can we actually 'know' the universe? My God, it's hard enough finding your way around in Chinatown. The point, however, is: Is there anything out there? And why? And must they be so noisy? Finally, there can be no doubt that the one characteristic of 'reality' is that it lacks essence. That is not to say it has no essence, but merely lacks it. (The reality I speak of here is the same one Hobbes described, but a little smaller.)

The message, I take it, is simply this: never mind mind, essence is not essential, and matter doesn't matter. We do better to focus on versions rather than worlds. Of course, we want to distinguish between versions that do and those that do not refer, and to talk about the things and worlds, if any, referred to; but these things and worlds and even the stuff they are made of—matter, anti-matter, mind, energy, or whatnot—are fashioned along with the things and worlds themselves. Facts, as Norwood Hanson says, are theory-laden[6]; they are as theory-laden as we hope our theories are fact-laden. Or in other words, facts are small theories, and true theories are big facts. This does not mean, I must repeat, that right versions can be arrived at casually, or that worlds are built from scratch. We start, on any occasion, with some old version or world that we have on hand and that we are stuck with until we have the determination and skill to remake it into a new one. Some of the felt stubbornness of fact is the grip of habit: our firm foundation is indeed stolid. Worldmaking begins with one version and ends with another.

3. Some Ancient Worlds

Let's look for a few moments at some early examples of worldmaking. The pre-Socratics, I have long felt, made almost all the important advances and mistakes in the history of philosophy. Before I consider how their views illustrate topics central to our present discussion, I must give you, much compressed, the inside story of that period of philosophy.

These philosophers, like most of us, started from a world concocted of religion, superstition, suspicion, hope, and bitter and sweet experience. Then Thales, seeking some unity in the jumble, noticed the sun drawing water and heating it to flame, the clouds condensing and falling and drying into earth—and, according to legend, the water at the bottom of a certain well. The solution dawned—indeed, the solution *was* solution: the world is water.

But Anaximander argued, "With earth, air, fire, and water all changing into one another, why pick water? What makes it any different from the other three? We have to find something neutral that all are made from." So he invented the Boundless, thus in one stroke inflicting upon philosophy two of its greatest burdens: infinity and substance.

Empedocles ruled the Boundless out-of-bounds. If there is no choice among the elements, we must take all four; what counts is how they are mixed. He saw that the real secret of the universe is confusion.

When Heraclitus asked for action, Parmenides responded with a stop sign, reducing philosophy to the formula "It is," meaning of course "It is not," or to make a short story long, "Look at the mess we have got ourselves into!"

Democritus, though, deftly rescued us. He replaced "It is" by "They are." The point is that if you slice things fine enough everything will be the same. All particles are alike; the way they are put together makes water or air or fire or earth—or whatever. Quality is supplanted by quantity and structure.

One issue between Thales and his successors reverberates all through philosophical history. Thales reduced all four elements to water; Anaximander and Empedocles objected that the four could as well be reduced to any of the other three. So far, both sides are equally right. Thales' acquacentric system is no better justified as against its three alternatives than a geocentric description of the solar system is justified as against its obvious alternatives. But Thales' critics went wrong in supposing that since none of the alternative systems is exclusively right, all are wrong. That we can do without any one of them does not mean that we can do without all, but only that we have a choice. The implicit ground for rejecting Thales' theory was that features distinguishing alternative systems cannot reflect reality as it is. Thus Empedocles insisted that any ordering among the four elements is an arbitrary imposition on reality. What he overlooked is that any organizing into elements is no less an imposition, and that if we prohibit all such impositions we end with nothing. Anaximander had grasped, and indeed embraced, this consequence and treated the four elements as derivative from a neutral and nugatory Boundless. The logical Parmenides concluded that if only something completely neutral can be common to the worlds of all alternative versions, only *that* is real and all else is mere illusion; but even he organized that reality in a special way: the It that is is One. Democritus, thus invited, promptly organized it differently, breaking it into small pieces—and off we were again.

Under much of this controversy concerning what can be reduced to what, lies the recurrent question what constitutes reduction. That water changes into the other elements does not, Anaximander objected, make them merely water; and neither, Empedocles in effect retorted, does construing the elements as made of a neutral substance make them merely neutral substance. Here are precursors of current campaigns, by friends and enemies of physical objects or phenomena or concreta or qualities or mind or matter, against or for dispensing with any of these in favor of others. Such campaigns characteristically spring from misunderstanding of the requirements upon and the significance of what is as much construction as reduction.

4. REDUCTION AND CONSTRUCTION

Debates concerning criteria for constructional definitions have often centered upon whether intensional or only extensional agreement is required between definiens and definiendum. The demand for absolute synonymy was grounded in the conviction that the definiens must be an explanation of the meaning of the definiendum. Trouble with the notion of meanings and even with the idea of exact sameness of meaning raised the question whether extensional identity might do, but this in turn proved too tight, for often multiple alternative definientia that are not coextensive are obviously equally admissible. For example, a point in a plane may be defined either as a certain pair of intersecting lines or as a quite different pair or as a nest of regions, etc.; but the definientia having these disjoint extensions surely cannot all be co-extensive with the definiendum.

Such considerations point to a criterion framed in terms of an extensional isomorphism that requires preservation of structure rather than of extension. Since a structure may be common to many different extensions; this allows for legitimate alternative definientia. The isomorphism in question is global, required to obtain between the whole set of definientia of a system and the whole set of their definitions of points, a definiens articulates its extension more fully than does the definiendum, and thus performs an analysis and introduces means for systematic integration.[7]

So conceived, definition of points in terms of lines or sets makes no claim that points are merely lines or sets; and derivations of the other elements from water makes no claim that they are merely water. Insofar as the definitions or derivations are successful, they organize the points and lines, or the four elements, into a system. That there are alternative systems discredits none of them; for there is no alternative but blankness to alternative systems, to organization of one kind or another. To his successors who complained that Thales was introducing artificial order and priorities, he might well have rejoined that that is what science and philosophy do, and that complete elimination of the so-called artificial would leave us empty-minded and empty-handed. With the reconception of the nature and significance of reduction or construction or derivation or systematization we give up our futile search for the aboriginal world, and come to recognize that systems and other versions are as productive as reproductive.

In the foregoing history of thought from Thales to Allen, several of the processes of worldmaking—or relation between worlds—that I discussed in Chapter 1 have been illustrated: *ordering,* in the derivation of all four elements from one; *supplementation,* in the introduction of the Boundless; *deletion,* in the elimination of everything else; and *division,* in the shattering of the One into atoms. Supplementation and deletion are also dramatically illustrated in the relation between the world of physics and a familiar perceptual world. Among other processes or relationships mentioned were *composition,* as when events are combined into an enduring object; *deformation,* as when rough curves are smoothed out; and *weighting* or emphasis. The last of these, less often noted and less well understood, yet especially important for what follows, needs some further attention here.

Worldmaking sometimes, without adding or dropping entities, alters emphasis; and a difference between two versions that consists primarily or even solely in their relative weighting of the same entities may be striking and consequential. For one notable example, consider the differences in what may be taken by two versions to be natural or relevant kinds—that is, to be the kinds important for description or investigation or induction. Our habitual projection of "green" and "blue" does not deny that "grue" and "bleen" name classes, but treats these classes as trivial.[9] To reverse this—to project "grue" and "bleen" rather than "green" and "blue"—would be to make, and live in, a different world. A second example of the effect of weighting appears in the difference between two histories of the Renaissance: one that, without excluding the battles, stresses the arts; and another that, without excluding the arts, stresses the battles (II:2). This difference in style is a difference in weighting that gives us two different Renaissance worlds.

5. FACT FROM FICTION

With all this variety, attention focuses on versions that are literal, denotational, and verbal. While that covers some—though I think far from all—scientific and quasi-scientific worldmaking, it leaves out perceptual and pictorial versions and all figurative and exemplificational means and all nonverbal media. The worlds of fiction, poetry, painting, music, dance, and the other arts are built largely by such nonliteral devices as metaphor, by such nondenotational means as exemplification and expression, and often by use of pictures or sounds or gestures or other symbols of nonlinguistic systems. Such worldmaking and such versions are my primary concern here; for a major thesis of this book is that the arts must be taken no less seriously than the sciences as modes of discovery, creation, and enlargement of knowledge in the broad sense of advancement of the understanding, and thus that the philosophy of art should be conceived as an integral part of metaphysics and epistemology.

Consider, first, versions that are visions, depictions rather than descriptions. On the syntactic side, pictures differ radically from words— pictures are not comprised of items from an alphabet, are not identified across a variety of hands and fonts, do not combine with other pictures or with words to make sentences. But pictures and terms alike denote—apply as labels—to whatever they represent or name or describe.[10] Names and such pictures as individual and group portraits denote uniquely, while predicates and such pictures as those in an ornithologist's guide denote generally. Thus pictures may make and present facts and participate in worldmaking in much the same way as do terms. Indeed, our everyday so-called picture of the world is the joint product of description and depiction. Yet I must repeat that I am here subscribing neither to any picture theory of language nor to any language theory of pictures; for pictures belong to nonlinguistic, and terms to nonpictorial, symbol systems.

Some depictions and descriptions, though, do not literally denote anything. Painted or written portrayals of Don Quixote, for example, do not denote Don Quixote—who is simply not there to be denoted. Works of fiction in literature and their counterparts in other arts obviously play a prominent role in worldmaking; our worlds are no more a heritage from scientists, biographers, and historians than from novelists, playwrights, and painters. But how can versions of nothing thus participate in the making of actual worlds? The inevitable proposal to supply fictive entities and possible worlds as denotata will not, even for those who can swallow it, help with this question. Yet the answer, once sought, comes rather readily.

"Don Quixote," taken literally, applies to no one, but taken figuratively, applies to many of us—for example, to me in my tilts with the windmills of current linguistics. To many others the term applies neither literally nor metaphorically. Literal falsity or inapplicability is entirely compatible with, but of course no guarantee of, metaphorical truth; and the line between metaphorical truth and metaphorical falsity intersects, but is no more arbitrary than, the line between literal truth and literal falsity. Whether a person is a Don Quixote (i.e., quixotic) or a Don Juan is as genuine a question as whether a person is paranoid or schizophrenic, and rather easier to decide. And application of the fictive term "Don Quixote" to actual people, like the metaphorical application of the nonfictive term "Napoleon" to other generals and like the literal application of some newly invented term such as "vitamin" or "radioactive" to materials, effects a reorganization of our familiar world by picking out and underlining as a relevant kind category that cuts across well-worn ruts. Metaphor is no mere decorative rhetorical device but a way we make our terms do multiple moonlighting service.[11]

Fiction, then, whether written or painted or acted, applies truly neither to nothing nor to diaphanous possible worlds but, albeit metaphorically, to actual worlds. Somewhat as I have argued elsewhere that the merely possible[12]—so far as admissible at all—lies within the actual, so we might say here again, in a different context, that the so-called possible worlds of fiction lie within actual worlds. Fiction operates in actual worlds in much the same way as nonfiction. Cervantes and Bosch and Goya, no less than Boswell and Newton and Darwin, take and unmake and remake and retake familiar worlds, recasting them in remarkable and sometimes recondite but eventually recognizable—that is *re-cognizable*—ways.

But what of purely abstract paintings and other works that have no subject, that do not apply to anything literally or metaphorically, that even the most permissive philosophers would hardly regard as depicting any world, possible or actual? Such works, unlike Don Quixote portraits or centaur pictures, are not literal labels on empty jars or fanciful labels on full ones; they are not labels at all. Are they, then, to be cherished in and for themselves only, as the pure-in-spirit uncontaminated by contact with any world? Of course not; our worlds are no less powerfully informed by the patterns and feelings of abstract works than by a literal Chardin still-life or an allegorical "Birth of Venus." After we spend an hour or so at one or another exhibition of abstract painting, everything tends to square off into geometric patches or swirl in circles or weave into textural arabesques, to sharpen into black and white or vibrate with new color consonances and dissonances. Yet how can what does not either literally or figuratively depict or describe or debate or denote or otherwise apply to anything whatever so transform our well-worn worlds?

We have seen earlier that what does not denote may still *refer* by exemplification or expression, and that nondescriptive, nonrepresentational works nevertheless function as symbols for features they possess either literally or metaphorically. Serving as samples of, and thereby focusing attention upon, certain—often upon unnoticed or neglected— shared or shareable forms, colors, feelings, such works induce reorganization of our accustomed world in accordance with these features, thus dividing and combining erstwhile relevant kinds, adding and subtracting, effecting new discriminations and integrations, reordering priorities. Indeed, symbols may work through exemplification and expression as well as through denotation in any or all of the various already mentioned ways of worldmaking.

Music obviously works in like ways upon the auditory realm, but it also participates in producing whatever conglomerate linguistic and nonlinguistic visual version we tend to take at a given moment as our 'picture of the world'. For the forms and feelings of music are by no means all confined to sound; many patterns and emotions, shapes, contrasts, rhymes, and rhythms are common to the auditory and the visual and often to the tactual and the kinesthetic as well. A poem, a painting, and a piano sonata may literally and metaphorically exemplify some of the same features; and any of these works may thus have effects transcending its own medium. In these days of experimentation with the combination of media in the performing arts, nothing is clearer than that music affects seeing, that pictures affect hearing, that both affect and are affected by the movement of dance. They all interpenetrate in making a world.

Exemplification and expression are of course functions not of abstract works exclusively but also of many descriptive and representational works, fictional and nonfictional. What a portrait or a novel exemplifies or expresses often reorganizes a world more drastically than does what the work literally or figuratively says or depicts; and sometimes the subject serves merely as a vehicle for what is exemplified or expressed. But whether alone or in combination, the several modes and means of symbolization are powerful instruments. With them, a Japanese haiku or five-line poem by Samuel Manashe can renovate and remodel a world; without them, the moving of mountains by an environmental artist would be futile.

The artist's resources—modes of reference, literal and nonliteral, linguistic and nonlinguistic, denotational and nondenotational, in many media—seem more varied and impressive than the scientist's. But to suppose that science is flatfootedly linguistic, literal, and denotational would be to overlook, for instance, the analog instruments often used, the metaphor involved in measurement when a numerical scheme is applied in a new realm, and the talk in current physics and astronomy of charm and strangeness and black holes. Even if the ultimate product of science, unlike that of art, is a literal, verbal or mathematical, denotational theory, science and art proceed in much the same way with their searching and building.

My outline of the facts concerning the fabricatin of facts is of course itself a fabrication; but as I have cautioned more than once, recognition of multiple alternative world-versions betokens no policy of laissez-faire. Standards distinguishing right from wrong versions become, if anything, more rather than less important. But what standards? Not only does countenancing unreconciled alternatives put truth in a different light, but broadening our purview to include versions and visions that make no statements and may even not describe or depict anything requires consideration of standards other than truth. Truth is often inapplicable, is seldom sufficient, and must sometimes give way to competing criteria.

NOTES

1. Paul A. Kolers, *Aspects of Motion Perception* (Oxford: Pergamon Press, 1972), p. 160.

2. See Nelson Goodman, *The Structure of Appearance* (Dordrecht: Reidel, 1977), third edition, pp. 26–28 (hereafter referred to as *SA*); see also Nelson Goodman, *Problems and Projects* (Indianapolis: Hackett, 1972), pp. 157–61. (hereafter referred to as *PP*).

3. And in others, especially in that the nominalist's doctrine requires constructional interpretation of every difference in terms of differences between individuals, while the physicalist's doctrine is less explicit, often requiring only some unspecified or at best causal connection between physical and other differences.

4. In the same spirit, although *SA* is committed to nominalism, its criterion for constructional definitions and its measurement of simplicity were, for comparative purposes, made broad enough to apply to platonistic systems as well. On the other hand, neither there nor here is any allowance made for departures from *extensionalism.*

5. Woody Allen, "My Philosophy," in *Getting Even* (1966), chap. 4, sec. 1.

6. In *Patterns of Discovery* (Cambridge University Press, 1958, chap. 1 and throughout.

7. See further *SA:* 1. In some circumstances, criteria even looser than extensional isomorphism may be appropriate.

8. See further chap. 7:2 below on convention and content.

9. Such loose platonistic talk should be taken as vernacular for a nominalistic formulation in terms of predicates.

10. On the general matter of the difference between linguistic and pictorial symbol systems, see Nelson Goodman, *Languages of Art* (Indianapolis: Hackett, 1976), second edition (hereafter referred to as *LA*), esp. pp. 41-34, 225-27. For further discussion of denotation by pictures, see my comments on a paper by Monroe Beardsley, in *Erkenntnis*, vol. 12 (1978), pp. 169-70.

11. On metaphorical truth, see further *LA*, pp. 68-70. On meaning-relationships between different fictive terms like "Don Quixote" and "Don Juan," see *PP*, pp. 221-38, and Israel Scheffler's important paper "Ambiguity: An Inscriptional Approach" in *Logic and Art*, R. Rudner and I. Scheffler, eds. (Indianapolis, 1972), pp. 251-72. Notice that since "Don Quixote" and "Don Juan" have the same (null) literal extension, their metaphorical sorting of people cannot reflect any literal sorting. How then can the metaphorical behavior of these terms be subsumed under the general theory of metaphor? In two closely interelated ways. The metaphorical sorting may reflect: (1) difference in literal extension between parallel compounds of the two terms—for example, "Don-Quixote-term (or picture)" and "Don-Juan-term (or picture)" have different literal extensions; or (2) difference in the terms that denote, and may be exemplified by, the two terms—for example, "Don Juan" is an inveterate-seducer-term while "Don Quixote" is not. In sum, "Don Quixote" and "Don Juan" are denoted by different terms (e.g., "Don-Quixote-term" and "Don-Juan-term") that also denote other different terms (e.g., "zany jouster" and "inveterate seducer") that in turn denote different people. If this is somewhat complicated, the component steps are all simple; and any trafficking with fictive entities is avoided.

12. Nelson Goodman, *Fact, Fiction, and Forecast* (Indianapolis: Hackett, 1977), third edition, pp. 49-58. I am by no means here letting down the bars to admit merely possible worlds, but only suggesting that some talk that is ostensibly 'about possible things' can be usefully reinterpreted as talk about actual things.

INTRODUCTION TO

Subjective, Objective, and Conceptual Relativisms

Having looked in detail at one type of cognitive relativism, we now turn to an essay which gives a classification of some types of cognitive relativism and puts forward the most frequent and most influential objection made to cognitive relativism—the charge that cognitive relativism is self-refuting.

Subjective relativism holds that "any assertion must be viewed in relation to the beliefs and attitudes of the particular individual making the assertion." Objective relativism holds that an assertion must be viewed in relation to "the nature of the total context in which the assertion is made." Because the items which comprise objective relativism's "total context"— such as purposes and points of view—are much like subjective relativism's "beliefs and attitudes," it is not easy to discern the difference between these two forms of relativism. Mandelbaum recognizes this and takes some pains to try to differentiate them. For example, he says that the objective relativist, but not the subjective relativist, "claims that such judgments will be concurred in by others who are similarly placed and share the same concerns." This is the "objective" element in objective relativism. Both of these forms of relativism are to be distinguished from conceptual relativism, which is the view that assertions are relative to "the intellectual or conceptual background which the individual brings to his problems from the cultural milieu to which he belongs." (We should note that Mandelbaum explicitly classifies Thomas Kuhn as a conceptual relativist, an interpretation of Kuhn which Gerald Doppelt rejects in his article later in this volume.) Whatever the similarities or differences among these three forms of relativism, they all have in common the claim that the truth or falsity of an assertion is to be judged by reference to the properties or situation of the person making the assertion. This sets cognitive relativism apart from absolutist views which hold that truth and falsity depend solely

30

on the relation between a statement and what that statement is about and not at all on the properties or situation of the person making the statement.

Mandelbaum criticizes these three versions of relativism in the same way, so we can focus on his criticism of the first type, subjective relativism, as an example. The problem arises, according to Mandelbaum, from the attempt by the subjective relativist to support his relativism by citing evidence of some kind. Such evidence "is only convincing so long as it is not itself interpreted relativistically, as a consistent subjective relativist would be forced to interpret it." Again, such evidence "must be taken to be true in a sense other than the only sense which the subjective relativist ascribes to the concept of truth." In other words, the relativist must take the statements which express the evidence for his relativism to be true in some absolute sense. But his relativism claims that all statements are true only in a relativistic sense. It claims that each statement is true "for him" or "for her" and not true "for everyone regardless of who they are," whereas the statements of evidence brought forward to support this claim must themselves be taken to be absolute truths—which, at a minimum, means "true for everyone regardless of who they are." The upshot is that the relativist contradicts himself by saying that all statements are only relatively true and then relying on the absolute truth of some statements in order to prove his point.

This criticism—that cognitive relativism is "self-contradictory" or "self-refuting"—is the criticism most often made of relativism and is usually taken to be devastating. A more common version of this charge of self-refutation focuses on the statement of the relativist's position, rather than on the evidence adduced for that position, in the following way. The relativist holds that each statement is at most relatively true (rather than absolutely true). Does this relativistic thesis apply to itself? If it does, then the relativist's position itself is only "relative" and "subjective" and need not be taken seriously by anyone who does not already subscribe to that position. If, on the other hand, the relativist's thesis does not apply to itself, then there is something which is absolutely true (namely, the relativist's own thesis), a position which blatantly contradicts that very thesis.

Let us examine Mandelbaum's version of the self-refutation objection more closely. Mandelbaum tells us that the evidence adduced by the relativist is convincing only if it is not taken relativistically. But convincing to whom? Perhaps it is supposed to be convincing to the relativist himself to persuade him to become a relativist. Before he is a relativist, he will presumably regard the evidence as absolutely true. There is no problem here since he is not yet a relativist and therefore is not making the evidence an exception to the relativist doctrine. After he becomes a relativist, he will naturally regard the evidence as relatively true—that is, true for him. But since he is now a relativist, that is all that is needed for the evidence to be convincing to him. A statement which is regarded by the relativist as true for himself will be as convincing to the relativist as anything could be.

Perhaps the person to be convinced by the evidence is the non-relativist, and the evidence is being cited by the relativist to the nonrelativist in an attempt to convince the nonrelativist to convert to relativism. In this case, for the evidence to be convincing, all that is necessary is that the evidence be regarded by the nonrelativist as true-for-himself. The evidence need not also be true in some absolute sense.

Furthermore, even if there is a problem for relativism when the relativist tries to convince the nonrelativist, this may not be a fundamental problem—not a problem which shows that relativism is somehow self-refuting. What it might show instead is that the relativist should not try to convince the nonrelativist because he will not succeed. This is very different from exhibiting some type of internal incoherence in relativism.

Mandelbaum's basic objection is that the relativist offers arguments to support his position and, in doing so, presupposes some statements to be absolutely true. It has just been suggested that in offering arguments, the relativist need only presuppose statements which are true-for-the-person-being-persuaded-or-convinced. But throughout this discussion so far, an assumption has been made—namely that when the relativist gives arguments to the nonrelativist, he is trying to convince the nonrelativist. Persuasion may be the nonrelativist's purpose in giving arguments, but it need not be the relativist's purpose. The giving of arguments can have many purposes. For example, the relativist may use the argumentative form in order to present his view in a logically ordered way so that his audience will better understand that view.[1]

To insist that the relativist should have the same purposes in argument as the nonrelativist might have is misguided. It is an example of a practice often followed by absolutist objectors to relativism—the practice of requiring the relativist to adopt ends and to satisfy standards which are appropriate to absolutism and then declaring relativism refuted when relativism fails to live up to the mark. Relativism may be more appropriately considered as a world-view which generates its own goals and standards.

NOTE

1. For a fuller discussion of the objection that cognitive relativism is self-refuting and of replies to this objection, see Jack W. Meiland, "On the Paradox of

Cognitive Relativism," *Metaphilosophy* 11:2 (1980). Nelson Goodman makes a brief but suggestive remark on one possible relativist use of argument in *Ways of Worldmaking*, p. 129.

Subjective, Objective, and Conceptual Relativisms*

Maurice Mandelbaum

Frequently, throughout the history of modern philosophy, it has been held that although claims to knowledge can be adequately defended against relativistic arguments, judgments of value cannot. Positions of this type were widely accepted in Anglo-American philosophy during the last half-century. To be sure, some philosophers have at all times attacked such a dichotomy, holding that arguments similar to those which justify a rejection of relativism is mistaken in both spheres. Recently, however, there has been an attack on the same dichotomy from the opposite direction. An increasing number of philosophers have accepted positions that lead to a relativization of judgments of fact as well as of judgments of value. This tendency has many independent roots, and those who accept it in one form or another may hold antithetical positions on a variety of other issues. I shall therefore not attempt to disentangle the presuppositions which underlie contemporary relativistic theories of knowledge, though I shall indicate some of them in passing; rather, I shall confine myself to showing that an acceptance of relativism in the theory of knowledge frequently—and perhaps always—involves a prior commitment to non-relativistic interpretations of at least *some* judgments concerning matters of fact. Consequently, whatever may be the case with respect to judgments of value, epistemological relativism may be said to be self-limiting.[1]

*Reprinted with permission of the author and publisher from *The Monist* 62:4 (1979): 403-23.

I

In order to proceed with the argument, it will be necessary to identify what various forms of "relativism" have in common. The most basic common denominator appears to be the contention that assertions cannot be judged true or false in themselves, but must be so judged with reference to one or more aspects of the total situation in which they have been made. The aspects of a particular assertion's context with respect to which it is treated as relative may be of various types; I shall single out three such types for discussion. The first holds that any assertion must be viewed in relation to the beliefs and attitudes of the particular individual making the assertion. As a consequence, one cannot speak of the truth or falsity of an assertion *simpliciter:* what should be understood is that the assertion is "true (or false) for him or for her." A relativism of this type may best be described as *subjective relativism,* the truth being relative to characteristics of the person making the assertion. Though a relativism of this sort has sometimes been accepted with respect to judgments of value (as uses of the *de gustibus* maxim remind us), it has rarely been applied in a wholesale manner when the truth or falsity of judgments of fact is at issue.

A second type of relativism is that which has been characterized as *objective relativism.* It takes as its point of departure the undoubted fact that whenever a person makes an assertion there is some reason for his making that assertion; further, it appeals to the fact that whenever an assertion is made, the person making that assertion occupies some particular position, or point of view, with reference to that with which his assertion is concerned; finally, it points out that any assertion refers only to some and not other aspects of that with which it is concerned. These three components in the knowledge relationship are not likely to be wholly independent of one another. A person's purposes will often determine with which aspects of an object he is concerned, and his purposes frequently depend upon the specific relationship in which he stands to that particular object. Consequently (the objective relativist argues), the truth of what is asserted cannot be judged independently of the context in which the assertion is made: all assertions are relative to the purposes of whoever makes the assertion, the point of view from which his judgment is made, and the aspect of the object with which he is concerned. While this leads an objective relativist to deny that assertions are either true or false *simpliciter,* his position is not identical with that of a subjective relativist. Unlike the subjective relativist, he would deny that what is taken to be true or false is primarily a function of the beliefs and attitudes of the particular person making the assertion: rather, it is relative to the nature of the total context in which the assertion is made. Also, unlike the subjective relativist, an objective reativist claims that such judgments will be concurred in by others who are similarly placed and share the same concerns. Thus, he claims that knowledge can be said to be objective in spite of its being relative to a particular context.

A third general form of relativism is that which I shall term *conceptual relativism*. Like objective relativism, it holds that judgments concerning matters of fact are to be interpreted with reference to the context in which they are made, not with reference to the individual who makes them. That which is relevant for a conceptual relativist is not, however, the individual's purposes or interests, nor the particular relationship in which he stands to the objects with which his judgments are concerned; rather, what is relevant is taken to be the intellectual or conceptual background which the individual brings to his problems from the cultural milieu to which he belongs. A relativism of this type has been brought to the forefront of attention by aspects of Wittgenstein's later work, by Benjamin Lee Whorf, by T.S. Kuhn, and more recently by Richard Rorty, among others. I shall attempt to show that in its appeal to what may be termed culture-bound interpretations of matters of fact, this type of relativism must rely on data which are not to be interpreted as themselves being culture-bound. In this case as in the others, I shall argue that those who attempt to establish relativism make claims that involve what I have elsewhere termed "the self-excepting fallacy," that is, the fallacy of stating a generalization that purports to hold of all persons but which, inconsistently, is not then applied to oneself.[2]

Let us first take the case of subjective relativism, and consider it briefly. A subjective relativist puts forward the claim that the judgments of fact which are made by others are always relative to their own interests, attitudes, and biases as these are reflected in antecedently held commitments or beliefs. Not only does he make this claim, but he attempts to support it by evidence. Yet, in order to do so, he must assume that he himself actually knows the interest, attitudes, and biases of others, and that, in addition, he knows that their assertions would have been significantly different had it not been for these particular interests, attitudes, and biases. Thus, when a historical relativist such as Charles A. Beard offers evidence in favor of his relativism by analyzing the role of bias in the historical writings of others, he fails to take seriously the fact that if his thesis were universally true it would also apply to his own analysis, thus destroying the evidence on which it was based.

To be sure, evidence *can* be gathered to show that there are many cases in which one can only understand why a person asserted what he did—and why he presumably took his assertion to be true—by understanding that his assertion was related to his own particular interests, attitudes, and biases. What must not be overlooked, however, is that evidence of this sort is only convincing so long as it is not itself interpreted relativistically, as a consistent subjective relativist would be forced to interpret it. Nor could a subjective relativist escape this criticism by appealing to some general Protagorean or Carneadean thesis instead of actual instances in which an individual's judgments are distorted: such general thesis are only convincing insofar as they are assumed to follow from psychological or ontological premises. Such premises, however, must be taken to be true in a sense other than the only sense which the subjective relativist ascribes to the concept of truth.

II

It is a less simple matter to single out the difficulties in objective relativism, but such difficulties nonetheless exist. I shall discuss them under three heads: first, with respect to the role of interest or purpose in judgments concerning matters of fact; second, with respect to the influence of the standpoint of the observer on the judgments he makes; and, third, the consequences which follow from the fact that any judgment is selective, dealing only with particular features or aspects of the object or situation judged. While there is in each case an element of truth in the contentions of the objective relativist, the conclusions which are claimed to follow from these facts will not successfully withstand scrutiny.

The term "objective relativism" was coined by Arthur E. Murphy in 1927, in an article entitled "Objective Relativism in Dewey and Whitehead."[3] As one notes in that article, what was most characteristic of the position was a belief that events and relationships, not objects, are the ultimate constituents of what there is. However, as the term suggests, it was on the epistemological consequences held to follow from this ontological position that attention was primarily focussed.[4] It is with these epistemological consequences that I shall here be concerned.[5]

No one, I take it, would be likely to deny that every judgment concerning a matter of fact issues from a situation in which the person making that judgment has an interest or a purpose related to that with which his judgment is concerned. One should, however, distinguish two ways in which such interests can presumably come into play. On the one hand, whatever is an object of knowledge may interest a person because it is instrumentally connected with some state of affairs that he would like to bring about or avoid; in such cases his present interest in the object depends upon a further purpose which is of interest to him. On the other hand, a person may presumably be interested in an object for no reason other than that it does in fact interest him. In that case his activity with respect to that object need not be said to be lacking in purpose; the purpose, however, will be one of appreciating, or exploring, or understanding, or explaining the particular object or state of affairs in which he is interested. Of course, these two basic types of interest need not be mutually exclusive: an individual's purposes in any situation may be of both types, and both may be simultaneously present. What the objective relativist underemphasizes, overlooks, or sometimes even denies, is that there are these two possible relations between an individual's interests and that with which his judgments are concerned; in the account of knowledge most characteristic of objective relativists, only the instrumental relationship, and not an interest in the object for its own sake, is stressed.[6]

In any case of Dewey at least, the objective relativist's stress on this aspect of judgments can be accounted for in terms of his acceptance of an instrumental view of mind. It is clear, however, that anyone holding such a view does so with the intention of claiming that this view is true independently of his own interests and purposes. Pushing this contention a step further, it may plausibly be argued that one reason why Dewey accepted as instrumental theory of mind was that he believed it to be demanded by evolutionary theory. As his famous essay on the influence of Darwinism on philosophy makes clear, Dewey derived great support for his own philosophic views from that which was revolutionary in Darwin's thought. At the same time, it was only because he regarded Darwin's theory as true, independently of the use to which he could put it, that Dewey could in fact use it in this way. In fact, in order to accept Darwin's theory as true, the only instrumental function that had to be attributed to it was that it had permitted Darwin and others to understand and explain a wide variety of facts with which biologists, paleontologists, philosophers, and theologians were concerned. Thus, it is my contention that the view of the knowledge relationship stressed by objective relativists such as Dewey, ultimately depends on regarding *some* assertions concerning matters of fact as true or false independently of any further uses to which those assertions can be put.

I now turn to consider the second aspect of the objective relativist's thesis: that judgments of matters of fact are always relative to the standpoint of the person judging. Here the notion of "a standpoint" can be conceived in either of two ways: temporally or spatially. Those objective relativists who have been primarily concerned with historical knowledge, rather than with sense-perception, have emphasized the relativity of our judgments with respect to *when* they are made, whereas those who have been primarily concerned with sense-perception, or with analogues to it, have frequently placed greater emphasis on the fact that different observers, looking at the same object, do so from different points of view.

Yet, no sharp line is to be drawn between these two approaches. Objective relativists are also apt to use the concept of "a point of view" in at least a metaphorical sense when dealing with historical knowledge; similarly, temporal factors may be taken into account in discussions of sense-perception when, for example, objective relativists refer to the epistemological implications of the Doppler-effect, or to those entailed by the finite velocity of light. Regardless of whether they emphasize the implications of temporal or of spatial relations, objective relativists hold that differences in standpoints are objective facts, and that they influence every judgment that it is possible for anyone to make. Whether this claim is consistent with an acceptance of relativism, as I have defined it, is what I propose to examine.

With respect to the influence of the temporal factor on judgments of the past, those objective relativists who are concerned with historical knowledge may stress either of two ways in which such influences are brought to bear. Each, however, depends on the fact that selection and interpretations are essential to the writing of history. The first and less radical of these arguments consists in the claim that what dominates the selection and interpretation of the past by those writing history in the present is to be found in present interests, *and* that those events on which interest will be focussed are events which the historian sees as in some way continuous with his present. Consequently, as the present changes, so will interpretations of the past.[7] This argument is flawed. It fails to take into account the basis on which historians are led to accept, reject, or modify the work of other historians. Even if one were to accept the fundamental premise of the argument—that historians are only interested in the past insofar as they see it as continuous with their present—it would be inconsistent with the ways in which historians actually assess the accounts of both their contemporaries and their predecessors. For example, historical accounts are criticized for claiming continuities among events which evidence fails to substantiate; furthermore, they are even more severely criticized for having neglected those aspects of the past which are discontinuous with what is characteristic of the historian's present. In short, it is in relation to accumulated evidence deriving from many sources, and not in relation to the historian's own present, that the works of past and present historians are actually judged. That this is so should not be suprising: the very notion of taking something as *evidence* involves treating it as not being self-referential, but as pointing beyond itself. Thus, even a historian who may be exceptionally immersed in present concerns, treats the evidence on which his account is based as referring not to his own situation but to something which occurred in the past. When later historians subsequently assess the reliability of his account, it is in relation to all the evidence at their disposal, and not merely in terms of whatever evidence his own situation led him to use. Thus, if an objective relativist is to take seriously criticism as it is practiced in the historical profession, he will have to enlarge his theory, allowing some assertions to be true or false with reference to accumulated evidence rather than in relation to the particular historical conditions out of which they arose. Since objective relativists such as Dewey and Randall do not in their own historical writings seem to deny that one interpretation of the past is better warranted than another, their actual critical practice is not consistent with the form of relativism they espouse.[8]

The second and more radical argument which objective relativists derive from the purported influence of a temporal factor on historical judgments rests on the claim that in fact the past itself undergoes significant change through what later develops. This thesis rests on the contention that what is incipient in any event cannot be recognized until the future unrolls, and the connections between that event and its consequences become apparent. As Randall said, "the history the historian will write, and the principle of selection he will employ, will be undergoing continual change, because the histories things themselves possess are continually changing, always being cumulatively added to. With the occurrence of fresh events, the meaning and significance of past events is always changing."[9] Therefore, a historian who attempts to write contemporary history is not likely to hit upon an adequate interpretation of the events with which he deals, since he will be too close in time to those events to grasp their actual outcomes. Nor will the work of a later historians prove to be more acceptable, since ever new consequences of the past will continue to appear in the future.[10] Therefore, contrary to fact, each historical inquiry will have to be evaluated with reference to its own standpoint only; as Randall said, "knowledge is 'objective' only *for* some determinate context: it is always knowledge of *the* structure and relations essential *for* that context. In historical knowledge, the context is always a teleological and functional one, pointing to a structure of means and ends, of 'means *for*' or 'relative *to*' ends and eventuations."[11]

Once again we must ask whether these assertions are to be applied to the contentions of the objective relativist himself. What obviously underlay Randall's thesis was a set of metaphysical assumptions which can be described as a modernized form of Aristotelianism. Randall, however, does not ask whether one is to view his acceptance of these assumptions as relative to his own historical situation. In that case, what would follow from them would presumably have to undergo change as the historical situation in philosophy changes. Yet, Randall defines metaphysics as "the investigation of existence as existence, an inquiry distinguished from other inquiries by a subject-matter of its own, the general characters and the

ultimate distinctions illustrated and exhibited in each specific and determinate kind of existence and existential subject-matter."[12] Given that
definition, one has a right to expect that such inquiries uncover a set of
categories which are objective, not only in the sense that they are nonarbitrary, but also as denominating the pervasive features of whatever
exists. Randall himself assuredly believed that his metaphysical categories
were, in principle, capable of doing this, since it was only because of his
insistence that process is the ultimate metaphysical category, and that the
world involves a pluralism of processes, that (like Dewey and Whitehead)
he initially accepted objective relativism. Yet, if objective relativism were to
be applied to this metaphysical position it would undercut that position's
claim to being true in any non-relative sense. Once again, then, it should be
apparent that even though it is always possible to show that *some*
assertions are indeed relative to the interests, purposes, and historically
conditioned circumstances of those who assert them, not all assertions can
consistently be interpreted in this way.

At this point an objective relativist might abandon a temporalistic
interpretation of what constitutes the standpoint to which judgments are
relative (except perhaps in the case of historical judgments), and might
instead appeal to the analogy of spatial location to indicate that to which
every judgment is relative. He might then hold that just as objects appear to
be of different shapes when viewed from different perspectives, or of
different sizes when viewed from different distances, so the truth of any
factual judgment is relative to the point of view from which that object is
seen. In metaphysical propositions, for example, one philosopher might
stress mobility and change whereas another might stress relative perma-
nence, and both might be correct if that which is judged does in fact have
both aspects: each judgment would then be true relative to those features of
the object to which the judgment had refernce. As McGilvary said in the
opening sentences of his Carus Lectures, "Every philosophy is the universe
as it appears in the perspective of a philosopher. It is a *Welt angeschaut* and
not *die Welt an und für sich*"[13] This statement, taken alone, may appear as
a relatively innocuous truism, but its consequences, as McGilvary developed them, were radical; and it was with these consequences that his book
as a whole was concerned. In his case, as in the case of Randall, one finds
that underlying his perspectival relativity there was a fundamental
metaphysical thesis. He stated this thesis as follows:

> Every particular in the world is a member of a context of particulars
> and is what it is only because of its context; and every character any
> member has, it has only by virtue of its relations to other members of
> that context. (p. 17)

He then interpreted this as implying that

> In a world of nature any 'thing' at any time is, and is nothing but, the
> totality of the relational characters, experienced or not experienced,
> that the 'thing' has at that time in whatever relations it has at that time
> to other 'things'. (p. 30)

From this it followed as a corollary that

> Every character which any thing has at any time it has only as it is a
> term of some relation in which at that time it stands to some other
> thing. (p. 36)

I do not believe that these metaphysical doctrines can be rendered harmless
by turning McGilvary's own perspectival theory against them; unlike
Randall's temporalistic version of objective relativism, McGilvary's perspectivism does not undercut his own metaphysical claims. Nevertheless, there
are important difficulties in his theory which must be brought to light.

One such difficulty is that to which Lovejoy continually referred in his
attack on objective relativism: that the doctrine dissolves the object
(whatever it is) into a set of perspectival views. Therefore, two persons
standing in different relations to what is ostensibly one and the same object
will not be encountering the same object at all. Where that is the case, their
views could not be said to be contradictory, and the question of whether
any of these diverse views is more correct than any other is not a question
that should arise. To this McGilvary would presumably have answered
through appealing to his basic realistic postulate: that we are living
organisms, and that there is presented to us in sense experience a real world
in which each of us does and must live.[14] While an appeal of this type would
not have satisfied Lovejoy, who would have insisted (and rightly, I believe)
that such a contention presupposes knowledge which is not restricted to the
knower's own standpoint,[15] let us grant that McGilvary's realistic assumption provides an escape from the danger than when two people claim to
know a particular object, what they know is not in any sense the same
object. Even so, a difficulty remains. Since the characters possessed by any
object are in all cases claimed to be dependent on its relations to other
objects, and since these relations vary indefinitely, it will possess many
characteristics that will appear to be incompatible. The same railroad
tracks will be parallel and convergent, the surface of the same coin will be
both circular and elliptical, depending on the position in which a percipient
organism stands (or might stand) in relation to it. The same person may be
kind or cruel, the same object a piece of brass or a work of art, the same

drug curative or poisonous, depending on what experiences define the characteristics of the object with which we are concerned. None of this need be troublesome so long as we find ways to explain why it is that the same object can take on characteristics that appear to be antithetical. This, however, involves offering explanations that appeal to differences between the various relations in which that object stands to other objects. Such explanations could not be given were our knowledge limited to the relations directly existing between these objects and ourselves. We must also know how they affect other persons, and how they affect other objects. This is the sort of knowledge which, for example, we acquire through physical and physiological optics; that knowledge is neutral with repsect to any one perspective, and through it we are in a position to explain the differences in perception which depend upon perspectival differences. Similarly, the physics of acoustics serves to explain why a train's whistle sounds as it does when the train is approaching and sounds differently as it recedes. In these explanations of the Doppler-effect, a standpoint is adopted which is free of these differing perspectival views, neither of which is adopted, though both are explained. Nor would one be entitled to take the perspective of the train's engineer as authoritative if one could not, through a knowledge of physics, reconcile what is given from his perspective with what is given from each of the other two points of view. Or, to choose an example of a different sort, it is necessary for us to gain non-perspectival knowledge of the characteristics of human beings in order to explain why some particular person may be kind to some and cruel to others, or kind under one set of circumstances and cruel under others. In order to made sense of his actions, we must somehow place ourselves within the perspective of that person himself, or we shall not understand how such contrary characteristics are elicited by different situations. The striving to justify this sort of transcendence of one's *own* perspective is evident even among some of the strongest defenders of perspectivism, as is evident both in Karl Mannheim's essay, "Wissenssoziologie,"[16] and in George Herbert Mead's paper, "The Objective Reality of Perspectives."[17] Both Mannheim and Mead in fact assumed that the theorist can escape the limitations of his own perspective, and this is but another example of what I have termed the self-excepting fallacy.

I come now to the third aspect of the objective relativist's position, the fact that every judgment is selective, and does not fully mirror all that an observer viewing an object is actually in a position to see. Thus, the knowledge we have of any object is limited not only by the position we occupy with respect to that object, but it is also limited by the focus of our interest on one rather than another of its characteristics. It is on this basis that the objective relativist argues that the object as we know it is not knowledge of what it may be like independently of us, but only what it is like for and to us.

In order to draw this conclusion from the undoubted fact that our attention is always selective, the objective relativist must assume that if we could simultaneously discern all of the characteristics of any object, no one of them would be exactly like what we take it to be when viewed independently of the others. This is surely not always the case. I may, for example, be so situated that I at first can see only one surface of an object, but when, later, I am able to view it from other angles, my conception of that surface may not have had to undergo change. Nor is this sort of independence of one characteristic of an object from its other characteristics always confined to simple cases of this sort. In coming to know a person, for example, I may first be struck by some trait, such as his shyness, and may only later come to discover that he is also exceptionally bright. While the fact that I know him to be bright as well as being shy will round out my picture of the person, and will provide additional insight into his character, this will not alter my view that he is in fact exceptionally shy, nor will my awareness of his shyness conceal the fact that he is exceptionally bright. To be sure, it is often the case that various characteristics possessed by a person, or by an object, are so related that if one were to attempt to describe one of these characteristics independently of its relations to the others that description might be not only inadequate but positively misleading. The existence of such cases does not, however, establish the objective relativist's thesis, since what they involve is a *correction* of the original judgment, not merely the substitution of one judgment for another. That which entitles one to view them as corrections is the fact that what has changed is not the relationship between the observer and that which he is observing; rather, it is the observer's discernment of a previously unrecognized relationship *within* the object itself.

An objective relativist might be inclined to challenge such an answer, asking why one should hold that the discernment of this relationship can be said to have yielded a more adequate view of the object, rather than merely a different one. To this there is, I believe, an obvious answer. While all objective relativists hold that judgments are relative to a particular standpoint, they do not hold that all are equally worthy of credence. For example, although a judgment regarding the past is made with reference to the relationships between that past and the present, not all judgments which purport to refer to the past are taken to be equally reliable: only those which refer to what did actually exist in the past are to be accepted.[18] Thus, even though every judgment is made from some point of view, and deals with only some aspects of an object which is seen from that point of view, it is not with reference to its point of view that we discriminate among judgments. Instead, we are forced to appeal to whatever judgments issue from a point of view which permits an observer to discern whatever qualities the object itself possesses. Thus, objective relativists, no less than those holding other epistemological positions, will have to appeal to tests which decide what characteristics particular objects do in fact possess. This involves an abandonment of the assumption that objects posses characteristics only insofar as they are seen from certain points of view, and with respect to certain purposes.

III

We now turn to a consideration of the even more radical thesis of conceptual relativism.[19] While its background is complex, one can isolate three convergent streams of influence which have been of special importance in establishing the widespread acceptance it enjoys today. The first stems from developments within the philosophy of science; the second from problems of method in the *Geisteswissenschaften*; the third from the ways in which certain perceptual phenomena, and also data drawn from comparative linguistics, have often been interpreted. I shall briefly—and admittedly inadequately—identify each of these factors.

With respect to the first, since the last quarter of the nineteenth century it has increasingly come to be recognized that scientific explanations are not uniquely determined by the observations from which they may have been derived, nor from those which are used as confirmatory evidence for them. While this conviction was an essential feature in the otherwise divergent views of Mach, Poincaré, and Duhem, among others, it failed to forestall the acceptance of the epistemological foundationalism which was characteristic of logical positivism. The acceptance of that form of foundationalism was, however, shaken by Quine's "Two Dogmas of Empiricism," in which it was claimed that in conflicts between observations and a theory it is not necessarily the theory that must be abandoned. Instead, these conflicting observations may be reinterpreted in terms of an alternative theory. In addition, logical positivism had been committed to drawing a sharp distinction between observational terms and theoretical terms, but that distinction came under increasingly severe attack, also serving to undermine the foundationalism characteristic of the positivist's position.

With respect to the second of the influences, a cognate issue arose in connection with the interpretation of texts, and also in connection with the interpretation of the character of a person or a historical period. Ast, Schleiermacher, and Dilthey identified this problem as "the hermeneutic circle."[20] The apparent circularity in interpretation arises because one can presumably only interpret any given portion of a text in terms of the whole of which it is a part, but one is only in a position to interpret that whole through experiencing its individual parts. Thus, the interplay of part and whole in all interpretations of texts, and in interpreting the character of persons or of historical periods, parallels the interplay of observation and theory in interpretations of nature. Here, too, the search for a rock-bottom and unassailable foundation of facts, on which interpretation is supposedly based, is lacking.

In addition to the problems ostensibly posed by the hermeneutic circle, the thought of those who were concerned with the methods of the *Geisteswissenschaften* was often deeply affected by subjective relativism, and sometimes by that form of objective relativism which stresses the role of ideological factors in determining the content of our systems of knowledge. In either case it was claimed that whatever individual facts could be objectively established would be insufficient to determine the account in which they were included. Instead, it was held that these facts were fitted into a structure which depended on the values which the inquirer himself had brought to the materials with which he sought to deal. Once again, this parallels the position of conceptual relativism when applied to the sciences: interpretations do not emerge directly from the facts in any given situation; rather, the facts cited are those which conform to some accepted interpretation.[21]

Turning now to the impact of psychology and comparative linguistics, we may note that conceptual relativism has been fostered by interpretations placed on our perception of reversible figures, such as the duck-rabbit figure made familiar through Wittgenstein's use of it; in addition, it has been fostered by the uses to which data derived from comparisons between Indo-European languages and native American languages have been put by Whorf and by others.

First, with respect to the question of the epistemological significance of reversible figures, one can see that if one takes such figures as paradigmatic of what occurs in all sense-perception, one would be tempted to accept conceptual relativism. It is, for example, natural to say when describing what one sees when one looks at the duck-rabbit figure that one sees it as a duck, or else as a rabbit. Similarly, in the reversible cube figure, one can describe what one sees as a cube seen from above, or as a cube seen from below. In such cases the same visual figure is seen in either of two ways, and each is no less legitimate than the other. Thus, what is directly presented to our sense organs does not uniquely determine in what ways we may describe it. When these cases are taken as paradigmatic for the analysis of perceptual experience (as they have been by such conceptual relativists as Hanson and Kuhn), attention is focussed on the question of "seeing *as,*" rather than on whatever is involved in the act of seeing itself. As a consequence, in many instances philosophic interest has been diverted from those traditional epistemological questions which had their roots in analyses of the specific conditions which are responsible for different persons (or for the same person at different times), attributing different properties to the same object. Many contemporary philosophers (unlike Locke, Berkeley, and Hume) would regard all such empirically oriented questions as lying wholly outside philosophical analysis. As a consequence, they are unlikely to ask in what ways reversible figures differ from non-reversible figures. However, unless it can be shown that there are no epistemologically relevant differences between reversible and nonreversible figures, it is odd to take the former as paradigmatic for analyses of perception generally.[22]

Furthermore, a blanket use of the concept "seeing as" conceals difficulties. It is perfectly normal to say that one sees the duck-rabbit figure first "as a duck" and then "as a rabbit." It is sometimes also perfectly normal to use the locution "seeing as" in cases in which one is not referring to reversible figures. For example, one can say that the astronomer looking at a photographic plate sees a point of light "as a star." However, there is no parallel between that case and what occurs with respect to reversible figures, except that the same locution has been used. In looking at the photographic plate, the astronomer can simultaneously recognize what he sees "as a point of light" and also "as a star," but what he sees is not a reversible figure. Rather, that which is seen can be described in either of two ways, each of which is equally applicable *at the same time.*[23] In a reversible figure, on the contrary, what I see at any one time is *either* a rabbit or a duck, not both. I do not see a rabbit which I also recognize to be a duck, nor a duck which I can equally well describe as a rabbit. Given this difference in the two types of case, the mere fact that the same locution is used does not justify the analogy which N.R. Hanson, T.S. Kuhn, and others, have drawn between reversible figures and the observational data used in the sciences.[24]

Having considered, and rejected, the ways in which reversible figures have recently been used in support of conceptual relativism, I now turn to a comparable argument that has its source in comparative linguistics. The most striking instance of epistemological conclusions being drawn from this source is Benjamin Lee Whorf's hypothesis that all natural languages include an implicit metaphysics, and that how the world appears to those using a language reflects the metaphysics contained in its grammatical structure. To choose merely one example of his formulation of this point, I shall cite the following:

The background linguistic system (in other words, the grammar) of each language is not merely a reproducing instrument for voicing ideas but rather is itself the shaper of ideas, the program and guide for the individual's mental activity, for his analysis of impressions, for his synthesis of his mental stock in trade.... The categories and types that we isolate from the world of phenomena we do not find there because they stare every observer in the face; on the contrary, the world is presented as a kaleidoscopic flux of impressions which has to be organized by our minds—and this means largely by the linguistic systems in our minds.[25]

Whorf's thesis was based on an analysis of differences in the grammatical structure of different languages, with reference, for example, to factors such as whether there are tenses representing past, present, and future in the language; or, to choose another example, whether or not sentences in the language are formed in terms of subject and predicate. That there are significant differences of this sort in the structure of different languages cannot be questioned. What must not be overlooked, however, is that the illustrations used by Whorf show that, in spite of linguistic differences, users of different languages in many cases refer to precisely the same objects and activities. For example, his illustrations in "Science and Linguistics" show that persons using Shawnee and persons using English are equally able to refer to cleaning a gun with a ramrod. Similarly, as is evident in his paper on "Language and Logic," it is possible in both the English and Nootka languages to refer to inviting people to a feast, though the grammatical structure of the two sentences is wholly different.

Nor is this situation confined to cases in which two alternative languages refer to relatively isolable objects or activities. As Whorf's own translations indicate, precisely the same situation obtains in those cases in which he seeks to deny that it does—for example, in how the world of nature is viewed by those using different languages. Comparing the views of nature of the Apache with those which ostensibly depend on the structure of Indo-European languages, he said:

The real question is: What do different languages do, not with artificially isolated objects but with the flowing face of nature in its motion, color, and changing form; with clouds, beaches, and yonder flight of birds? For as goes our segmentation of the face of nature, so goes our physics of the cosmos.[26]

Then, speaking of the Apache, he continues:

Such languages, which do not paint the separate-object picture of the universe to the same degree as do English and its sister tongues, point toward possible new types of logic and possible new cosmical pictures.

Yet, even though Whorf was brought up on Indo-European languages, with the logic of his thinking presumably dependent on the grammatical structure of these languages, he was able to understand how nature appeared to the Apache. In short, as a linguist, he was not bound by his own grammar, but stood outside both his own language and theirs. In doing so he was not only able to understand both languages, but was able, using English, to explicate the world-views implicit in other languages. It follows, then, that conceptual relativism, as represented by Whorf, is not universally applicable: at least he and other linguists are not entrapped within it.

And how, we may ask, does the linguist escape? It is, I submit, because he takes statements made in each language to be referential, and in each case seeks to establish that to which they refer. If it were the case that every statement in a language received its meaning solely through other expressions used within that language, each language would be self-enclosed, and no equivalence of meaning between statements in any two languages could be established. Thus, contrary to fact, neither Whorf nor anyone else could effect even a rough translation from one language to another. What breaks the circle is a recognition of the intentionality inherent in all uses of language, and the possibility of offering ostensive definitions of the meanings of many words, phrases, and sentences which occur in a given language. It is on these foundations that any person must ultimately rely when learning a language. It is only later, after having acquired knowledge of two or more languages, that anyone is in a position to compare their lexicons, grammatical structures, and modes of expression. Such comparisons are of interest, and perhaps suggest that those who use a particular language will be likely to single out for attention aspects of the environment which may not so readily be noticed by those whose language possesses a very different form. Conceptual relativism, however, goes beyond a recognition that this may be the case. In its linguistic form, it holds that the influence of language on thought is so pervasive and so compelling that, insofar as it is a question of truth or falsity, one cannot legitimately compare statements made in one language with those made in another: the truth of each must be assessed within the framework provided by the conceptual system implicit in the structure of the language used. In short, paraphrasing Kuhn, one might say that the Whorfian hypothesis contends that different languages are incommensurable, for they serve to structure different worlds. It is *this* contention that must be rejected.

As we have seen, if the Whorfian thesis were accepted without limitation, Whorf himself would have been unable to draw the contrasts he drew between different languages: in order to draw them he initially had to assume that the same objects and activities were being referred to in both languages. Therefore, it cannot be the case that how the world appears to those who speak a particular language is in *all* respects determined by the language they speak. While varying grammatical forms may lead to varying ways of classifying objects and relating them to one another, languages presuppose a world of extra-linguistic objects to which the speakers of a language refer. Since, however, it is possible to refer to the same aspects of this world when using radically different languages (as Whorf's own practice established that one can), it cannot be maintained that those whose thought is expressed in different languages do not share a common world.

As we shall now see, objections of a similar sort can be raised when Kuhn speaks of scientific theories which are based on different paradigms as being incommensurable because they structure different worlds. To be sure, his thesis is less all-embracing than was Whorf's, for he confined his attention to what occurs within science, thus excluding any discussion of the more general world-pictures.[27] Furthermore, in speaking of scientific theories he explicitly acknowledged that historians of science *are* in a position to compare these theories (just as linguists are in a position to compare languages); he also held that scientists themselves are able to do so. Nevertheless, he held that merely being able to recognize the point of view from which another theory was formulated does not serve to establish true communication between those holding different theories.[28] Although he then outlined various stages in a process of persuasion which could lead from the acceptance of an old paradigm to the adoption of a new one, he nevertheless insisted that, in the end, it is only through a "gestalt-switch," that is, a "conversion," that the new comes to be established.

In this discussion, and throughout his analyses of scientific procedures, Kuhn was forced to assume that rival theories do in fact include reference to some of the same sets of facts, although placing different interpretations on them.[29] Were this not the case, there would be no conflict whatsoever between them: they would in no sense be *rival* theories, since each would pass the other by, without contact. That there is in fact rivalry concerning the proper interpretation of the same data was acknowledged by Kuhn when he said, "Before the group accepts it, a new theory has been tested over time by the research of a number of men, some working within it, others within its traditional rival."[30] Nevertheless, he placed relatively little emphasis on this stage in scientific conflicts. While he would surely admit that particular conflicts are sometimes resolved by an appeal to further facts, as is the case when hypotheses of limited generality are tested, what he emphasized were those clashes in which differences between an old and a new interpretation of many of the same data rested on the use of basically different conceptual frameworks. To the question of how such differences can be adjudicated, Kuhn's answer is that they cannot be: one theory simply supplants the other. In this connection he quotes Planck's dictum: "A new scientific theory does not triumph by convincing its opponents and making them see the light, but rather because its opponents eventually die, and a new generation grows up that is familiar with it."[31]

It cannot be denied that there usually is a deep, ingrained conservatism in those who uphold an earlier theory, but it is nevertheless also necessary to account for the fact that those in the new generation convert to the new theory. As I have indicated, Kuhn uses terms such as "gestalt-switch" and "conversion" to indicate the change that occurs when a revolution has taken place, but this treatment of the mechanisms needed for such a change are not, I believe, adequately analyzed.[32] To be sure, he stresses the role of anomalies in the normal science of the preceding period, but such anomalies only arise because the world of nature does not in all respects conform to what the theory had originally anticipated. Consequently, if a new theory is able, without strain, to incorporate what were formerly regarded as anomalies, and especially if the new interpretation of them constitutes an important component within the new theory, that fact alone would explain much of its appeal. What this indicates, however, is that scientific theories are not to be considered as self-enclosed systems; rather, each claims to depict and explain features of the world which are what they are, independently of it. This point is not, of course, in any sense novel; it is perhaps for that reason that Kuhn failed to place any emphasis on it. Had he done so, however, his account of what is involved in scientific inquiry, and how scientific change occurs, would have been far less radical than it now appears to be.[33] As I shall next indicate, in his account of what makes one scientific theory more acceptable than another, Kuhn did in fact appeal to the way the world is, but since he failed to make such appeals clear and explicit, the most striking feature of his position is his claim that alternative scientific theories are incommensurable.

As examples of passages in which an appeal is made to the world as it is, independently of theory, consider the following. "Successive paradigms tell us different things about the population of the universe and about the population's behavior."[34] Also, Kuhn acknowledges that scientific theories "attach to nature" at various points.[35] Furthermore, in discussing pre-revolutionary and post-revolutionary paradigms, he holds that even in the case of those who accept differing paradigms "both their everyday and most of their scientific world and language are shared."[36] To be sure, although each of these statements suggests that no scientific theory is wholly self-enclosed, in the same passages Kuhn immediately qualifies his statements in ways which stress the interpretive role played by an accepted theoretical framework. For example, the different things we learn from different theories reflect the structure of the theory, not merely what is found in nature; similarly, while all scientific theories "attach to nature" at some points, there may be large interstices between these points which can only be filled by theory, and will be differently filled by different theories; finally, while there may be much that is shared by those who accept differing theories, the acceptance of one rather than another way of interpreting what is experienced depends not on an appeal to nature but on how rival theories structure nature.[37]

Faced by what appear to be these conflicting strains in Kuhn's epistemology, I suggest that it is enlightening to turn to what he says concerning the criteria to be used in evaluating any scientific theory. In a previously unpublished lecture, now found in *The Essential Tension,* he lists five such criteria which, as he says, "play a vital role when scientists must choose between an established theory and an upstart competitor. Together with others of much the same sort, they provide the shared basis for theory choice."[38] I shall quote his characterizations of these criteria, at least three of which—and perhaps all five—contain an implicit appeal to facts which are theory-independent. In order to direct attention to this aspect of these criteria, I shall italicize those phrases which I take to be most significant in this respect. Kuhn says:

> First, a theory should be accurate: within its domain, that is, consequences deducible from a theory should be in demonstrated *agreement with the results of existing experiments and observations.* Second, a theory should be consistent, not only internally or with itself, but also with currently accepted theories applicable to *related aspects of nature.* Third, it should have broad scope: in particular, a theory's consequences should extend far beyond the particular observations, laws, or subtheories it was initially designed to explain. Fourth, and closely related, it should be simple, bringing order to phenomena that in its absence would be individually isolated and, as a set, confused. Fifth, . . . a theory should be fruitful of new research findings; it should, that is, *disclose new phenomena or previously unnoticed relationships among those already known.*

Kuhn does not intend this list to be exhaustive, and he is insistent that it should not be interpreted as providing an algorithm capable of un-ambiguously determining which of two theories is to be granted precedence. In this connection he points out that these criteria are imprecise, and that individuals may differ as to how they apply them in particular cases; furthermore, in particular cases there may be conflict between them. Consequently, he does not regard them as *rules* to be followed, but rather as *values* which guide but do not dictate the choices scientists make.[39]

With this one can have no quarrel, but it is worth noting that there are a number of passages which show that Kuhn does not actually regard each of these criteria as equally fundamental.[40] For example, he frequently stresses *accuracy*. Yet, accuracy is a relational attribute: there must be something (presumably observations of one sort or another) with respect to which a theory is judged to be accurate or lacking in accuracy; yet Kuhn does not specify what this is. To pursue this point, we may note that among the passages which stress accuracy, some single out the importance of quantitative formulations;[41] others stress accuracy of prediction, which Kuhn characterizes as being "probably the most deeply held value."[42] In fact, he holds that if one substracts "accuracy of fit to nature" from the list of criteria, "the enterprise may not resemble science at all, but perhaps philosophy instead."[43] With respect to accuracy we may also note that Kuhn claims that "with the passage of time, scientific theories taken as a group are obviously more and more articulated. In the process, they are matched to nature at an increasing number of points and with increasing precision."[44] Finally, it is important to recall that in discussing scientific change Kuhn emphasized the role of anomalies in preparing the way for paradigm shifts. An anomaly, however, only exists when observations are apparently at odds with what an otherwise entrenched theory would lead one to expect: in short, at such points the theory ceases to be accurate. If, however, a theory were to be treated as wholly self-enclosed, there actually would not be anything to designate as an anomaly.

It is at this point that one can see the tension, and indeed the vacillation, within Kuhn's epistemology. On the one hand, his criteria are, as he says, "all standard criteria for evaluating the adequacy of a theory;" otherwise, he tells us, he would have discussed them more fully in *The Stucture of Scientific Revolutions*.[45] On the other hand, however, the standard interpretation of these criteria falls within what Kuhn called "the traditional epistemological paradigm" which emphasizes the fundamental character of observation in scientific procedures, whereas Kuhn himself argues that observation is *not* foundational since it is always theory-laden. This tension can be concretely illustrated in contrasting two possible interpretations of the criterion of accuracy, as Kuhn formulates it. As we have seen, he said that accuracy demands that "consequences deducible from a theory should be in demonstrated agreement with the results of existing experiments and observations." To interpret this passage one must, however, know what are to be taken as "*the results*" of an experiment or observation. If these "results" are how an experiment or observation is interpreted when seen from the point of view of an antecedently accepted theory, then they cannot serve as an adequate test of that theory. It is only if they are initially taken to be neutral with respect to alternative theories that they provide a test for those theories. According to Kuhn's epistemology, however, no observation or experiment is in fact theoretically neutral.

How is one to escape this dilemma? The answer, I suggest, lies in considering what led Kuhn into it. On the one hand, he did not with to deny or fundamentally reinterpret the standard criteria actually used by scientists in theory-choice, and these criteria include, among other elements, a reliance on the role of observation and experiment in confirming a theory. On the other hand, he insisted that the foundationalist epistemology of the positivistic interpretation of scientific procedures failed to do justice to the ways in which theory-construction can alter the *significance* of the supposedly "hard data" that observation and experiment supply. However, these two theses are not, in themselves, incompatible. What led Kuhn so to regard them was his acceptance of the view that "observation" is never controlled by that which is observed, but depends upon the prior experience of the observer, and that, as a consequence, seeing is never merely *seeing,* but is always "*seeing as. . . .* " He derived this view from an unqualified acceptance of conclusions drawn from various psychological experiments which he mistakenly identified with Gestalt-psychology,[46] and from the faulty assumption that reversible figures furnish reliable clues to what occurs in perception generally. If, however, one were to abandon these psychological assumptions, a rejection of positivistic foundationalism would be entirely compatible with ascribing to observation and experiment a role no less important than that ascribed to them by the positivist tradition.

The path to this reconciliation lies in an acceptance of the now familiar view that in a scientific theory what is to be confirmed is the theory itself, not its individual components, taken individually. But how is one to test a theory taken as a whole? To attempt to match each of two theories, taken as wholes, with "the way the world is" would be futile if both theories were relatively comprehensive in what they included.[47] This was the sort of difficulty which Kuhn stressed: each scientific theory had its own way of organizing its data, and each differed from the other in how it did so. Nevertheless, one can test a theory as a whole in a way other than attempting to *test* it *as a whole.* Every theory includes observational elements, and also holds that these elements are related to one another in certain definable ways: the theoretical aspect of a theory lies precisely in this—in the relations it ascribes to the observations and experiments included within it. Therefore, one can test the adequacy of a theory as a whole by attempting to show whether or not the ascribed connections among observables, as deducible from the theory, do or do not exist; and whether their relations have been accurately determined. In addition, of course, a theory is tested through seeking out new observational or experimental data which, if the theory were true, could be immediately absorbed by it, or which, alternatively, would call for adjustments in it. If absorption or adjustments were to fail, this would ultimately lead to abandonment of the theory.

Although crudely drawn, this picture, I submit, is consistent with what was fundamental in traditional views of theory-confirmation, but does not involve the foundationalism which Kuhn attributed to positivistic philosophies of science. In this respect it admits what Kuhn attempted to establish: that no set of observational or experimental data, taken individually, can either falsify or adequately confirm a scientific theory. Yet, unlike Kuhn's position with respect to that point, it does not commit one to the view that scientific theories can successfully resist the impact of new observational and experimental data. If a view such as that which I propose were to be accepted, it would follow that even the most comprehensive scientific theories are not to be construed as self-enclosed systems, with the acceptance of one rather than another resting solely—or even largely—on sociological and psychological factors. Instead, the chief factor inducing scientific change would be located in those further inquiries that uncover relationships in nature which previous inquiry had failed to reveal.

It is, then, my contention that what is generally taken to be Kuhn's position, and what he tends to emphasize in that position, is not ultimately tenable. As in the case of Whorf and others, the conceptual relativism which he apparently sought to establish was not established; like Whorf, he was forced to relate alternative conceptual systems to various points of contact with what lay outside those systems, and it was with respect to that which was thus "outside" that the systems themselves were interpreted and judged. If what I have briefly suggested concerning the role of observational and experimental data in confirming scientific theories is sound, that which was held in common by Mach, Poincaré, and Duhem with respect to the role played by theory in the sciences need not be taken as establishing conceptual relativism. What I have suggested concerning the relation of whole and part in confirmation procedures in the domain of science can, in my opinion, also be applied to the so-called hermeneutic circle. Consequently, I believe that issues concerning interpretation within the *Geisteswissenschaften* do not pose a unique sort of problem, but that is another question that I cannot here address.

NOTES

1. I attempted to establish a similar point with respect to skepticism regarding the senses in *Philosophy, Science, and Sense-Perception* (Baltimore: John Hopkins Press, 1964), ch. 3.

2. "Some Instances of the Self-Excepting Fallacy," *Psychologische Beiträge* 6 (1962): 383-86.

3. *Philosophical Review* 36 (1927): 121-44. Reprinted, along with a further essay, "What Happened to Objective Relativism?" in *Reason and the Common Good* (Englewood Cliffs, N.J.: Prentice-Hall, 1963).

4. The same may be said with respect to E.B. McGilvary's Carus Lectures, *Toward a Perspective Realism* (La Salle, Ill.: Open Court, 1956). Murphy wrote an extended review of McGilvary's book in *Journal of Philosophy* 54 (1959): 149-65. He was sympathetic but critical, and reiterated his belief that objective relativism is untenable.

5. As the example of C.D. Broad illustrates, one can accept the ontological thesis underlying objective relativism but not accept its supposed epistemological consequences.

6. This parallels a criticism made by Lovejoy with reference to the application of objective relativism to historical studies. (Cf. "Present Standpoints and Past History," *Journal of Philosophy* 36 [1939]: 477-89.)

For his more extended criticism of objective relativism, cf. *The Revolt against Dualism* (Chicago: Open Court, 1930), especially chs. 3 and 4.

7. For example, J.H. Randall says, "A 'history' thus always involves the relation between an outcome in a present, and the past of that present. It will have both a determinate 'focus' in a 'present,' and a past from which that focus selects what has a bearing on that particular history." (*Nature and Historical Experience* [New York: Columbia University Press, 1958], p. 36.)

8. In an essay on Hobbes, Dewey wrote:

> It is the object of this essay to place the political philosophy of Hobbes in its historical context. The history of thought is peculiarly exposed to an illusion of perspective. Earlier doctrines are always getting shoved, as it were, nearer our own day. (*Studies in the History of Ideas* [New York: Columbia University Press, 1918], I: 236.)

Yet, in the *Journal of Philosophy* in 1938, he espoused what would appear to be a diametrically opposed position, which is reiterated in *Logic: The Theory of Inquiry* (New York: Henry Holt, 1938), where he says, "historical inquiry . . . is controlled by the dominant problems and conceptions of the period in which it is written" (p. 236).

With respect to the relation between Randall's theory and his practice, one may note that in "Controlling Assumptions in the Practice of American Historians" (written with George Haines, IV), the position of objective relativism was stated as follows: "knowledge can be objective only *for* a determinate context; it is always a knowledge of the relations essential for that context." However, only five sentences later we find the following: "It is the aim of this essay to illustrate [that thesis] in terms of the principles of selection and interpretation *actually employed* by certain of the major historians of the last two generations." (*Theory and Practice in Historical Study,* Social Science Research Council, Bulletin 54, p. 23. Italics added.) In short, it was assumed possible to discover the controlling assumptions actually employed by other historians, not how such assumptions appear to later historians from the point of view of their own controlling assumptions. A few pages later we also find the following: "These salient facts of the institutional development of the historical profession in the United States have been emphasized, because they provide the framework indispensible for understanding the assumptions and principles of selection American historians have actually employed" (p. 27). Once again, Randall's own practice seems not to have been covered by the principle of objective relativism that he held to be universally true.

9. *Nature and Historical Experience,* p. 39. As is well known, the same point is stressed in G.H. Mead's *Philosophy of the Present* (Chicago: Open Court, 1932).

A similar view, though based on entirely different metaphysical presuppositions is to be found in F.H. Bradley's essay, "What Is the Real Julius Caesar?" in *Essays on Truth and Reality* (Oxford: Clarendon Press, 1914). We may also note that Bergson held that the future alters the past, as when he said:

> Nothing hinders us today from associating the romanticism of the nineteenth century to that which was already romantic in the classicists. But the romantic aspect of classicism is only brought [about] through the retroactive effect of romanticism once it has appeared. If there had not been a Rousseau, a Chateaubriand, a Vigny, a Victor Hugo, not only should we never have perceived, but *there would never really have existed,* any romanticism in the earlier classical writers. (*The Creative Mind* [New York: Philosophical Library, 1946], p. 23.)

10. Cf. Randall, *Nature and Historical Experience,* p. 42.

11. *Nature and Historical Experience,* pp. 60–61. Cf. p. 54. For another statement of the position held by objective relativists, cf. *Theory and Practice in Historical Study: A Report of the Committee on Historiography,* Social Science Research Council Bulletin 54 (1946): 22–23.

12. *Nature and Historical Experience,* p. 144.

13. *Toward a Perspective Realism,* p. 1.

14. Cf. *Toward a Perspective Realism,* p. 15. Though McGilvary did take note of Lovejoy's *Revolt against Dualism,* his only extended discussion of Lovejoy concerned the interpretation of Einstein's theory of relativity, not Lovejoy's criticism of objective relativism. (Cf. *Toward a Perspective Realism,* ch. 10.)

15. Cf. *Revolt against Dualism,* p. 120.

16. Reprinted as an appendix to *Ideology and Utopia* (New York: Harcourt, Brace, 1936). Especially relevant are pp. 270–72.

17. *Proceedings of the Sixth International Congress of Philosophy* (New York: Longmans Green, 1927), pp. 75–85.

18. In this connection we may quote Randall, adding italics to signal the points

at which reference is made to the actual past, not its continuity with the present:

> "Objective relativism" means concretely: The history of anything is *what has happened* and becomes relevant in the envisaged past of that thing. The understanding of that history consists in looking backward from a "focus," *tracing the continuities or persistences of materials to be found in that history, uncovering the operations of the various factors and processes that have in the past modified and reconstructed those materials,* and understanding those modifications in terms of the best scientific knowledge available today. (*Nature and Historical Experience,* p. 61.)

19. I have been unable to determine when, and by whom, this term was first used, but one source which has doubtless contributed to the frequency of its recent occurrence is to be found in Donald Davidson's "On the Very Idea of a Conceptual Scheme," *American Philosophical Association, Proceedings and Addresses* 47 (1973–74): 5–20 (this volume, pp. 66–80). In the various uses to which the term has been put, there have been some variations in its extension, but so far as I am aware it has in all cases been used to refer to positions which strongly resemble one another.

20. Cf. Richard E. Palmer, *Hermeneutics* (Evanston: Northwestern University Press, 1969).

21. For a recent example of this point of view in historiography, cf. Wolfgang J. Mommsen, "Social Conditioning and Social Relevance," *History and Theory* 17, 4 (Beiheft 17): 22.

22. The oddity here does not depend on the fact that reversibility occurs less frequently than non-reversibility. Rather, one should note that reversibility as it occurs in vision does not occur in any of the other sense modalities; it is thus a doubtful example to use as a paradigm for what is involved in all cases of perceiving. One should also note that it is extremely difficult to construct reversible figures. Unless one comes upon them by chance, one must in fact understand the general principles underlying visual organization, *and be able to negate them,* in order to construct such figures. Finally we may note that those optical illusions which have in the past been regarded as most important for epistemology have *not* been reversible figures. This is readily intelligible. Epistemologically important illusions are always, at the time, experienced as veridical; we later find that they conflict with other perceptual experiences which were also regarded as veridical. In the case of reversible figures, however, no comparable conflict is engendered: we simply see that the figure *is* reversible, that it can be seen in either of two ways, neither of which need be taken to be better justified than the other. If we are puzzled by such figures, we are only puzzled as to why they are in fact reversible. (For a similar point, cf. Israel Scheffler, "Vision and Revolution: A Postscript on Kuhn," *Philosophy of Science* 39 [1972]: 372.)

23. Similar situations obtain with respect to touch and to our other sense modalities. I can, for example, designate what I hold in my hand as being a solid, cylindrical object, or as being my pen; I can say that I hear a train or that I hear a train's whistle, etc. Both descriptions are in these cases (as in the photograph of a star) applicable at the same time, and there is not the involuntary alteration in them that is to be found in reversible figures.

24. Cf. N.R. Hanson, *Patterns of Discovery* (Cambridge: The University Press, 1958), ch. 1, and T.S. Kuhn, *The Structure of Scientific Revolutions*, 2d. enlarged edition (*International Encyclopedia of Unified Science*, vol. II, no. 2. [Chicago: University of Chicago Press, 1970]), pp. 85, 111, 126f.

25. Benjamin Lee Whorf, "Science and Linguistics," in *Language, Thought, and Reality*, ed. by J.B. Carroll (Cambridge: Technology Press of Massachusetts Institute of Technology, 1956), pp. 212–13.

It is perhaps worth noting that Whorf recognizes at least one possible exception to the view that it is language which structures experience. That exception is to be found in our experience of space. However, Whorf held that even in this case our *concepts* of space (Newtonian space, Euclidean space, etc.) are linked to other concepts which are language-dependent. (Cf. "Relation of Habitual Thought and Behavior to Language," in *Language, Thought, and Reality*, p. 158f.) Whether there are other aspects of experience not directly tied to linguistic structures remains an open question. My criticism of the Whorfian hypothesis suggests that there may be, but my argument will not presuppose that there are.

It is worth noting that Kuhn also accepts the assumption that the world is originally presented as being without structure, as being—in William James's phrase—"a bloomin', buzzin' confusion." (*Structure of Scientific Revolutions*, p. 113.)

26. "Languages and Logic," in *Language, Thought, and Reality*, pp. 240–41.

27. Not all who have adopted Kuhnian concepts have been equally restrained. It is perhaps worth noting that Kuhn acknowledges having received early stimulation from Whorf's theory, but mentions no special indebtedness to him (*Structure of Scientific Revolutions*, p. vi). In *The Essential Tension* (Chicago and London: University of Chicago Press, 1977) Whorf is mentioned, but noncommitally (p. 258).

28. *Structure of Scientific Revolutions*, pp. 202–3.

29. Kuhn rejects this phraseology, which he associates with "the traditional epistemological paradigm." Instead of referring to what occurs in a scientific revolution as providing a new *interpretation* of some of the same facts that had been included within the theories of the previous periods, he describes what happens as the opening up of a new world: a seeing of different things than had previously been seen. (Cf. *Structure of Scientific Revolutions*, pp. 120–23, 111, and 150.) Since, as Kuhn acknowledges (p. 150), he has not yet worked out the epistemological consequences of this position (which is formulated by him chiefly in metaphors), I shall continue to speak of facts and their interpretation. However, the argument which follows does not, I believe, rest on my use of this terminology.

The same rejection of any dichotomy between facts and their interpretation was stressed by N.R. Hanson in ch. 1 of *Patterns of Discovery*.

30. *Essential Tension*, p. 332.

31. *Structure of Scientific Revolutions*, p. 151. For Kuhn's comparable analysis, ibid., p. 203.

32. Cf. my "Note on T.S. Kuhn's *Structure of Scientific Revolutions*," *The Monist* 60 (1977): 442–52.

33. In fact, Kuhn acknowledged that no new and adequate epistemological

paradigm has as yet developed; therefore, he found that he was unable wholly to give up the traditional one. On the other hand, he also found himself unable to accept it (*Structure of Scientific Revolutions*, p. 126). As I shall later suggest, his dilemma was not inescapable.

34. *Structure of Scientific Revolutions*, p. 103.

35. *Essential Tension*, p. 290.

36. *Structure of Scientific Revolutions*, p. 201.

37. In this connection Kuhn says, "There is, I think, no theory-independent way to reconstruct phrases like 'really there'; the notion of a match between the ontology of a theory and its 'real' counterpart in nature now seems to me illusive in principle" (*Structure of Scientific Revolutions*, p. 206).

38. From "Objectivity, Value Judgment, and Theory Choice," *Essential Tension*, p. 332.

39. *Essential Tension*, pp. 322–25 and 330–31. In *Structure of Scientific Revolutions* (pp. 184–86), he also spoke of the criteria used by scientists as "values." It is of interest that he held that criteria such as accuracy "do much to provide a sense of community to natural scientists as a whole," and he considered such criteria as being "relatively, though not entirely, stable from one time to another and from one member to another in a particular group." (p. 185).

40. In fact, at the end of the same essay, he adds a parenthetical remark concerning the application of the five criteria to problems of theory-choice. He says, "Accuracy and fruitfulness are the most immediately applicable, perhaps followed by scope. Consistency and simplicity are far more problematic. (*Essential Tension*, p. 339.)

41. For example, *Structure of Scientific Revolutions*, pp. 153f. and 185.

42. *Structure of Scientific Revolutions*, p. 185; cf. *Essential Tension*, pp. 222f. and 331f.

43. *Essential Tension*, p. 331. For another instance in which he uses the locution of a fit between a theory and facts, *Structure of Scientific Revolutions*, p. 147.

44. *Essential Tension*, p. 289. As is well known, Kuhn wrestled time and again with the problem of whether or not there is progress in science. The interpretation of his views on this matter is not of primary importance for the present discussion. It is to be noted, however, that he rather consistently holds that the theories of successive periods become "vastly more powerful and precise" than those of their predecessors (*Essential Tension*, p. 30; also, cf. pp. 288–89). What he *rejects* is that such growth is continuous, and that it is incrementally cumulative, suffering no losses when one paradigm is given up for another. What he does *not* reject is that changes over time represent long-term gains—not stasis, mere alteration, nor retrogression.

45. *Essential Tension*, p. 322.

46. This is pointed out in my article on Kuhn cited in n 32 above.

47. This point has already been stressed by Quine in his "Two Dogmas of Empiricism," where he signalized it in the following striking fashion:

> Physical objects are . . . convenient intermediaries—not by definition in terms of experience, but simply as irreducible posits comparable, epistemologically,

to the gods of Homer. For my part I do, qua lay physicist, believe in physical objects and not in Homer's gods; and I consider it a scientific error to believe otherwise. But in point of epistemological footing the physical objects and the gods differ only in degree and not in kind. (*From a Logical Point of View* [Cambridge: Harvard University Press, 1953], p. 44.)

Kuhn acknowledges a debt to this essay (*Structure of Scientific Revolutions*, p. vi). For Quine's later statement of his position, which would appear to be less extreme, cf. *Word and Object* (Cambridge, Mass.: M.I.T. Press, 1960), ch. 1 (especially sections 5 and 6) and ch. 2 (especially sections 7 and 10).

On the Very Idea of a Conceptual Scheme

Mandelbaum uses the expression 'conceptual relativism' to designate the view that the evaluations of statements should be relative to the intellectual and conceptual background against which they are made. The relativism which Donald Davidson attacks in his "On the Very Idea of a Conceptual Scheme" is a particular version of this general position. This version adopts the Kantian distinction between what is given to the mind through sensation on the one hand and the concepts which the mind uses to organize this given on the other hand. Different people can use different sets of concepts (or different "conceptual schemes") to organize the given. Moreover, different conceptual schemes may well employ or contain different concepts of truth and of reality, so that what counts as true or real in one scheme may not count as true or real in another scheme. As Davidson puts it, "Reality itself is relative to a scheme"; and he might well have added that truth is relative to a scheme too. If reality is relative to a scheme, there might well be as many realities as there are schemes rather than one shared reality. Consequently, there is no possibility of selecting the single "correct" scheme by determining which scheme renders a shared reality correctly. This is the variety of conceptual relativism which Davidson criticizes.

Davidson attacks this type of relativism at its very foundation by arguing that the idea of a conceptual scheme is not intelligible. He tries to show that we could not determine that a conceptual scheme embodied in a particular language is a different scheme from that embodied in some other language. In arguing in this manner Davidson is presupposing that the criteria of identity and individuation of ϕ's is an essential part of a person's having the concept of a ϕ. If a person cannot determine whether what is before him is the same chair or two different chairs when he can see clearly, then he does not have any criteria of individuation for chairs. And if he has no criteria of individuation for chairs, then he does not know what a chair is; he does not have the concept of a chair. Similarly, if no criteria of individuation for conceptual schemes are available or usable, then the concept of a conceptual scheme itself is empty and unusable, and this variety of conceptual relativism collapses.

One apparent way of determining that conceptual schemes are different would be to take a neutral stance by divesting oneself of all conceptual schemes and then comparing schemes to one another. Davidson regards this procedure as impossible. Because conceptual schemes are embedded in langauges, to divest oneself of all conceptual schemes would require giving up the use of language. But language is necessary for thought. Hence, if one gave up the use of language, one could not engage in the kind of thinking required for comparison and differentiation of conceptual schemes.

How, then, could we ever determine that a conceptual scheme is different from our own? We might suspect that a group of people did have a conceptual scheme different from our own if we could not understand what they said—that is, if we could not translate their linguistic expressions into English expressions. This lack of translatability might well be due to their organizing their perceptions differently from the way in which we organize our perceptions, just as a difference in conceptual schemes would entail. Davidson points out that there is another possibility which can account for this situation: those people have beliefs quite different from our own. He uses the example of a person who says "Look at that handsome yawl!" as a ketch sails by. Is this person using the word 'yawl' to express a concept different from the concept which we use it to express? Or is he using this word to express our concept and simply has the false belief that a yawl is sailing by? Because a group of people might have false beliefs (that is, what we take to be false beliefs) rather than a different conceptual scheme, our difficulty in understanding what they say does not, by itself, justify us in taking them to have a different conceptual scheme from our own.

Kendall Walton puts this type of point in a somewhat different way. Walton points out that the reason why we do not understand these people might be that they are describing "kinds of facts which we are completely unaware of. Speakers of the language might simply have a form of sense-perception, a sixth sense, which we lack, and they might lack our senses. So the difference between their language and ours may reflect a difference of data rather than anything which could reasonably count as different ways of ordering or experiencing data."[1] Walton puts the conclusion in the form of a dilemma. If the language of the other group is translatable into English, then it cannot express a conceptual scheme radically different from our own, for, by using the resources of our own conceptual scheme, we can say and think everything which that group can say and think. If their language is not translatable into English, we cannot be justified in thinking that it expresses a different conceptual scheme, since it may express a quite different range of facts or beliefs instead. Moreover, if we cannot translate their language, we cannot have reason to believe that their language expresses the same facts as ours but in different ways; we would have no way of telling that the facts were the same as our facts so as to isolate the difference as one of conceptual scheme.

Richard Rorty characterizes this type of argument as "verificationist" because it asks what concrete situation would count as the presence of a conceptual scheme very different from our own. What situation, if it were to occur, would verify the presence of a different conceptual scheme? Davidson's claim is that there is no such situation and that consequently the idea of a conceptual scheme is meaningless. But, it can be retorted, all that his arguments show is that we have no criterion of the presence of a different conceptual scheme; different conceptual schemes may still exist even though we have no such criterion. The Davidsonian would reply to this that it is not enough simply to make this claim. We must also give some reason for believing that the claim is true. Rorty thinks that such a reason can be provided, so that the notion of a conceptual scheme different from our own turns out not to be an empty notion. He points out that since classical Greek times, new concepts have come into use. Moreover, there is now difficulty in knowing how to translate some Greek sentences. Let us extrapolate from our present situation to a civilization of the far future, a Galactic civilization. "It is rational to expect that the incommunicably and unintelligibly novel will occur, even though, ex hypothesi, we can neither write nor read a science-fiction story that describes Galactic civilization."[2] The differences between the classical Greeks and ourselves, extended to an extreme degree, amount to a difference in conceptual schemes.

Walton challenges Davidson's verification argument in a different way. Walton describes a society A which classifies birds differently from the way we do. A's species of birds are natural classes for them; the members of society A recognize birds as belonging to these species just by looking at them, whereas we can categorize birds as they do only by using rules which are arbitrary to us. Walton argues that A's classifications and ours are not "mere reflections of the facts, nor transparent patterns superimposed on them for convenience of communication; they are comparable neither to the outlines of continents on a map, nor to the arbitrary lines of latitude and longitude. They are better construed as forms or concepts through or by means of which we and A experience the facts. . . . They embody two alternative ways of ordering the data of experience."[3]

The situations imagined by both Rorty and Walton purport to provide intelligible bases on which it can be justifiably believed that different conceptual schemes can exist. If either or both have succeeded in this, then the notion of a conceptual scheme itself is not a wholly empty notion, and conceptual relativism had been provided with some defense against attacks on this flank.

NOTES

1. Kendall Walton, "Linguistic Relativity," in G. Pearce and P. Maynard, eds., *Conceptual Change* (Dordrecht, Holland: D. Reidel, 1973), p. 4.
2. Richard Rorty, "The World Well Lost," *Journal of Philosophy* 69 (1972): 656. Although Rorty finds this extrapolation meaningful and reasonable, he does not himself simply reject Davidson's position. Instead he finds Davidson's view and the view supported by the extrapolation to be two sides of a Kantian-style antinomy.
3. Walton, "Linguistic Relativity," p. 17.

On the Very Idea of a Conceptual Scheme*

Donald Davidson

Philosophers of many persuasions are prone to talk of conceptual schemes. Conceptual schemes, we are told, are ways of organizing experience; they are systems of categories that give form to the data of sensation; they are points of view from which individuals, cultures, or periods survey the passing scene. There may be no translating from one scheme to another, in which case the beliefs, desires, hopes and bits of knowledge that characterize one person have no true counterparts for the subscriber to another scheme. Reality itself is relative to a scheme: what counts as real in one system may not in another.

Even those thinkers who are certian there is only one conceptual scheme are in the sway of the scheme concept; even monotheists have religion. And when someone sets out to describe "our conceptual scheme," his homey task assumes, if we take him literally, that there might be rival systems.

Conceptual relativism is a heady and exotic doctrine, or would be if we could make good sense of it. The trouble is, as so often in philosophy, it is hard to improve intelligibility while retaining the excitement. At any rate that is what I shall argue.

We are encouraged to imagine we understand massive conceptual change or profound contrasts by legitimate examples of a familiar sort. Sometimes an idea, like that of simultaneity as defined in relativity theory, is so important that with its addition a whole department of science takes on a new look. Sometimes revisions in the list of sentences held true in a

*Reprinted with permission of the author and publisher from *Proceedings of the American Philosophical Association* 47 (1973–74): 5–20.

discipline are so central that we may feel that the terms involved have changed their meanings. Languages that have evolved in distant times or places may differ extensively in their resources for dealing with one or another range of phenomena. What comes easily in one language may come hard in another, and this difference may echo significant dissimilarities in style and value.

But examples like these, impressive as they occasionally are, are not so extreme but that the changes and the contrasts can be explained and described using the equipment of a single language. Whorf, wanting to demonstrate that Hopi incorporates a metaphysics so alien to ours that Hopi and English cannot, as he puts it, "be calibrated," uses English to convey the contents of sample Hopi sentences. Kuhn is brilliant at saying what things were like before the revolution using—what else?—our postrevolutionary idiom. Quine gives us a feel for the "pre-individuative phase in the evolution of our conceptual scheme," while Bergson tells us where we can go to get a view of a mountain undistorted by one or another provincial perspective.

The dominant metaphor of conceptual relativism, that of differing points of view, seems to betray an underlying paradox. Different points of view make sense, but only if there is a common coordinate system on which to plot them; yet the existence of a common system belies the claim of dramatic incomparability. What we need, it seems to me, is some idea of the considerations that set the limits to conceptual contrast. There are extreme suppositions that founder on paradox or contradiction; there are modest examples we have no trouble understanding. What determines where we cross from the merely strange or novel to the absurd?

We may accept the doctrine that associates having a language with having a conceptual scheme. The relation may be supposed to be this: if conceptual schemes differ, so do languages. But speakers of different languages may share a conceptual scheme provided there is a way of translating one language into the other. Studying the criteria of translation is therefore a way of focussing on criteria of identity for conceptual schemes. If conceptual schemes aren't associated with languages in this way, the original problem is needlessly doubled, for then we would have to imagine the mind, with its ordinary categories, operating with a language with *its* organizing structure. Under the circumstances we would certainly want to ask who is to be master.

Alternatively, there is the idea that *any* language distorts reality, which implies that it is only wordlessly if at all that the mind comes to grips with things as they really are. This is to conceive language as an inert (though necessarily distorting) medium independent of the human agencies that employ it: a view of language that surely cannot be maintained. Yet if the mind can grapple without distortion with the real, the mind itself must be without categories and concepts. This featureless self is familiar from theories in quite different parts of the philosophical landscape. There are, for example, theories that make freedom consist in decisions taken apart from all desires, habits and dispositions of the agent; and theories of knowledge that suggest that the mind can observe the totality of its own perceptions and ideas. In each case, the mind is divorced from the traits that constitute it; a familiar enough conclusion to certain lines of reasoning, as I said, but one that should always persuade us to reject the premisses.

We may identify conceptual schemes with languages, then, or better, allowing for the possibility that more than one language may express the same scheme, sets of intertranslatable languages. Languages we will not think of as separable from souls; speaking a language is not a trait a man can lose while retaining the power of thought. So there is no chance that someone can take up a vantage point for comparing conceptual schemes by temporarily shedding his own. Can we then say that two people have different conceptual schemes if they speak languages that fail of inter-translatability?

In what follows I consider two kinds of case that might be expected to arise: complete, and partial, failures of translatability. There would be complete failure if no significant range of sentences in one language could be translated into the other; there would be partial failure if some range could be translated and some range could not (I shall neglect possible asymmetries.) My strategy will be to argue that we cannot make sense of total failure and then to examine more briefly cases of partial failure.

First, then, the purported cases of complete failure. It is tempting to take a very short line indeed: nothing, it may be said, could count as evidence that some form of activity could not be interpreted in our language that was not at the same time evidence that that form of activity was not speech behavior. If this were right, we probably ought to hold that a form of activity that cannot be interpreted as language in our language is not speech behavior. Putting matters this way is unsatisfactory, however, for it comes to little more than making translatability into a familiar tongue a criterion of languagehood. As fiat, the thesis lacks the appeal of self-evidence; if it is a truth, as I think it is, it should emerge as the conclusion of an argument.

The credibility of the position is improved by reflection on the close relations between language and the attribution of attitudes such as belief, desire and intention. On the one hand, it is clear that speech requires a multitude of finely discriminated intentions and beliefs. A person who asserts that perseverance keeps honor bright must, for example, represent himself as believing that perseverance keeps honor bright, and he must intend to represent himself as believing it. On the other hand, it seems unlikely that we can intelligibly attribute attitudes as complex as these to a speaker unless we can translate his words into ours. There can be no doubt that the relation between being able to translate someone's language and being able to describe his attitudes is very close. Still, until we can say more about *what* this relation is, the case against untranslatable languages remains obscure.

It is sometimes thought that translatability into a familiar language, say English, cannot be a criterion of languagehood on the grounds that the relation of translatability is not transitive. The idea is that some language, say Saturnian, may be translatable into English, and some further language, like Plutonian, may be translatable into Saturnian, while Plutonian is not translatable into English. Enough translatable differences may add up to an untranslatable one. By imagining a sequence of languages, each close enough to the one before to be acceptably translated into it, we can imagine a language so different from English as to resist totally translation into it. Corresponding to this distant language would be a system of concepts altogether alien to us.

This exercise does not, I think, introduce any new element into the discussion. For we should have to ask how we recognized that what the Saturnian was doing was *translating* Plutonian (or anything else). The Saturnian speaker might tell us that that was what he was doing or rather, we might for a moment assume that that was what he was telling us. But then it would occur to us to wonder whether our translations of Saturnian were correct.

According to Kuhn, scientists operating in different scientific traditions (within different "paradigms") "live in different worlds." Strawson's *The Bounds of Sense* begins with the remark that "It is possible to imagine kinds of worlds very different from the world as we know it."[1] Since there is at most one world, these pluralities are metaphorical or merely imagined. The metaphors are, however, not at all the same. Strawson invites us to imagine possible non-actual worlds, worlds that might be described, using our present language, by redistributing truth values over sentences in various systematic ways. The clarity of the contrasts between worlds in this case depends on supposing our scheme of concepts, our descriptive resources, to remain fixed. Kuhn, on the other hand, wants us to think of different observers of the same world who come to it with incommensurable systems of concepts. Strawson's many imagined worlds are seen (or heard)—anyway described—from the same point of view; Kuhn's one world is seen from different points of view. It is the second metaphor we want to work on.

The first metaphor requires a distinction within language of concept and content: using a fixed system of concepts (words with fixed meanings) we describe alternative universes. Some sentences will be true simply because of the concepts or meanings involved, others because of the way of the world. In describing possible worlds, we play with sentences of the second kind only.

The second metaphor suggests instead a dualism of quite a different sort, a dualism of total scheme (or language) and uninterpreted content. Adherence to the second dualism, while not inconsistent with adherence to the first, may be encouraged by attacks on the first. Here is how it may work.

To give up the analytic-synthetic distinction as basic to the understanding of language is to give up the idea that we can clearly distinguish between theory and language. Meaning, as we might loosely use the word, is contaminated by theory, by what is held to be true. Feyerabend puts it this way:

> Our argument against meaning invariance is simple and clear. It proceeds from the fact that usually some of the principles involved in the determinations of the meanings of older theories or points of view are inconsistent with the new . . . theories. It points out that it is natural to resolve this contradiction by eliminating the troublesome . . . older principles, and to replace them by principles, or theorems, of a new . . . theory. And it concludes by showing that such a procedure will also lead to the elimination of the old meanings.[2]

We may now seem to have a formula for generating distinct conceptual schemes. We get a new out of an old scheme when the speakers of a language come to accept as true an important range of sentences they previously took to be false (and, of course, vice versa). We must not describe this change simply as a matter of their coming to view old falsehoods as truths, for a truth is a proposition, and what they come to accept, in accepting a sentence as true, is not the same thing that they rejected when formerly they held the sentence to be false. A change has come over the meaning of the sentence because it now belongs to a new language.

This picture of how new (perhaps better) schemes result from new and better science is very much the picture philosophers of science, like Putnam and Feyerabend, and historians of science, like Kuhn, have painted for us. A related idea emerges in the suggestion of some other philosophers, that we could improve our conceptual lot if we were to tune our language to an improved science. Thus both Quine and Smart, in somewhat different ways, regretfully admit that our present ways of talking make a serious science of behavior impossible. (Wittgenstein and Ryle have said similar things without regret.) The cure, Quine and Smart think, is to change how we talk. Smart advocates (and predicts) the change in order to put on the scientifically straight path of materialism; Quine is more concerned to clear the way for a purely extensional language. (Perhaps I should add that I think our *present* scheme and language are best understood as extensional and materialist.)

If we were to follow this advice, I do not myself think science or understanding would be advanced, though possibly morals would. But the present question is only whether, if such changes were to take place, we should be justified in calling them alterations in the basic conceptual apparatus. The difficulty in so calling them is easy to appreciate. Suppose that in my office of Minister of Scientific Language I want the new man to stop using words that refer, say, to emotions, feelings, thoughts and intentions, and to talk instead of the physiological states and happenings that are assumed to be more or less identical with the mental riff and raff. How do I tell whether my advice has been heeded if the new man speaks a new language? For all I know, the shiny new phrases, though stolen from the old language in which they refer to physiological stirrings, may in his mouth play the role of the messy old mental concepts.

The key phrase is: for all I know. What is clear is that retention of some or all of the old vocabulary in itself provides no basis for judging the new scheme to be the same as, or different from, the old. So what sounded at first like a thrilling discovery—that truth is relative to a conceptual scheme—has not so far been shown to be anything more than the pedestrian and familiar fact that the truth of a sentence is relative to (among other things) the language to which it belongs. Instead of living in different worlds, Kuhn's scientists may, like those who need Webster's dictionary, be only words apart.

Giving up the analytic-synthetic distinction has not proven a help in making sense of conceptual relativism. The analytic-synthetic distinction is however explained in terms of something that may serve to buttress conceptual relativism, namely the idea of empirical content. The dualism of the synthetic and the analytic is a dualism of sentences some of which are true (or false) both because of what they mean and because of their empirical content, having no empirical content. If we give up the dualism, we abandon the conception of meaning that goes with it, but we do not have to abandon the idea of empirical content: we can hold, if we want, that *all* sentences have empirical content. Empirical content is in turn explained by reference to the facts, the world, experience, sensation, the totality of sensory stimuli, or something similar. Meanings gave us a way to talk about categories, the organizing structure of language, and so on; but it is possible, as we have seen, to give up meanings and analyticity while retaining the idea of language as embodying a conceptual scheme. Thus in place of the dualism of the analytic-synthetic we get the dualism of conceptual scheme and empirical content. The new dualism is the foundation of an empiricism shorn of the untenable dogmas of the analytic-synthetic distinction and reductionism—shorn, that is, of the unworkable idea that we can uniquely allocate empirical content sentence by sentence.

I want to urge that this second dualism of scheme and content, of organizing system and something waiting to be organized, cannot be made intelligible and defensible. It is itself a dogma of empiricism, the third dogma. The third, and perhaps the last, for if we give it up it is not clear that there is anything distinctive left to call empiricism.

The scheme-content dualism has been formulated in many ways. Here are some examples. The first comes from Whorf, elaborating on a theme of Sapir's. Whorf says that:

> ... language produces an organization of experience. We are inclined
> to think of language as a technique of expression, and not to realize
> that language first of all is a classification and arrangement of the
> stream of sensory experience which results in a certain world-
> order... In other words, language does in a cruder but also in a
> broader and more versatile way the same thing that science does...
> We are thus introduced to a new principle of relativity, which holds
> that all observers are not led by the same physical evidence to the same
> picture of the universe, unless their linguistic backgrounds are similar,
> or can in some way be calibrated.[3]

Here we have all the required elements: language as the organizing force, not to be distinguished clearly from science; what is organized, referred to variously as "experience," "the stream of sensory experience," and "physical evidence"; and finally, the failure of intertranslatability ("calibration"). The failure of intertranslatability is a necessary condition for difference of conceptual schemes; the common relation to experience or the evidence is what is supposed to help us make sense of the claim that it is languages or schemes that are under consideration when translation fails. It is essential to this idea that there be something neutral and common that lies outside all schemes. This common something cannot, of course, be the *subject matter* of contrasting languages, or translation would be possible. Thus Kuhn has recently written:

Philosophers have now abandoned hope of finding a pure sense-datum language ... but many of them continue to assume that theories can be compared by recourse to a basic vocabulary consisting entirely of words which are attached to nature in ways that are unproblematic and, to the extent necessary, independent of theory ... Feyerabend and I have argued at length that no such vocabulary is available. In the transition from one theory to the next words change their meanings or conditions of applicability in subtle ways. Though most of the same signs are used before and after a revolution—e.g. force, mass, element, compound, cell—the ways in which some of them attach to nature has somehow changed. Successive theories are thus, we say, incommensurable.[4]

"Incommensurable" is, of course, Kuhn and Feyerabend's word for "not intertranslatable." The neutral content waiting to be organized is supplied by nature.

Feyerabend himself suggests that we may compare contrasting schemes by "choosing a point of view outside the system or the language." He hopes we can do this because "there is still human experience as an actually existing process"[5] independent of all schemes.

The same, or similar, thoughts are expressed by Quine in many passages: "The totality of our so-called knowledge or beliefs ... is a man-made fabric which impinges on experience only along the edges ... ",[6] "... total science is like a field of force whose boundary conditions are experience";[7] "As an empiricist I ... think of the conceptual scheme of science as a tool ... for predicting future experience in the light of past experience."[8] And again:

We persist in breaking reality down somehow into a multiplicity of identifiable and discriminable objects ... We talk so inveterately of objects that to say we do so seems almost to say nothing at all; for how else is there to talk? It is hard to say how else there is to talk, not because our objectifying pattern is an invariably trait of human nature, but because we are bound to adapt any alien pattern to our own in the very process of understanding or translating the alien sentences.[9]

The test of difference remains failure or difficulty of translation: "... to speak of that remote medium as radically different form ours is to say no more than that the translations do not come smoothly."[10] Yet the roughness may be so great that the alien has an "as yet unimagined pattern beyond individuation."[11]

The idea is then that something is a language, and associated with a conceptual scheme, whether we can translate it or not, if it stands in a certain relation (predicting, organizing, facing or fitting) to experience (nature, reality, sensory promptings). The problem is to say what the relation is, and to be clearer about the entities related.

The images and metaphors fall into two main groups: conceptual schemes (languages) either *organize* something, or they *fit* it (as in "he warps his scientific heritage to fit his ... sensory promptings"[12]). The first group contains also *systematize, divide up* (the stream of experience); further examples of the second group are *predict, account for, face* (the tribunal of experience). As for the entities that get organized, or which the scheme must fit, I think again we may detect two main ideas: either it is reality (the universe, the world, nature), or it is experience (the passing show, surface irritations, sensory promptings, sense data, the given).

We cannot attach a clear meaning to the notion of organizing a single object (the world, nature etc.) unless that object is understood to contain or consist in other objects. Someone who sets out to organize a closet arranges the things in it. If you are told not to organize the shoes and shirts, but the closet itself, you would be bewildered. How would you organize the Pacific Ocean? Straighten out its shores, perhaps, or relocate its islands, or destroy its fish.

A language may contain simple predicates whose extensions are matched by no simple predicates, or even by any predicates at all, in some other language. What enables us to make this point in particular cases is an ontology common to the two languages, with concepts that individuate the same objects. We can be clear about breakdowns in translation when they are local enough, for a background of generally successful translation provides what is needed to make the failures intelligible. But we were after larger game: we wanted to make sense of there being a language we could not translate at all. Or, to put the point differently, we were looking for a criterion of languagehood that did not depend on, or entail, translatability into a familiar idiom. I suggest that the image of organizing the closet of nature will not supply such a criterion.

How about the other kind of object, experience? Can we think of a language organizing *it?* Much the same difficulties recur. The notion of organization applies only to pluralities. But whatever plurality we take experience to consist in—events like losing a button or stubbing a toe, having a sensation of warmth or hearing a oboe—we will have to individuate according to familiar principles. A language that organizes *such* entities must be a language very like our own.

Experience (and its classmates like surface irritations, sensations and sense data) also makes another and more obvious trouble for the organizing idea. For how could something count as a language that organized *only* experiences, sensations, surface irritations or sense data? Surely knives and forks, railroads and mountains, cabbages and kingdoms also need organizing.

This last remark will no doubt sound inappropriate as a response to the claim that a conceptual scheme is a way of coping with sensory experience; and I agree that it is. But what was under consideration was the idea of *organizing* experience, not the idea of *coping with* (or fitting or facing) experience. The reply was apropos of the former, not the latter, concept. So now let's see whether we can do better with the second idea.

When we turn from talk of organization to talk of fitting we turn our attention from the referential apparatus of language—predicates, quantifiers variables and singular terms—to whole sentences. It is sentences that predict (or are used to predict), sentences that cope or deal with things, that fit our sensory promptings, that can be compared or confronted with the evidence. It is sentences also that face the tribunal of experience, though of course they must face it together.

The proposal is not that experiences, sense data, surface irritations or sensory promptings are the sole subject matter of language. There is, it is true, the theory that talk about brick houses on Elm Street is ultimately to be construed as being about sense data or perceptions, but such reductionistic views are only extreme, and implausible, versions of the general position we are considering. The general position is that sensory experience provides all the *evidence* for the acceptance of sentences (where sentences may include whole theories). A sentence or theory fits our sensory promptings, successfully faces the tribunal of experience, predicts future experience, or copes with the pattern of our surface irritations, provided it is borne out by the evidence.

In the common course of affairs, a theory may be borne out by the available evidence and yet be false. But what is in view here is not just actually available evidence; it is the totality of possible sensory evidence past, present and future. We do not need to pause to contemplate what this might mean. The point is that for a theory to fit or face up to the totality of possible sensory evidence is for that theory to be true. If a theory quantifies over physical objects, numbers or sets, what it says about these entities is true provided the theory as a whole fits the sensory evidence. One can see how, from this point of view, such entities might be called posits. It is reasonable to call something a posit if it can be contrasted with something that is not. Here the something that is not is sensory experience—at least that is the idea.

The trouble is that the notion of fitting the totality of experience, like the notions of fitting the facts, or being true to the facts, adds nothing intelligible to the simple concept of being true. To speak of sensory experience rather than the evidence, or just the facts, expresses a view about the source or nature of evidence, but it does not add a new entity to the universe against which to test conceptual schemes. The totality of sensory evidence is what we want provided it is all the evidence there is; and all the evidence there is is just what it takes to make our sentences or theories true. Nothing, however, no *thing,* makes sentences and theories true: not experience, not surface irritations, not the world, can make a sentence true. *That* experience takes a certain course, that our skin is warmed or punctured, that the universe is finite, these facts, if we like to talk that way, make sentences and theories true. But this point is put better without mention of facts. The sentence "My skin is warm" is true if and only if my skin is warm. Here there is no reference to a fact, a world, and experience, or a piece of evidence.[13]

Our attempt to characterize languages or conceptual schemes in terms of the notion of fitting some entity has come down, then, to the simple thought that something is an acceptable conceptual scheme or theory if it is true. Perhaps we better say *largely* true in order to allow sharers of a scheme to differ on details. And the criterion of a conceptual scheme different from our own now becomes: largely true but not translatable. The question whether this is a useful criterion is just the question how well we understand the notion of truth, as applied to language, independent of the notion of translation. The answer is, I think, that we do not understand it independently at all.

We recognize sentences like "'Snow is white' is true if and only if snow is white" to be trivially true. Yet the totality of such English sentences uniquely determines the extension of the concept of truth for English. Tarski generalized this observation and made it a test of theories of truth: according to Tarski's Convention T, a satisfactory theory of truth for a language L must entail, for every sentence s of L, a theorem of the form "s is true if and only if p" where "s" is replaced by a description of s and "p" by s itself if L is English, and by a translation of s into English if L is not English.[14] This isn't, of course, a definition of truth, and it doesn't hint that there is a single definition or theory that applies to languages generally. Nevertheless, Convention T suggests, though it cannot state, an important feature common to all the specialized concepts of truth. It succeeds in doing this by making essential use of the notion of translation into a language we know. Since Convention T embodies our best intuition as to how the concept of truth is used, there does not seem to be much hope for a test that a conceptual scheme is radically different from ours if that test depends on the assumption that we can divorce the notion of truth from that of translation.

Neither a fixed stock of meanings, nor a theory-neutral reality, can provide, then, a ground for comparison of conceptual schemes. It would be a mistake to look further for such a ground if by that we mean something conceived as common to incommensurable schemes. In abandoning this search, we abandon the attempt to make sense of the metaphor of a single space within which each scheme has a position and provides a point of view.

I turn now to the more modest approach: the idea of partial rather than total failure of translation. This introduces the possibility of making changes and contrasts in conceptual schemes intelligible by reference to the common part. What we need is a theory of translation or interpretation that makes no assumptions about shared meanings, concepts or beliefs.

The interdependence of belief and meaning springs from the interdependence of two aspects of the interpretation of speech behavior: the attribution of beliefs and the interpretation of sentences. We remarked before that we can afford to associate conceptual schemes with languages because of these dependencies. Now we can put the point in a somewhat sharper way. Allow that a man's speech cannot be interpreted without knowing a good deal about what he believes (and intends and wants), and that fine distinctions between beliefs are impossible without understood speech; how then are we to interpret speech or intelligibly to attribute beliefs and other attitudes? Clearly we must have a theory that simultaneously accounts for attitudes and interprets speech—a theory that rests on evidence which assumes neither.

I suggest, following Quine, that we may without circularity or unwarranted assumptions accept certain very general attitudes towards sentences as the basic evidence for a theory of radical interpretation. For the sake of the present discussion at least we may depend on the attitude of accepting as true, directed at sentences, as the crucial notion. (A more full-blooded theory would look to other attitudes towards sentences as well, such as wishing true, wondering whether true, intending to make true, and so on). Attitudes are indeed involved here, but the fact that the main issue is not begged can be seen from this: if we merely know that someone holds a certain sentence to be true, we know neither what he means by the sentence nor what belief his holding it true represents. His holding the sentence true is thus the vector of two forces: the problem of interpretation is to abstract from the evidence a workable theory of meaning and an acceptable theory of belief.

The way this problem is solved is best appreciated from undramatic examples. If you see a ketch sailing by and your companion says, "Look at the handsome yawl," you may be faced with a problem of interpretation. One natural possibility is that your friend has mistaken a ketch for a yawl, and has formed a false belief. But if his vision is good and his line of sight favorable it is even more plausible that he does not use the word "yawl" quite as you do, and has made no mistake at all about the position of the jigger on the passing yacht. We do this sort of off the cuff interpretation all the time, deciding in favor of reinterpretation of words in order to preserve a reasonable theory of belief. As philosophers we are peculiarly tolerant of systematic malapropism, and practised at interpreting the result. The process is that of constructing a viable theory of belief and meaning from sentences held true.

Such examples emphasize the interpretation of anomalous details against a background of common beliefs and a going method of translation. But the principles involved must be the same in less trivial cases. What matters is this: if all we know is what sentences a speaker holds true, and we cannot assume that his language is our own, then we cannot take even a first step towards interpretation without knowing or assuming a great deal about the speaker's beliefs. Since knowledge of beliefs comes only with the ability to interpret words, the only possibility at the start is to assume general agreement on beliefs. We get a first approximation to a finished theory by assigning to sentences of a speaker conditions of truth that actually obtain (in our own opinion) just when the speaker holds those sentences true. The guiding policy is to do this as far as possible, subject to considerations of simplicity, hunches about the effects of social conditioning, and of course our common sense, or scientific, knowledge of explicable error.

This method is not designed to eliminate disagreement, nor can it: its purpose is to make meaningful disagreement possible, and this depends entirely on a foundation—*some* foundation—in agreement. The agreement may take the form of wide spread sharing of sentences held true by speakers of "the same language," or agreement in the large mediated by a theory of truth contrived by an interpreter for speakers of another language.

Since charity is not an option, but a condition of having a workable theory, it is meaningless to suggest that we might fall into massive error by endorsing it. Until we have successfully established a systematic correlation of sentences held true with sentences held true, there are no mistakes to make. Charity is forced on us;—whether we like it or not, if we want to understand others, we must count them right in most matters. If we can produce a theory that reconciles charity and the formal conditions for a theory, we have done all that could be done to ensure communication. Nothing more is possible, and nothing more is needed.

We make maximum sense of the words and thoughts of others when we interpret in a way that optimizes agreement (this includes room, as we said, for explicable error, i.e. differences of opinion). Where does this leave the case for conceptual relativism? The answer is, I think, that we must say much the same thing about differences in conceptual scheme as we say about differences in belief: we improve the clarity and bit of declarations of difference, whether of scheme or opinion, by enlarging the basis of shared (translatable) language or of shared opinion. Indeed, no clear line between the cases can be made out. If we choose to translate some alien sentence rejected by its speakers by a sentence to which we are strongly attached on a community basis, we may be tempted to call this a difference in schemes; if we decide to accommodate the evidence in other ways, it may be more natural to speak of a difference of opinion. But when others think differently from us, no general principle, or appeal to evidence, can force us to decide that the difference lies in our beliefs rather than in our concepts.

We must conclude, I think, that the attempt to give a solid meaning to the idea of conceptual relativism, and hence to the idea of a conceptual scheme, fares no better when based on partial failure of translation than when based on total failure. Given the underlying methodology of interpretation, we could not be in a position to judge that others had concepts or beliefs radically different from our own.

It would be wrong to summarize by saying we have shown how communication is possible between people who have different schemes, a way that works without need of what there cannot be, namely a neutral ground, or a common coordinate system. For we have found no intelligible basis on which it can be said that schemes are different. It would be equally wrong to announce the glorious news that all mankind—all speakers of language, at least—share a common scheme and ontology. For if we cannot intelligibly say that schemes are different, neither can we intelligibly say that they are one.

In giving up dependence on the concept of an uninterpreted reality, something outside all schemes and science, we do not relinquish the notion of objective truth—quite the contrary. Given the dogma of a dualism of scheme and reality, we get conceptual relativity, and truth relative to a scheme. Without the dogma, this kind of relativity goes by the board. Of course truth of sentences remains relative to language, but that is as objective as can be. In giving up the dualism of scheme and world, we do not give up the world, but reestablish unmediated touch with the familiar objects whose antics make our sentences and opinions true or false.

NOTES

1. Peter Strawson, *The Bounds of Sense* (London, 1966), p. 15.

2. Paul Feyerabend, "Explanation, Reduction, and Empiricism," in *Scientific Explanation, Space, and Time: Minnesota Studies in the Philosophy of Science*, vol. 3 (Minneapolis, 1962), p. 82.

3. Benjamin Lee Whorf, *Language, Thought and Reality: Selected Writings of Benjamin Lee Whorf*, ed. J.B. Carroll (New York, 1956), p. 55.

4. Thomas Kuhn, "Reflection on my Critics," in *Criticism and the Growth of Knowledge*, eds. I. Lakatos and A. Musgrave (Cambridge, 1970), pp. 266, 267.

5. Paul Feyerabend, "Problems of Empiricism," in *Beyond the Edge of Certainty*, ed. R.G. Colodny (Englewood Cliffs, New Jersey, 1965), p. 214.

6. W.V.O. Quine, "Two Dogmas of Empiricism," reprinted in *From a Logical Point of View*, 2nd edition (Cambridge, Mass., 1961), p. 42.

7. *Ibid.*

8. *Ibid.*, p. 44.

9. W.V.O. Quine, "Speaking of Objects," reprinted in *Ontological Relativity and Other Essays* (New York, 1969), p. 1.

10. *Ibid.*, p. 25.

11. *Ibid.*, p. 24.

12. "Two Dogmas of Empiricism," p. 46.

13. These remarks are defended in my "True to the Facts," *The Journal of Philosophy* 66 (1969): 748–64.

14. Alfred Tarski, "The Concept of Truth in Formalized Languages," in *Logic, Semantics, Metamathematics* (Oxford, 1956).

True For

We have already seen several of the ways in which that form of cognitive relativism known as "conceptual relativism" can be attacked. Mandelbaum regards it as self-refuting, while Davidson holds that it depends essentially on the allegedly empty notion of conceptual scheme.

A third type of attack can be levelled against a notion of truth to which conceptual relativists are allegedly committed. Relativists sometimes say that a certain statement may be true *for* Jones and at the same time false *for* Smith. This notion of truth as "truth-for" is called "relative truth" and is usually distinguished from "absolute truth." Ordinarily, when we regard some statement as true, we do not add any qualifiers but instead think of the statement as true for everyone. Of course, even the notion of relative truth, or "true for," can allow a statement to be true for everyone: if a statement is true for Jones, true for Smith, and so on until everyone is included, then the statement is true for everyone. But when the relativist says that a statement is true for everyone, he means that the statement is true *because* of some personal characteristic of the persons involved— background, conceptual scheme used by each person, etc.—while the absolutist is saying that the statement is true for everyone *regardless* of their personal characteristics.

What is meant by saying that a statement is true *for* Jones? The charge against the conceptual relativist is that he can give no intelligible account of this notion of relative truth. Chris Swoyer believes that in whatever manner the relativist explains the notion of relative truth, that notion must resemble our ordinary, absolutist, notion of truth in order to be philosophically interesting. Relativists certainly invite this attitude by using the word 'true' in the first place, suggesting that they want relative truth to be a variety of truth. What are some of the features of truth in general which relative truth must have in order to be a variety of truth? It is reasonable to suggest that any concept of truth must allow the possibility (1) that there are now true propositions which no one now believes and (2) that some propositions which all or some people believe are in fact false. However, this way of phrasing these conditions is misleading because it implies, by using the word 'true' without qualification, that relative truth and other forms of truth must meet conditions stated in terms of absolute truth. So we must reformulate the conditions as follows: (1′) that there are now propositions which are true-for-X but which X does not now believe and (2′) that some propositions which X believes are in fact false-for-X. Conditions like these are intended to insure that there is a large gap between belief and truth of any kind. We think that this gap exists between belief and absolute truth—which is to say that a statement can be believed and yet not be true in the absolute sense. Such a gap should exist in the case of relative truth too. For if all that the relativists mean by saying that statement S is true for Jones is that Jones believes S, they have chosen a very misleading and needlessly circuitous way of saying that Jones believes S. Yet the difficulty is that, as Swoyer points out, in the first extended discussion in philosophical literature of the notion of relative truth, Plato claims that the relativist (specifically Protagoras) collapses the gap between belief and truth by taking belief to be a sufficient condition of relative truth. Swoyer insists that we must break with this hallowed philosophical tradition; otherwise, to talk of relative truth is only to talk about belief in an indirect way.

Fortunately the advent of conceptual relativism, unknown in Plato's time, allows this clean break to be made with the Platonic tradition. Different conceptual schemes may contain and employ different concepts and criteria of truth, and there is no scheme-independent way of determining which is the "correct" concept or "correct" set of criteria. Consequently, when we say that a statement is true, we must somehow indicate which concept or criteria we are employing. We can do this by saying that the statement is "true for Jones" where what we mean by this is that the statement is true according to the concept or criteria embedded in the conceptual scheme or framework employed by Jones (rather than that the statement is believed by Jones).

Swoyer distinguishes between two senses of the notion of relative truth as it pertains to conceptual relativism: (1) the strong sense—that in which a proposition can be true relative to one conceptual framework and false relative to another; (2) the weak sense—that in which a proposition can be true in one conceptual framework and inexpressible (hence neither true nor false) in another. He then raises a serious objection to truth's being relative in the strong sense: if the two conceptual frameworks are indeed different, no translation between them may be possible; hence a statement S which is true in one framework may not even be expressible in the other framework;

in this case S cannot be true in one framework and false in the other. But now suppose that such a translation were possible. Then the statement "S is true in framework F_1 and false in framework F_2" is itself either absolutely true or relatively true. If it is absolutely true, the game is up because the notion of relative truth becomes parasitic upon the notion of absolute truth; if it is relatively true, then we are using the notion of relative truth to explain itself, resulting in no enlightenment.

Strikingly, Swoyer does not regard this line of objection as a blow to conceptual relativism itself. Instead, he sees it as discrediting a theory of truth which conceptual relativism can slough off with no loss to itself. Relative truth in the weak sense survives, so far as Swoyer's objection is concerned. And it still makes sense to talk about alternative conceptual frameworks and about the difficulty of determining which framework renders the truth (in an absolute sense of 'truth'), even if no claims can be made about relative truth. Perhaps the most important point to emerge from Swoyer's discussion is that strong doctrines of relative truth are harmlessly detachable from conceptual relativism.

Other forms of cognitive relativism may have even less need of a strong doctrine of relative truth. In the next paper in this volume Gerald Doppelt gives an interpretation of Thomas Kuhn's philosophy of science which illustrates this point.

True For

Chris Swoyer

Truth is the Achilles' heel of relativism. At least since Plato's attack on the Protagorean doctrine of *homo mensura,* truth has been a focal point in criticisms of relativism. Yet relativism involves more than just truth; such seemingly diverse topics as conceptual change and incommensurability in the philosophy of science, ontological relativity, and the problem of understanding alien cultures or distant historical epochs all lead back to a concern with relativistic motifs. Such a list indicates relativism's importance but tells us little about what the doctrine involves. Many, indeed, have thought that it involves little more than paradox, and some have even found it unintelligible. Thus Donald Davidson tells us that "relativism is a heady and exotic doctrine, or would be if we could make good sense of it."[1] Whether standard treatments have made good sense of the doctrine is a question well calculated to inspire debate, but, in any case, I believe that relativism deserves a more sober and detailed hearing than it has received at the hands of many.

Discussions of relativism are often vague and impressionistic. This is so in part because many characterizations of relativism are to be found in the writings of opponents of the doctrine who sketch the view perfunctorily in order to have a target for criticism. Such writers have had the day largely because the label 'relativistic' is widely regarded as pejorative, and few philosophers have been willing to mount an explicit defense of relativism. Consequently, although various relativistic motifs are easily found in recent literature, the authors in whose work they occur often spend much of their time attempting to avoid the seemingly relativistic consequences of their views. For this reason it is useful to view the relativist as an ideal type that various thinkers approach more or less closely.

84

Earlier in this century the special theory of relativity was sometimes taken as a model for relativism, though because of misunderstandings of the theory this often led only to confusion. Nevertheless, there is something to be said for the paradigm. On Einstein's view such qualities as mass and velocity, once believed to be invariant or absolute, are now seen to be relative to inertial frameworks. To say that such qualities are relative is to say that they call for one more argument place or parameter than was formerly thought to be needed, and as a first approximation we may view relativism as the thesis that some concept ϕ requires relativization to some parameter π. I shall speak of relativization to conceptual frameworks, setting aside for the moment questions about their nature. Since there are many candidates for ϕ, relativism is not one thesis but many. A defense of relativism is most interesting, however, if ϕ is something that is often regarded as an absolute or invariant feature of experience, language, or thought, and a traditional list of such candidates includes truth, concepts, logic, standards of rationality, and moral principles. To be sure, these notions are related in numerous ways, but clarity is to be gained by avoiding their conflation.

My concern here will be with relativism with respect to truth. Truth provides a useful starting point for a discussion of relativism for several reasons. It is important because opponents of the doctrine usually make it the focal point of their criticisms. And although those of a more relativistic persuasion typically begin with considerations about concepts, meaning, or perception rather than with truth, their views do appear to lead rather naturally to conclusions about it which leave them open to such attacks. Moreover, despite the existence of a number of well-known arguments against the claim that truth is relative, a number of able thinkers have been drawn to the view that it is, and it is important to try to see why this is so. Finally, work is needed on the topic because until we find a clearer picture of a relativistic conception of truth than we currently have, discussions of the claim that relativism is self-refuting or otherwise incoherent are bound to be less conclusive than we would hope them to be.

To provide background for later discussion I shall first examine the general motivations for relativism and the nature of conceptual frameworks; less attention has been devoted to these topics than they deserve, so I shall spend some time on them. I then turn to recent work on theories of truth with an eye to relating it to the motivations for relativism. We will investigate plausible conditions of adequacy for a theory of relativistic truth and will see that, quite apart from standard charges that such a notion is self-contradictory, the very nature of the relativist's position makes it quite difficult for him to formulate coherently a claim to the effect that truth is relative. I conclude by noting some implications of our discussion for other aspects of relativism.

MOTIVATIONS

Most forms of relativism, and the motivation for them, can be viewed in terms of a fairly simple model which, despite differences in interest, general orientation, and terminology, is reflected in the work of a number of philosophers. We can think of the general argument for relativism as involving two stages: first, a defense of a constructivistic epistemology according to which the knower somehow organizes or constitutes what is known and, second, an argument that there is no uniquely correct way of doing this.

The first stage owes an obvious debt to Kant. According to this tradition, knowledge and perception are *constructive* processes. Far from being a *tabula rasa,* the mind organizes or conceptualizes some sort of input, which may be construed in a variety of ways, ranging from a manifold of empirical intuitions or sense data to physical stimulations of sensory receptors. It matters little to such a view whether or not there is a given element in experience, so long as what is given is, like the qualia of C.I. Lewis, simply content and not, as in Russell's discussion of acquaintance, knowledge. For relativism can grant that some sort of sensory content is given in experience which can then be organized or subsumed under concepts in alternative ways. But a relativist may reject the notion of the given altogether, holding that by the time anything enters experience it already possesses some conceptual component. Views of the latter sort may make for a more thoroughgoing version of the doctrine, but relativism does not require them.

The critical point is that all knowledge involves a framework of concepts; there is, in Quine's phrase, no "neutral cosmic exile" from which one can read off the nature of the world as it is "in itself." All knowledge is perspectival, theory-laden, dependent upon a framework of concepts which somehow allows us to sort out or organize the input. Hence there are no neutral facts, for the facts as we know them are correlative with the set of concepts we employ.[2]

Such views, however, need not be incompatible with the claim that *only one* conceptual framework is correct, or even possible. The second step on the road to relativism involves the Hegelian move of attacking the putative a priori character of our modes of thought. There are several strategies which have been adopted in an attempt to do this. One involves attacking the correspondence theory of truth and the view that the world possesses a unique structure which our beliefs and theories might somehow match. The criticisms here are familiar ones to the effect that the notion of correspondence is elusive and that since there is no neutral access to facts untinged by thought, talk of the things to which truths correspond is empty. Another typical ploy is to argue that our ways of picking out and individuating things depend on our concepts, especially our sortals, and that reality, whatever it is, *underdetermines* the way in which we think about it. Thus there is no unique "way the world is";[3] "a variety of different conceptual schemes can with equal validity be superimposed upon the order of 'empirical fact'."[4]

Other arguments for the second step turn upon more empirical considerations. Some stress the fact that differences in beliefs, expectations, and the like can influence perception, as is demonstrated by phenomena connected with various perceptual illusions. It is also frequently noted that members of different cultures may employ different systems of classification, even for such quotidian concerns as colors. And it is now a commonplace that once well-entrenched scientific and everyday beliefs have changed. It is mildly ironic that such arguments, drawn from more fledgling sciences, have recently been employed in an effort to undermine physics' claims to objectivity. But they are of value in showing that knowledge and reality are not connected in the simple way that we might naively have supposed them to be. Such arguments may also be useful in locating some of the *mechanisms* that might be involved in modes of thought rather different from our own. We have never observed the evolution of radically different species, but extrapolation of the operation of certain genetic mechanisms gives content to talk of full-blown evolution. And similar extrapolation may be useful in explaining the notion of alternative conceptual frameworks.

The most immediate difficulty with the two-stage argument is that it is very difficult to present it without relying on metaphors and very general notions like the structure of the world. But its pervasiveness suggests that the picture is important and that it is worth trying to understand. Moreover, as we will see, the real difficulties with the doctrine of relative truth do not result from the use of metaphors or generalities.

RELATIVE TO WHAT?

Before turning to truth, something needs to be said about conceptual frameworks. As I shall understand it, the notion of a conceptual framework has much in common with such things as *Weltanschauungen*, categorical schemes, and, perhaps, even forms of life. The notion of a conceptual framework or scheme is a theoretical one designed to help us understand and explain thought and action, and its use is to be justified by its success in doing so. Like the related theoretical notions of culture and society, that of a conceptual framework will involve a certain amount of idealization, for it is doubtful that the basic features of thought of any very large group of people, especially if it is highly diversified and heterogenous, could be set out literally without countless quantifications. But far from being a defect, such idealization is a standard feature of theoretical concepts and is one of the things that make them useful.

While things like truth, concepts, or standards of rationality are viewed by relativists as functions of conceptual frameworks, frameworks are themselves standardly held to be determined by something else. For generality we may view frameworks as the dependent variable and construe different relativistic positions as offering candidates for the independent variables. For example, it has been argued that our framework is grounded in the biological makeup of our species, a claim Husserl entitled *anthropologism;* that different historical periods or different cultures give rise to differnt frameworks, views often labeled *historicism* and *cultural relativism* respectively; or, following the lead of such thinkers as Cassirer, Whorf, and Winch, that fundamental differences between languages bring with them differences in frameworks. It may even be that economic and social factors, religion, or one's scientific views play some role in shaping one's thought, as is suggested by Marx, Durkheim, and Kuhn respectively. We therefore want a broad notion of a conceptual framework, for our interest is with relativism in general, and all of these views are species of it.

An important feature of relativism emerges from the above considerations. With the exception of anthropologism, relativism is at heart an empiricist view, for it holds that we acquire a framework in the process of language acquisition, acculturation, or the like. So, few actual relativistic positions involve a Protagorean relativism with each individual the measure; rather, conceptual frameworks are typically regarded as the common property of those who share a language, culture, or location in history. Thus the relativist with respect to truth would be likely to view truth as absolute and objective *within a framework;* only truth *simpliciter* would be regarded as relative.[5]

This leaves open the way in which frameworks are to be individuated. It is unreasonable to demand necessary and sufficient conditions for something's being a conceptual framework, for we can find concepts quite intelligible without being able to specify these, as is evinced by such time-worn examples as games and tables. Nor is it fruitful at the outset to follow certain critics of relativism in saying that two groups of people possess different conceptual frameworks only if they are unable to communicate with, or translate, each other.[6] For while we may find arguments which would lead us to conclude that this is in fact the case, few relativists would accept such a characterization.[7] Moreover, it would rule out from the beginning many interesting questions about relativism.

A better strategy is to begin with some reasonably clear examples, real or imaginary, of putative cases of conceptual frameworks different from our own, for example, the Hopi as interpreted by Whorf or the Azande as characterized by Evans-Pritchard. While these examples may not involve anything so dramatically different from our ways of thinking about the world as do more exotic cases, they do provide a foothold for discussion. And if we can isolate the features which make them seem different, those with a taste for the bizarre can extrapolate on the basis of them.

The Hopi are said to view time as a elation between events rather than in terms of duration, to articulate their world in terms of events rather than objects, and to think it possible that one can influence objects in the external world merely by thinking about them.[8] This example involves beliefs and concepts different from our own, but clearly not just any differences in beliefs or concepts justify talk of different world-views. Some differences matter more than others, but which? Without attempting to define the notions, let me suggest that one moral to be drawn from an examination of such examples is that there are differences in what may be called basic beliefs and central concepts. Basicness and centrality are, of course, matters of degree, but some fairly clear examples can be given which cast light on the notions. Central concepts have much in common with the items on traditional lists of categories: among our central concepts are those of object, cause, and person. And a basic belief is one that is so fundamental that a person could not abandon it without surrendering many other beliefs as well. These may embody rather specific claims, for example that most events have causes, that others have minds, that some things which aren't actual are possible, or more general standards for explanation and intelligibility, as that induction by enumeration is a reasonable way to gather evidence. It remains an open question as to how large a difference in such beliefs or concepts is needed to justify talk of different world-views. As with similar questions concerning the individuation of languages or cultures, we are confronted with matters of degree, and our purposes may very well play a role in deciding about particular examples.[9]

TRUTH

Twentieth-century philosophy is sometimes said to have taken the linguistic turn, and under the influence of Tarski, Carnap, and more recent writers this turn has taken a semantic twist. The relevant notion here is that of referential semantics, and it is important for us because its concepts of reference and satisfaction play a key role in theories which provide quite precise definitions or characterizations of the truth predicates for a number of languages. The initial work was done by Tarski, although it has gained in interest in light of recent attempts by Davidson and others to deal with fragments of natural languages within a Tarskian framework.[10] And the approach is especially important because it is the only really general and systematic treatment of truth that we have.

Tarski's project was to formulate explicit definitions of truth for various formalized languages in higher-order metalanguages. He began by proposing a *condition of adequacy*—Convention T—which any acceptable theory that defines a truth predicate for a language must satisfy. The theory must have as a theorem, for each sentence of the language under investigation, an instance of the scheme

T   X is true in $OL \leftrightarrow$ p,

where OL is the object language, 'X' is replaced by a structural-descriptive name of a sentence of OL, and 'p' is replaced by its translation into the metalanguage [CTFL, 187–188].

Tarski took the notion of translation as primitive and defined truth. By contrast, Davidson and others have worked on theories—not explicit definitions—of truth for various fragments of natural languages, and much of their work can be viewed as reversing the direction of explanation in an effort to elicit such notions as meaning and translation from an antecedently understood concept of truth. Since our present concern is not with meaning or interpretation, however, what is important for us is that such work shows how a Tarski-style approach can be accommodated to parts of natural language.

It will be useful to roughly outline one way in which Tarski's general strategy can be implemented. Suppose our goal is to provide a finite theory that specifies the conditions under which the infinitely many sentences of OL are true. We conduct our business in a metalanguage, ML, which includes names for every expression of OL as well as their translations into ML. If the object language is a fragment of a natural language, the metalanguage may be just that fragment plus some semantical and syntactical terms.

Suppose *OL* is a fragment of English which has been given a canonical first-order formulation, that *ML* includes *OL,* and that its names of expressions of object-language expressions are represented by drawing a line over them. Since predicates can do the work of individual constants and functors, we will assume that the only nonlogical constants of *OL* are predicates.

We begin by providing a recursive definition of *satisfaction.* This can be done by laying down a few standard axioms asserting that there are denumerably infinite sequences of objects and that these have certain properties. We then specify a basis clause for each predicate of *OL*. For example, a sequence *s* satisfies a predication of $\overline{red}$ with the variable x_i just in case the i_{th} member of *s* is red, and basis clauses are given in this way for each primitive predicate of *OL*. A recursion is then specified along roughly the following lines: a sequence *s* satisfies a conjunction just in case it satisfies both conjuncts; it satisfies a negation just in case it does not satisfy the sentence negated; and it satisfies an existential quantification with respect to the i_{th} variable just in case there is at least one sequence, differing from *s* in at most the i_{th} place, which satisfies the expression resulting from the deletion of the quantifier. Finally, a sentence is true just in case it is closed and is satisfied by all sequences. This definition of truth conforms to T, and the recursive definition can in general be upgraded to an explicit one with the aid of some set theory.

What, now, of relativism? Tarski did not attempt to provide a definition of *true-in-L,* for variable L, but gave us definitions of the truth predicates for particular languages. Nor is this merely an artifact of theory. We can imagine that the same string of marks, or the same accoustic production, is by happenstance a sentence of two distinct languages; it might even be true in one, false in the other [CTFL, 153]. But clearly neither contradiction nor relativism threaten, for we simply view the sentence as true in one language, false in the other. On Tarski's account it is (closed) *sentences* which are true or false, for his definitions were devised for languages free of demonstratives. Natural languages, however, contain many constructions like "I see that now," and their existence is often thought to require the relativization of the truth predicates to utterances of sentences, speakers, times and objects demonstrated. This complicates matters but clearly does not make truth relative in a way which bears on relativism. Nor does the relativization of truth (in a language) to an interpretation, for this merely involves various ways of assigning extensions to the nonlogical vocabulary of the language.

What does relativism of an interesting sort require? To avoid unnecessary complications, let us restrict attention to unambiguous sentences free of all indexical constructions. As a first approximation we can then say that relativism would result if a sentence S could be true in L for some speakers of L, false for others, or if a correct translation manual paired a sentence S of L with a sentence S′ of L′, and S were true in L, S′ false in L′. A situation of either sort would involve what I shall call *strong relativism* and may be contrasted with a weaker version of the doctrine, according to which a sentence could be true in the language of one framework and simply inexpressible in that of another. It should be stressed that neither thesis involves an empirical claim that there *actually* are cases of different frameworks which provide instances of strong or weak relativism; the two doctrines merely affirm the coherence and intelligibility of the notions of strong and weak relative truth.

Clearly Tarski's work lends no support to a strong version of relativism. Indeed, Sir Karl Popper goes so far as to claim that it shows this thesis to be false. He tells us, for example, that Tarski's work affords an *"absolute and objective"* definition of truth, and he has frequently appealed to it in his attacks on relativism.[11] One reason it is useful for such purposes, he tells us, is that it is a correspondence theory of truth. Yet in the passages where we would expect arguments to show that this is so, we instead find stipulations; for example, we are told that students understand the theory more readily if we "take 'truth' as a synonym for 'correspondence with the facts'."[12] And his claim that the theory is *objective* is defended primarily by contrasting it with "subjective theories" of truth, that is, theories which rely upon such epistemic notions as belief [*C&R,* 225]. Just how much this claim would rule out is not entirely clear, however, for even classical coherence theories did not appeal to such notions. It is true that Tarski sometimes speaks of his definitions as characterizing an *absolute* concept of truth, though his purpose in doing so is not to champion any sort of metaphysical doctrine, but to contrast this concept with the notions of truth in a structure or model [CTFL, 199]. Indeed, there is at least one sense in which Tarski's definitions are not absolute, for they are relativized to languages.

It is, in fact, rather misleading to speak of Tarski's *theory* without qualification, and Popper's tendency to do so may account for the rather sweeping character of some of his remarks.[13] But in the end Popper's defense of his claims on behalf of Tarski's work boils down to the assertion that if S and S′ are sentences of L and L′ respectively, T a correct translation manual from L into L′, and T(S) = S′, then S′ is true in L′ just in case S is true in L [*OK,* 225]. Unfortunately the claim about translation, like those concerning correspondence, is merely asserted, and although it has a great deal of intuitive plausibility, it must be supported by argument if it is not to beg the question against the relativist.

Despite Popper's lack of argument at key points, a defense of similar views can be found in the work of writers who have linked Tarski's work to theories of reference in a defense of realism. Realism involves the thesis that there is a way the world is and that our theories can in principle succeed in capturing it. At the turn of the century such realists as Moore and Russell talked of correspondence to the facts. But facts have fallen out of favor, and correspondence as traditionally conceived is acknowledged to be an extremely problematic notion. As elsewhere, discussion of such matters has undergone a semantic turn. The general idea, defended in one way or another by such writers as Davidson, Putnam, and Field, is this.[14] We do not need facts to make talk of correspondence intelligible; rather, we can give it a sense by linking it to such semantic notions as satisfaction or reference. Facts are dispensed with in favor of the (typically) extramental, extralinguistic objects in the sequences which satisfy our sentences. The resulting theory is realistic insofar as it depends on the way the world is; semantic relations are, after all, *word-world* connections. Some writers go a step further, explicating semantic notions in terms of a causal theory of reference. One may then attempt to avoid relativism of many sorts by arguing that whatever the senses of intentions (if any) of the expressions of a language, truth depends on reference—and *that* is objective. Moreover, frameworks of various sorts are not regarded as incommensurable, for reference affords an objective connection between language and reality which makes translation and comparison between the languages in which they are couched possible.[15]

The relativist, however, is not likely to see such views as significant improvements over classical correspondence theories. For although the contemporary claims are far more precise and rigorous articulations of realism than were their predecessors, and although these presentations are sometimes backed by an appeal to the explanatory value of realism, the relativist will still maintain that we have no framework-independent access to reality and, indeed, that talk of objective relations between terms and their referents in the world is no clearer in the end than talk of correspondence to facts.[16] In neither case have we any reason for thinking that the world comprises a unique set of factors or of objects, and the detailed arguments against the recent formulations of realism would parallel those against the old.

Whether or not one finds the newer versions of realism plausible will thus depend in large measure on how he views older versions of the doctrine. If one sees the latter as intuitively compelling but involving a few key terms which need clarification, he will find the recent work attractive. On the other hand, if one sees the standard arguments against realism as pointing to deep difficulties unlikely to be remedied by formal emendations, he will doubtless be skeptical about the metaphysical significance of more recent work. The arguments advanced by the various disputants are well-known, so we need not rehearse them here. Instead, having seen how a realist's account of truth might run, let us turn to questions about relative truth.

TRUE FOR

Relativistic views of truth are commonly attacked on the grounds that they are self-refuting or that their very formulation presupposes a theory of absolute truth. I will argue below that careful statements of relativism with respect to truth are less vulnerable to such objections than is frequently supposed; at present, however, I am concerned with slightly different issues, so let us set this problem aside for the moment.[17]

Relativism with respect to truth involves the locution 'true for', and the first question we must ask is whether we can make sense of it. Often it is unproblematic, as when we say that it is true for John that social choice theory is difficult. This is simply an infelicitous way of saying that the subject is difficult for John. More objectionable is the conflation of 'true for' with 'believes that', for to say that it is true for Ralph that God exists, where this means—as it usually does—that Ralph believes in the existence of the Deity, can easily lead to a simple-minded confusion of metaphysical and epistemological considerations. But while relativism may in the end rest on the thesis that such considerations can not be separated, and may even do so because of confusions, the confusions are more subtle than this.

Talk of belief and truth is likely to call to mind Plato's discussion in the *Theaetetus,* where he attributes to Protagoras roughly the view that

P $\forall x$ (x believes that p $\rightarrow$ X is true for x).[18]

As unpromising as P is as a statement of relativism—or of anything else— Plato proceeds to drop the qualifying phrase 'for x' at a critical stage in the argument [*Theaetetus,* 171-72], thus saddling Protagoras with an even more vulnerable view:

P' $\forall x$ (x believes that p $\rightarrow$ X is true).

What is surprising is that a number of more recent objections to relativism have been raised against a form of the doctrine suggested by **P'**.

It is said, for example, that a relativistic conception of truth leads to violations of the laws of excluded middle and noncontradiction. Suppose, for instance, that everyone is suspending belief with respect to S. Neither S nor its negation will be believed, and so at least one substitution instance of the law of excluded middle will not be true. Worse, if one person believes S, another its negation, we have both S and its contradictory coming out true, and on virtually any account of falsity it follows that S is both true and false.

The answer to such objections, of course, lies on the face of **P'**: such criticisms beg the question against relativism in their implicit reliance upon an absolute theory of truth. **P** is not open to such objections, for if *a* and *b* are different people, the assertion that S is true-for-*a*, false-for-*b* is not inconsistent. Laws of logic get relativized to agents, and so long as we do not have S being both true and false for the same agent, we escape contradiction.

We may yet find violations of the law of excluded middle, for if *a* has no beliefs one way or another about S, then neither it nor its negation will be true for him. This is not so serious, for it merely signals the need for relativized truth-value gaps, a relativistic counterpart of suggestions made by such writers as Frege and Strawson. But worse is in store, for even if we assume that our agents do not believe all of the logical consequences of their beliefs, it is a rare person indeed who does not explicitly harbor a few inconsistent beliefs. And, assuming a relativized version of standard logic, this will make every sentence true for such an agent. (If the agent has bizarre beliefs about logical consequence, this may not follow, but equally unpalatable results are likely to.) Furthermore, changes of belief lead to changing truth (-for) values for a single sentence. Finally, the possibility of mistaken beliefs, even in one's relativized world, is ruled out. Such difficulties show, I think, that if someone's believing something makes it true for him, then our notion of *true for* does not come close enough to *truth* to be of any philosophical interest at all.

But if we recall that most relativists would have us relativize truth to conceptual frameworks rather than to individuals, we can escape such difficulties. For example, on Whorf's view all (normal) native speakers of Hopi share the Hopi world-view. Now we have intentionally left the notion of a conceptual framework general in order to be able to accommodate it to various specific views about relativism. But since most of thse views involve a social component, let us require that a conceptual framework be social, that is, shared and intersubjective for the group whose framework it is. Thus we no longer speak of sentences being true for particular individuals but, rather, true for *groups* of people or, better, true in a conceptual framework.

To maintain generality we must avoid requiring a one-to-one correspondence between languages and frameworks. For many relativists, Whorf included, would happily concede that speakers of different languages can share the same framework, provided their languages and cultures are sufficiently similar. On the other hand, some relativists would hold that two speakers of the same language can have different world-views, provided that they have very different and far-reaching beliefs about religion, science, or the like.

We can thus speak of sentences being true (in L) for a conceptual framework F, though for most purposes we do not need to mention the language. And by analogy with *speakers* of a language, we may talk of *users* of a framework. We now see how Sam's believing S need not make S true for him, or anyone else, for he may be a user of F, believe S, and yet S might be false in F. But an analogue of P seems to remain, for if all, or most, of the users of F believe S, then surely S is true in F.

But the relativist *need* not be seen as holding either that truth is merely a matter of what the majority of people take to be the case, on the one hand, or as trying to show that most of our accepted truths are false, on the other. Nothing *forces* us to view relativism in this way; we could instead follow those who characterize the doctrine in such a way that it is quite obviously absurd or incoherent. But there is little point in doing so. For if we adopt the latter approach, there is little hope of explaining why relativism has captivated so many. More important, if the doctrine is to be of genuine philosophical interest—if only as a foil against which to evaluate other positions—we must strike a delicate balance, trying to formulate it as plausibly as we can, without so diluting it that it no longer deserves the name. And since one way to do this might be to clarify the notion of relative truth, let us ask about conditions of adequacy for an account of this notion. Given the state of the art, we cannot reasonably expect necessary and sufficient conditions, much less anything comparable in precision to **T**. But I think that we can find some general constraints to place on the notion of relative truth that are illuminating.

The relativist is best viewed as advancing a thesis about the nature of, not the criteria for, truth. Like Berkeley, he treats as many everyday facts as possible with respect, while according them a new and arresting philo-sophical interpretation. And there are certain phenomena which the serious relativist must try to save, on pain of denying many common-sense truisms. Thus he must be impressed by the fact that we intuitively suppose that there are many things which are true even though no one believes them, and that there are other things that most of us believe which might turn out to be false. Most Western Europeans in the early sixteenth century believed that the earth was flat, but they were wrong. The discovery that it was not flat changed one of their beliefs. But there is reason to resist the conclusion that it changed their conceptual framework, since it was in terms of concepts and standards of evidence of their framework that they came to change this belief. So mistaken beliefs within a framework, even ones shared by most of its users, are possible. The relativist who stresses the social nature of frameworks thus goes part way with the realist, for he acknowledges that S may be true in F even if none of the users of F ever discover this and, indeed, even if most of them believe it to be false. But the relativist and realist part company over the question of whether some extramental, extralinguistic reality uniquely determines all truth.

If one's merely thinking something so does not make it so (for him), the relativist must allow that there are some constraints on what can be true in a framework. What are they? One, I think, is a framework-independent "world" which, though it underdetermines the ways in which we can think about it, nevertheless places some constraints on experience and thought. It provides the input which can be "conceptualized" or "organized" in a multiplicity of ways. Like Aristotle's prime matter or Kant's thing-in-itself, such a notion is nearly empty, for, by the relativist's own lights, it can not be experienced or described in a neutral way; it is a limiting notion, entering into experience only as mediated by concepts, language, or the like, and of course one of the chief tasks facing the relativist is to make this concept intelligible to us. The important point here, however, is that something of this sort must be postulated if the relativist's picture is to avoid the slide into subjective idealism; indeed, only by appeal to it can he account for the possibility of intraframework communication and objectivity.

Whatever the nature of this notion of "the world"—and it is undeniably problematic—it alone cannot explain the constraints on truth in a framework, since it is said to underdetermine concepts, beliefs, and truth. The relativist also needs a notion we might call *collateral commitment*. The basic beliefs and concepts of a framework involve a collateral commitment to additional truths in the framework. Some of these commitments may be hypothetical, to the effect that if future experience is of a certain sort, then such and such is the case. Among other things, collateral commitments may involve logical and evidential relations. If logic is not relative to frameworks, for example, then if S is true in F, any standard logical consequence of S will also be true in F. Likewise, assuming a framework involves the notion of laws, some basic beliefs of F may nomologically imply further sentences which will be true in F, regardless of the opinions of F's users.[19]

Although some, even many, of the things believed true by users of F could turn out to be false in F, not all of them could be. In particular, not all, and on some accounts not any, of its basic beliefs could be false in F. Whether any of a framework's basic beliefs could be false depends on how frameworks are individuated. It is not implausible to hold that basic beliefs are essential properties of a framework, so that if a basic belief of a framework were given up, the framework would change. But one might instead treat frameworks as analogous to cluster concepts, so that few, if any, basic beliefs are essential to a framework, although a large portion of them must be maintained if it is to retain its identity. There is something to be said on behalf of each approach, and the issues involved in choosing between them are interesting, but for our purposes either characterization of frameworks will do.

The picture we have thus far is one in which "the world," together with the central concepts and basic beliefs of a framework, somehow determine truth in that framework. We can see more clearly how this sort of picture often leads to a relativism with respect to truth if we recall the relativistic argument that our concepts, language, or the like somehow help to constitute the world as we know it. A typical example of this picture can be found in Mannheim's remark that the world "as 'world' exists only with reference to the knowing mind, and the mental activity determines the form in which it appears."[20] Now if one is to move from the view that large differences in concepts or beliefs can lead to a relative notion of truth, he must interpret such remarks in a very strong way; indeed, he must conclude that the only notion of the world that has significant content is that of the world *as known* and that this is in part literally created by the central concepts and basic beliefs we employ. Truth then indeed has something to do with the world—not with an independent world-in-itself, however, but with a world as constituted by someone's mode of thought. In short, worlds are seen to be relative to frameworks; truth involves the (or a) world; hence, it too becomes relative. using the notion of correspondence loosely, we can then view truth in F as correspondence to the facts of F's world; it remains a semantic notion, but it now involves a word-*relativized* world relation.

The view presented in the last few pages is, I think, a serviceable sketch of the notion of relative truth. On the one hand, it saves such obvious phenomena as the fact that someone's believing something is neither a necessary nor sufficient condition for its being true and that, for many beliefs, the fact that they are held by most members of a given culture, linguistic community, or the like is neither a necessary nor sufficient condition for their being true for that group. On the other hand, the picture *is* relativistic in that it is motivated by the relativist's constructivistic epistemology and leads to a picture of truth as depending on a world which is itself relative to a conceptual framework. It thus merits the appellation 'relativistic', while avoiding many of the weaknesses of common accounts of such doctrines.

RELATIVE TRUTH

To be sure, the picture is not lacking in difficulties, but our task was to find the most plausible version of relative truth that we could, not to devise a version free of problems. We need not dwell on its defects here, however, for we will see that even if we grant the relativist his picture of the world as partially fashioned by concepts or language, it is still quite difficult to develop the view that truth could be relative in the strong sense.

If different frameworks are couched in different languages, then since sentences in one language are typically not to be found in another, a given sentence can not receive different truth values in each. But although a sentence S of L typically will not be found in a framework couched in L', the translation of S into L' may be. We may thus view translation as central to our discussion, regarding cases—if there are any—of distinct frameworks couched in the same language as involving homophonic translation.

Familiar cases of translation, of course, do not involve any interesting relativity of truth. For example, "Kant ist gestorben" is true in German just in case "Kant is dead" is true in English. Here the referent of 'Kant' in both languages is the same, as is the extension of the two predicates. With more complicated sentences this will not be so obvious, but the same sorts of principles will often be involved. In this example we have viewed speakers of German and English as sharing a common world, so that the talk of frameworks is idle. But now let us imagine that Whorf's Hopi possesses a conceptual framework different from our own.[21] If the difference in frameworks makes it impossible in principle to translate between Hopi and English, then there will be no S of E and S' of H such that S = T(S'). Thus truth here would not be relative in the strong sense simply because there would be nothing which could be true in one framework and false in the other, though it would be relative in our weaker sense, since the truths of one framework would be inexpressible in the other. A number of recent writers would object that in such an event we would have no reason to suppose that the Hopi had a language and world-view at all, and, indeed, that little sense could be given to the claim that they did. This need not worry us unduly, however, for the first claim is far from obvious, while the second is verificationistic.[22]

In any case, such figures as Whorf, Winch, Feyerabend, and Kuhn, who come nearer our ideal type of the relativist than most, have believed that translation in such cases is possible. Indeed, Whorf's attribution of an alternative framework to the Hopi was largely based on what he took his translation of them to reveal. And, of course, the most interesting claims about the relativity of truth are those which purport to give examples that allegedly show a clash between world-views and hint at resulting deep and troubling questions concerning objectivity and justification. So let us see what happens if we agree that such translation is, at least in principle, possible.

Taking stock, we have granted the relativist (1) and (2) and are concerned to discover the status of (3):

(1) The world, as experienced, known, and knowable, is partially constituted by the framework through which it is known.

(2) Translation between different frameworks is, in principle, possible.

(3) Truth is relative in a strong sense.

(2) is a necessary condition for (3), for if truth is relative in a strong sense, there must be something which is true in one framework, false in another. Now if (1) holds, cases might arise in which we would find the enterprise of translation difficult; a principle of charity—that is, the assumption that those we wish to translate agree with us on many matters—may well be required for translation to work in practice. But, as a thought experiment, let us imagine an omniscient translator. In circumstances where (3) held, could not he simply pair the sentences of the two frameworks that express this something they share which can vary in truth value, thus obtaining at least a partial translation?

Hopes for this fade quickly, however, for the notion of an omniscient translator leads back to standard objections that talk of relative truth implicitly relies on a notion of absolute truth; truth for an omniscient being seems to be *the* truth, period. Thus this approach has to be abandoned, and the relativist seems forced to acknowledge that the claim that something is true in F, false in F′, may *itself* be true in one framework, false in another. And with this admission we appear to lose all grip on the claim that truth is relative.

Some have attempted to argue that while most things are true only in a relative sense, a few are true absolutely. It is sometimes thought, for example, that Engels and Lenin held a view rather like this in order to exempt Marxist theory from the strictures of their own historical relativism. Clearly a similar move might be made in an attempt to likewise exempt the relativisitic thesis itself, along with discussions of the status of the truth values of sentences in various frameworks. But such a strategy is unpromising for a number of familiar reasons; for our purposes, it should suffice to point out just how badly it comports with the general picture that led to relativism in the first place.

The relativist with respect to truth will do better to grant at the outset that all truth is relative. His strategy should then be to seek to minimize the significance of this admission by arguing that at least most of his audience shares his framework. For if the relativist can convince the would-be objectivist that his seemingly objective concepts and beliefs presuppose the same framework as the relativist's, the latter can then argue for relativism in the context of the framework they share. The project of showing the objectivist that his beliefs depend upon a comon core of beliefs and standards and that relativism is reasonable according to them would not be easy to carry out. But unless a defense of this sort can be mounted, relativism with respect to truth will never get off the ground. Indeed, such considerations indicate that the relativist should resist individuating frameworks narrowly; the more widely his framework is shared, the more sense he can make of relativism with respect to truth.

If the relativist can make such a position plausible, he can then add that his claims are no worse off than most of the other things we hold true. And if relativism's claims are as secure as the myriad claims that are on solid ground for us normally, what more could be demanded? As Spengler put it, "the claim of higher thought to possess general and eternal truths falls to the ground," adding that his own philosophy is "able to express and reflect only the Western soul . . . and that soul only in its present civilized phrase."[23] Or, in Quine's words, "I philosophize from the vantage point only of our own provincial conceptual scheme . . . true; but I know no better" [*OR*, 25]. Relativism may seem less exciting when viewed in this light, but it does give us an answer to the question: In whose framework is it true that S is true in F, T(S) false in F'? The answer is, of course, our own.

Continuing our policy of giving the relativist the benefit of the doubt in an effort to leave him with the strongest position possible, let us grant that the above line of argument can be filled out in a reasonably plausible way. It still does not follow that truth is relative in the strong sense. Put simply, the problem is that to get a strong version of relativism we need *some one thing* that could be true in F, false in F'. And whatever its exact nature, it will surely involve meanings. We need not demand anything so strong as strict synonymity, but unless two sentences have roughly the same meaning, there will be no justification for speaking of something that is true in one framework and false in another. Yet if F and F' involve "different worlds," as a natural interpretation of the strong relativistic conception of truth requires, how can a sentence of F mean, even roughly, the same thing as one if F'? The problem is that the sentences of F and F' are *about* different things, and any move from F to F' seems simply to involve a change of subject.

The word 'about' is elusive, but we can sharpen the point in the following way. Suppose that the constituents of a sentence of F and those of F′ have the same extensions, as in our German-English example above. We are no longer concerned simply with different, yet similar, languages, however, for in the present case the extensions of the terms in the two languages involve objects in "different worlds." Hence it is most unclear how there could be an overlap in the extension of their terms, even one of a very complicated sort. Nor, for the same reason, is it easy to make sense of users of different frameworks having *de re* beliefs *about* the same things. Unlike the case where two languages involve a common framework, we can no longer even speak of two languages categorizing things in *the* world differently. Here, by the relativist's own lights, the worlds themselves differ. Nor does it help to suppose that the sentences of the two frameworks have the same sense, for sense determines reference, and this leaves us with our original difficulty.

That this difficulty is not simply a result of our emphasis on reference can be brought out by examining the matter from a different perspective. This view is holistic, though not excessively so, and has the added benefit of dashing any hopes that appeal to some sort of coherence theory of truth might solve the problem just encountered. The argument here turns on the claim that the content of a belief is fixed by other beliefs and concepts, and that it cannot remain intact if they change radically. Radical changes in beliefs, at least central ones, will affect the very concepts in terms of which beliefs are expressed. Likewise, large changes in central concepts will affect beliefs, for such concepts are constitutive of them. For example, our concept of a person is partially determined by beliefs we hold about intentional action, responsibility, material bodies, and the like. Thus, a basic belief will be intimately related to central concepts and, through them, to other beliefs. My belief that there are other persons is tied to my concept of a person, and through it to further belief, for example, that persons have material bodies, that they can think, and so on indefinitely. But if this is so, it is difficult to see how the users of different frameworks could entertain the same beliefs.

We have tried two accounts and encountered the same difficulty; the relativist seems unable to tell a convincing story about *what it is* that can be true in a relative sense. We have thus far brushed aside questions concerning the nature of the bearers of truth-values, uncritically taking them to be sentences or the beliefs they express. But it has been argued that the bearers of truth-values are propositions, judgments, statements, utterances, and so on, and perhaps one of these can solve our problem. Propositions as conceived by the Frege-Church tradition in semantics are not likely to be useful here, however, for they are thought to be abstract,

extralinguistic entities with unchanging truth-values; moreover, an ontology compromising objective propositions that can be grasped by thinkers
ill accords with the spirit of relativism. And the subtle problems involved in
choosing among the remaining notions are overshadowed by a similar
difficulty in each case. How can a statement, judgment, or utterance made
by a user of F be the same statement, judgment, or utterance as that made
by a user of F? As before, the problem involves specifying *identity
conditions* for something across frameworks, and the only way to do so
seems to be in terms of shared meanings, beliefs, and concepts.

IMPLICATIONS

Let us take stock. Our relativist began with considerations about the
constructive nature of knowledge and experience, and pointed out that
alternative concepts, beliefs, and languages might lead rather to different
constructions. He then concluded that in some sense different worlds are
possible. But if this is so, truth cannot reside in a correspondence with a
neutral world of facts, for no such world exists. Truth does indeed involve
the way the world is, but since *this* is relative to a framework, truth too is
relative.

This is often taken to mean that truth can be relative in the strong
sense, a view which is indeed heady and exotic. But either different
frameworks involve very different worlds or they do not. If they do, a move
from one framework to another is, if possible at all, more akin to acquiring
a first language than it is to normal cases of translation. Thus a sentence S
of F will not be true in F while its counterpart is false in F' simply because
no counterpart of S exists in F'. On the other hand, if F and F' are
sufficiently similar to contain some one thing of the sort required for
translation, they will involve many of the same objects and concepts, and
the picture that tempted us to view truth as relative dims.

It may appear that a similar argument shows that if two allegedly
different frameworks are sufficiently alike for one to be translated into the
other, then they are not really distinct at all. For translation of another
framework (or its language) into ours requires that we express whatever it
is that is translated in terms of our language or framework. So, if F can be
translated into our framework (let us call it E), the concepts and
mechanisms of reference of F can be expressed in E. And although this may
not be possible in any simple or straightforward way, if they can be
expressed in our language and framework at all, then we understand them,
for we understand the English into which they are translated. Hence we do
not come to understand anything radically new, and the frameworks were
not really so different after all.[24]

Despite apparent parallels with the argument about truth, this argument does not, I think, tell against relativism as expressed in (1). For even if we can somehow express others' concepts in our language, it does not follow that we can actually use them to articulate our world; there is a large gap between being able to translate another tongue and being able to use it in the way in which its speakers do. Consider a beginning student of a foreign language. Armed with his German dictionary, he can express German sentences in English, but he cannot think in German. Or take the case of John, who is familiar only with Cartesian coordinates. Positions expressed in Polar coordinates can easily be converted to Cartesian ones, yet John has access to talk about Polar coordinates only in a rather indirect way; he has to perform the conversion before he can usefully think about them. In short, there is a difference between having the ability to express certain things and actually being able to use these things directly in one's thought.

Our examples are trivial but point to the fact that there is a difference between the expressibility of concepts and their accessibility. Accessibility has to do, not with what *could* be used, but with what *is* used, and this is what concerns the relativist. The temptation to overlook the difference between expressibility and accessibility is encouraged, I think, by a tendency to view natural languages as formal calculi. If one does this, then expressibility will be likened to explicit definability, and such definitions are, of course, noncreative and eliminable. If I define a new predicate in a first-order language, then I could already express anything that I can now express with it. But for those who like formal models, a better analogy than that of a definitional extension of a theory is furnished by an extension involving new nonlogical axioms. This underscores the fact that translation of a foreign idiom into our own may stretch or enrich ours. Moreover, in actual cases there are degrees of translatability, and we may lose a good deal in translation. Hence in some cases translation between two frameworks may be possible even if the users of the two frameworks think about the world in quite different ways.

This does not mean that truth goes relative, however, for unlike questions about the use of concepts, questions about truth *do* depend heavily upon logical considerations. Although a concept might be expressible in two different frameworks without being used by users of each, truth (in a framework) does not likewise depend on accessibility. To take a simple example, consider a first-order theory in which we define a new n-place predicate θ^n in terms of some very complicated sentence in n free variables. Then a sentence containing θ^n may be much more accessible to us than one in which the term is replaced by its definiens. But the truth conditions of the two will be the same. Frameworks, of course, are not first-order theories, but something like this will have to hold for them as well, on pain of changing the subject from truth to something else.

CONCLUSION

Where does this leave us? I have tried to trace several relativistic motifs and the motivations behind them and to see how these might be connected with the doctrine that truth is relative. The picture of relativism that emerged is compatible with the view that truth might be relative in a weak sense, that is, there could be things that were true in one framework which were not expressible and a fortiori not true in another. This is not to say, of course, that there in fact are alternative frameworks or that if there are there are actually things in one which resist translation into others. Nor, even if there are, does it follow that truth is relative in a strong sense.

A stronger form of relativism requires that one and the same thing can be true in one framework and false in another. And here we saw that a difficulty arises in trying to maintain simultaneously that two frameworks are sufficiently different for one thing to be true in one while false in the other *and* that they are sufficiently alike to share something which could thus vary in truth value. For if the frameworks are radically different, they deal with different worlds and have little subject matter in common. As we imagine one or both evolving to become more like the other, we can begin to make more sense of their containing resources for expressing the same thing, but less sense of their assigning it different truth values. Nor is it at all clear what it would mean to catch this change in the middle, at a point where talk of strongly relative truth could be given a modicum of sense. The general difficulty is simply that a strong version of relativism is most naturally stated, *first,* in terms of something that can be shared by different frameworks and, *second,* in the form of the claim that this something can receive different truth-values in those frameworks. The first point may be elaborated by appeal to propositions, shared meanings, or shared objects of reference. But none of these fit well with the second aspect of the thesis, for the very picture that lends plausibility to talk of relative truth leaves little room for them.

What morals can we draw from our discussion? To begin with, questions about the relativity of truth are more complicated than is often supposed. It is quite difficult to state even rough conditions of adequacy for a strongly relativistic conception of truth, for the notion pulls us in opposite directions at the same time. But our conclusions do not tell against all versions of relativism. Indeed, by giving the relativist the benefit of the doubt at nearly every stage, we have seen that his claims that our knowledge of the world is colored by our concepts, that these might have been quite different, and the like, do not lead to the conclusion that truth is relative in a strong sense. And such relativistic themes thus receive a partial vindication by being dissociated from an extremely problematic doctrine of truth.

NOTES

1. Donald Davidson, "On the Very Idea of a Conceptual Scheme," *Proceedings and Addresses of the American Philosophical Association* 47 (1973/74): this volume, pp. 66–80.

2. This picture can be found in various guises in a wide range of philosophers: it is reflected in such remarks as: *"gerade Tatsachen gibt es nicht, nur Interpretationen. Wir können kein Faktum an sich feststellen,"* Friedrich Nietzsche, *Nietzsches Werke in Drei Banden* (Munich: Carl Hanser Verlag, 1958), p. 903; facts are "essentially ideational," Paul Feyerabend, *Against Method* (London: Humanities Press, 1975), p. 38, cf. p. 19 and passim; "what is real and what is unreal shows itself in the sense that language has," Peter Winch, "Understanding a Primitive Society," in B. Wilson, ed., *Rationality* (N.Y.: Harper & Row, 1970), p. 82; "categorical schemata ... are tools the knower uses in coping with what comes to him," they "make the world," Nelson Goodman, *Problems and Projects* (Indianapolis: Bobbs-Merrill, 1972), pp. 416 and 419.

3. Goodman, *Problems and Projects,* pp. 31ff.

4. Nicholas Rescher, *Conceptual Idealism* (Oxford: Basil Blackwell, 1972), p. 9. Although their remarks are illustrative of relativism themes, many of the authors cited in footnotes 2-4 would not find relativism congenial as a general doctrine.

5. Cf. Kuhn: "If I am right, then 'truth' may, like 'proof', be a term with only intra-theoretical applications," in "Reflections on My Critics," in I. Lakatos and A. Musgrave, eds., *Criticism and the Growth of Knowledge* (Cambridge: Cambridge University Press, 1970), p. 266.

6. Thus Davidson: "The failure of intertranslatability is a necessary condition for difference of conceptual schemes," in "On the Very Idea of a Conceptual Scheme," p. 12; this volume, p. 72; see also Sir Karl Popper, "Normal Science and Its Dangers," in Lakatos and Musgrave, *Criticism and the Growth of Knowledge,* p. 56.

7. Even those who speak of incommensurability between frameworks deny that interframework communication is impossible: see Thomas Kuhn, *The Structure of Scientific Revolutions* (2nd ed.; Chicago: University of Chicago Press, 1970), pp. 202-3; Feyerabend, *Against Method,* p. 251; see also Winch, "Understanding a Primitive Society," pp. 102-4.

8. Benjamin Whorf, *Language, Thought and Reality* (Cambridge: M.I.T. Press, 1956), pp. 139-40; on events, pp. 59, 147, 215; on thought's efficacy, 495. This

example is only intended as an illustration of the sorts of things that might be involved in the case of an alternative framework; in fact Whorf's empirical claims about the Hopi are almost certainly false.

9. To say this much is of course only to pose the problem for investigation. The topics of the last several pages are treated at greater length in my *Conceptual Relativism* (Ph.D. Dissertation, University of Minnesota, 1976) and in *Relativism* (in preparation).

10. The classic paper, first published in 1933, is Alfred Tarski's "The Concept of Truth in Formalized Languages" (hereafter [CTFL], in *Logic, Semantics, Meta-mathematics* (Oxford: Clarendon Press, 1956). Davidson's program is outlined in "Truth and Meaning," *Synthese* 17 (1967): 304-23; for a more recent discussion, with some afterthoughts, see his "Reply to Foster," in G. Evans and J. McDowell, eds., *Truth and Meaning* (Oxford: Clarendon Press, 1976).

11. Karl Popper, *Conjectures and Refutations* (hereafter [*C&R*]) (London: Hutchison, 1963), p. 224. Relativsm is Popper's *bête noire;* a typical example of his use of Tarski's work in attacking it can be found in *The Open Society and Its Enemies,* vol. 2 (Princeton: Princeton University Press, 1966), addendum to the 4th ed., esp. pp. 369-70.

12. *C&R,* p. 224; cf. Karl Popper, *Objective Knowledge* [*OK*] (Oxford: Oxford University Press, 1972), pp. 44-45.

13. Susan Haack has noted some of these points in "Is It True What They Say about Tarski?" *Philosophy* 51 (1976): 323-36.

14. Donald Davidson, "True to the Facts," *Journal of Philosophy* 66 (1969): 748-64; Hilary Putnam, "Explanation and Reference" and "Language and Reality," in *Mind, Language and Reality* (Cambridge: Cambridge University Press, 1975); and Hartry Field, "Theory Change and the Indeterminancy of Reference," *Journal of Philosophy* 70 (1973): 462-81.

15. See Israel Scheffler, *Science and Subjectivity* (Indianapolis: Bobbs-Merrill, 1967), chap. 3; Putnam, "Explanation and References" and "Language and Reality" and Field, "Theory Change." Although these authors are concerned primarily with comparison of scientific theories, their views are easily generalized to other areas.

16. I take this to be one of the things involved in Quine's thesis of ontological relativity. He tells us that ontology is *doubly relative,* first to some background theory or language, and second to some choice of translation manual from object language into background language, *Ontological Relativity and Other Essays* [*OR*] (N.Y.: Columbia University Press, 1969), passim. the first relativity is what I have in mind here; the second involves Quine's thesis of the indeterminancy of translation. Quine, however, opposes full-blown relativism because he believes that there is, by and large, no fact of the matter about the conceptual scheme of others. It is not that the native mind is inscrutable; there simply is "nothing to scrute." *OR,* p. 5; cf. *Word and Object* (Cambridge: M.I.T. Press, 1960), p. 58 and, on Whorf and Cassirer, p. 77.

17. Also, for replies to some of the standard objections of this sort, see Jack W. Meiland, "On the Paradox of Cognitive Relativism," *Metaphilosophy* 11 (1980).

18. Here 'X' and 'p' function as they did in **T**. Two historical points are worth

noting. First, Plato's conditional represents something stronger than material implication, for he uses it to support counterfactual conditionals [*Theaetetus,* 171a]. Second, as M.F. Burnyeat argues in "Protagoras and Self-Refutation in Plato's *Theaetetus,*" *Philosophical Review* 85 (1977): 172-95, the implication actually runs from right to left as well as from left to right. I shall ignore these matters, as well as problems arising from the opaque context in **P**, for the formula raises plenty of difficulties quite apart from these.

19. Since beliefs can, at least typically, be expressed in sentences, I will often speak of basic beliefs having truth values and entailing other sentences or belief regarding this as shorthand for talk about the corresponding sentences. If different frameworks can have different logics, the relation of logical consequence involved in any given case must be that of the framework in question.

20. Mannheim, *Ideology and Utopia* (N.Y.: Harcourt Brace and World, 1936), p. 66; cf. Kuhn's talk about adherents to different paradigms living in "different worlds," *The Structure of Scientific Revolutions,* chap. 10 and passim.

21. In what follows I shall make the simplifying assumption that languages and frameworks are in a one-to-one correspondence, thus allowing talk of truth in F, rather than truth in L (in F). This has the added advantage of allowing us to speak simply of translation from one framework to another; where necessary, such shorthand can be expanded.

22. Indeed, certain sorts of behavioral evidence could justify attributions of a language and world-view to others *even if* we could not succeed in translating their language. Or so I argue in *Conceptual Relativism,* chap. 5; see also Jonathon Bennett, *Linguistic Behavior* (Cambridge: Cambridge University Press, 1976), chap. 4 and passim, and Robert Stalnaker, "Propositions," in a. MacKay and D. Merrill, eds., *Issues in the Philosophy of Language* (New Haven: Yale University Press, 1976), p. 82.

23. Oswald Spengler, *The Decline of the West,* vol. 1 (N.Y.: Alfred Knopf, 1966), p. 46.

24. This is a version of an argument given by Barry Stroud in "Conventionalism and the Indeterminancy of Translation," in D. Davidson and J. Hintikka, eds., *Words and Objections* (Dordrect: D. Reidel, 1969).

INTRODUCTION TO
Kuhn's Epistemological Relativism

Much of the discussion of cognitive relativism in recent years has focused on conceptual relativism. And in large part this recent interest in conceptual relativism is due to the philosophy of science of Thomas Kuhn. Kuhn is prominently mentioned in Mandelbaum's and Davidson's attacks on conceptual relativism earlier in this volume. Kuhn's revolutionary work, *The Structure of Scientific Revolutions,* has elicited the interest of thinkers in many fields and continues to be discussed intensively twenty years after its publication. Much of the discussion has been critical of his views: he has been accused of picturing science, and perhaps all intellectual work, as irrational and totally lacking in objectivity. Israel Scheffler takes the consequences of Kuhn's work to be quite extreme: "Independent and public controls are no more, communication has failed, the common universe of things is a delusion, reality itself is made by the scientist rather than discovered by him. In place of a community of rational men following objective procedures in the pursuit of truth, we have a set of isolated monads, within each of which belief forms without systematic constraints."[1]

Although Kuhn believes that the charge of relativism against him is misleading, he does explicitly state views which nonrelativists find distressing: "There is, I think, no theory-independent way to reconstruct phrases like 'really there'; the notion of a match between the ontology of a theory and its 'real' counterpart in nature now seems to me illusive in principle."[2] This is, surely, a type of relativism in making reality relative to a theory. But what type of relativism is it? Is it conceptual relativism, as Scheffler and many others claim, or is it some other type?

Many of Kuhn's critics hold Kuhn to be a conceptual relativist because they understand what Kuhn calls "paradigms" to involve sets of concepts or conceptual schemes. For example, Newtonian mechanics and Einstein-ian mechanics exemplify two different paradigms and employ quite different concepts. As Kuhn says, "Newtonian mass is conserved; Einsteinian is convertible with energy. Only at low velocities may the two be measured in the same way, and even then they must not be conceived to be the same. . . . This need to change the meaning of established and familiar concepts is central to the revolutionary impact of Einstein's theory."[3] Because these two types of mechanics employ different concepts and thus structure the world differently, they do not talk about the same things even when the same words (such as 'mass') are used by the two theories. The same words express different concepts. For this reason Newtonian laws are not limiting cases of Einstein's laws, and one theory cannot be reduced to the other. "The transition from Newtonian to Einsteinian mechanics illustrates with particular clarity the scientific revolution as a displacement of the conceptual network through which scientists view the world."[4] This heavy emphasis on *conceptual* shifts during scientific revolutions supports the interpretation of Kuhn as a conceptual relativist.

If Kuhn is a conceptual relativist, then his position is subject to serious difficulties, some of which are summarized by Doppelt. For example, we normally take some scientific theories to be competitors and hence about the same subject-matter. But if different theories employ different concepts to structure the world differently, in what way can these theories be about the same subject-matter? We normally think that science makes progress over the years. But if different theories cannot have the same subject-matter, there can be no progress along a continuous dimension.

Doppelt feels that whatever the intrinsic merit of these objections, they are not objections to Kuhn. For Kuhn should not be interpreted as a conceptual relativist. Although Doppelt does not put his position in these terms, he sees Kuhn as a type of value relativist, where the values in question are "cognitive values." The expression 'cognitive values' will seem to many to be a contradiction in terms, especially in the context of science. Science is commonly taken to be an objective enterprise, where this means in part that science is "value-free." The acceptance and rejection of scientific theories is regarded as dictated by the observational and experimental data, a procedure from which the scientists' values, prejudices, and desires are rigidly excluded. But Kuhn points out that nature presents the scientist with many puzzles and problems to be solved and that the solving of some of these problems can be considered more important than the solving of others. Rival paradigms deem different problems to be important. As Doppelt puts it, "Even though rival paradigms share some of the same problems, they do not weigh their importance in the same way, assigning them different orders of significance and priority in the achievement of what will count as the success of a paradigm." He cites Kuhn's example of pre-Daltonian chemistry which aimed at explaining the observable qualities of chemical substances and the qualitative changes they undergo during reactions as compared with Daltonian chemistry which emphasized quantitative problems concerning weight relations and proportions in reactions. The two paradigms differ in what is considered important to explain. Judgments of importance and significance are value judgments. And judgments about the importance of one or another cognitive element may be termed judgments about cognitive values.

To put this point in a more general way, Kuhn emphasizes the role of criteria of adequacy in science. All theoreticians must employ some criteria of adequacy so that they know when they have been successful. Deciding which problems are the important problems is only one of the issues for the theoretician. The theoretician must also decide what type of results one should aim at. For example, should one aim to develop general laws? Should one instead aim at systematic description or classification? Different decisions about these issues result in different ways of doing science—indeed, different modes of inquiry generally. Doppelt's interpretation of Kuhn has the great virtue of bringing this essential but generally ignored aspect of science to the fore. The role of cognitive values is all too likely to be overlooked because this role imports a significant and ineradicable element of subjectivity into an activity usually regarded as objective. If two scientists differ over the importance of a given problem or over the goal of inquiry, no "objective" method can be used to settle these ultimate disagreements. And yet their views on such matters play a direct and substantial role in their ways of doing science.

Thus, on Doppelt's interpretation, too, Kuhn's position appears to have the features characteristic of cognitive relativism. There appears to be no paradigm-independent way of determining which paradigm is best or which gives the most accurate picture of nature. There seems to be no rational way of settling disputes among scientists about the proper way to do science. But, though Doppelt's Kuhn is as relativistic as Scheffler's Kuhn, Doppelt's Kuhn is not subject to the same objections as Scheffler's Kuhn. For example, while scientists who employ quite different conceptual schemes cannot communicate with one another, scientists who differ in their cognitive values may nevertheless employ the same concepts and therefore may communicate. Moreover, two paradigms different in their cognitive values can base their conclusions on the same data. Is scientific development a rational process according to Doppelt's interpretation? This depends on what is meant by 'rational'. A scientist is able to give reasons for switching from one paradigm to another; these reasons derive from the cognitive values embedded in the new paradigm. But the scientist cannot deny that reasons can also be given for choosing quite different paradigms, so that the reasons he gives for his choice need not be coercive or compelling for everyone. Moreover, switching from one paradigm to another involves a conversion to different cognitive values, a conversion which may be viewed as nonrational.

Kuhn argues that in the switch from one paradigm to another something is inevitably lost. The new paradigm focuses attention on new problems and treats it as a matter of no significance that the new way of doing science offers no solutions to the old problems as the previous paradigm did. Nevertheless, not having solutions to the old problems does represent a loss and throws doubt on any claim that science has progressed by the shift to the new paradigm. Doppelt makes an important distinction between (1) short-run relativism—the view that shifts of paradigm incur such losses as well as make gains—and (2) long-run relativism—the view that some losses are permanent and never made up regardless of how many new paradigms arise. Short-run relativism may be true, but this does not entail that losses are permanent. Doppelt believes that none of Kuhn's arguments show that there is no possibility of a paradigm's some day arising which provides solutions simultaneously to all of the problems previously considered significant. If this were to happen, should we say that this paradigm gives us the absolute truth about nature? Doppelt does not discuss this question. But we suggest that for a paradigm to be justifiably so regarded, it would have to provide solutions for all possible problems, not just those historically considered important. Otherwise, someone could easily maintain that the unsolved problems are the important problems which must be solved if a theory is to be considered adequate.

Readers will perhaps differ over the accuracy of Doppelt's interpretation of Kuhn. But this disagreement should not blind us to the fact that Doppelt has correctly focused attention on the significance of cognitive values in scientific theorizing and, in this way, on a very important type of cognitive relativism.

NOTES

1. Israel Scheffler, *Science and Subjectivity* (Indianapolis: Bobbs-Merrill, 1967), p. 19.
2. Thomas Kuhn, *The Structure of Scientific Revolutions* (2nd ed.; Chicago: University of Chicago Press, 1970), p. 206.
3. Ibid., p. 102.
4. Ibid.

Kuhn's Epistemological Relativism: An Interpretation and Defense*

Gerald Doppelt

I

It is generally acknowledged that Thomas Kuhn's *The Structure of Scientific Revolution* [1] develops one of the most original, powerful, and provocative conceptions of science to emerge as an alternative to the positivist tradition in recent times. Yet I think it is fair to say that the most interesting and radical philosophical claims concerning science advanced by Kuhn have generally been found wanting and rejected by influential voices in Anglo-American philosophy of science. On one hand reviewers grant that Kuhn's work has brought into perspective important dimensions of the historical development of scientific theory neglected or obscured in positivist accounts; on the other hand they have tried to show that this historical perspective does not support the epistemological arguments Kuhn purports to draw from it (e.g. see [1]). The central focus of this criticism is Kuhn's epistemological relativism and its underlying arguments for what he calls the 'incommensurability' of rival scientific paradigms.

Dudley Shapere and Israel Scheffler have developed some of the most persuasive criticism of Kuhn's relativism and in the process defended several features of a positivist account of scientific development. In this

*Reprinted with permission of the author and publisher from *Inquiry* 21 (1978): 33–45, 49–52, 60–66, 68–69, 71–77, 80–82, 84–86 (Universitetsforlaget, Oslo-Bergen-Tromso, publishers).

paper, I want to reconstruct one of their central lines of argument and the interpretation of Kuhn on which it rests;[1] in essence, I will argue that this account of Kuhn fails to do justice to the main line of epistemological argument in his position which lends it far more plausibility, internal coherence, and systematic import than the former conveys. My larger aim is to expose an aspect of Kuhn's critique of the positivist model of scientific progress which I find powerful, and which has not commanded sufficient attention in my estimation. The interpretation of Kuhn I offer leaves open the question of whether his relativist account of scientific development is ultimately correct. But if my interpretation is sound this question cannot be resolved by purely philosophical argumentation but rather requires an examination of actual cases of scientific revolution to test Kuhn's own use of scientific examples.

The radical thrust of Kuhn's relativism is the denial of the view, shared by positivists, practising scientists, and the layman, that later or contemporary scientific theories constitute more rational, faithful, comprehensive, and deep accounts of the way the world is than their predecessors. Interelated to this claim is Kuhn's rejection of the view that the explanatory superiority (on balance) of one paradigm over another relative to a common set of criteria constitutes the decisive reason actually at work in scientists' transition from an established theory to its revolutionary alternative. Kuhn's relativism hinges on his key argument that competing and historically successive scientific theories are 'incommensurable' with one another: that they are *in some sense* sufficiently different, disparate, incongruous relative to one another to block the possibility of comparative evaluation on the same scale of criteria.

A careful reading of Kuhn's works reveals that the incommensurability of rival scientific paradigms is grounded in the incommensurability, disparity, or incongruity between the following of their respective elements: (1) their scientific concepts, or theoretical language; (2) their observational data, or mode of scientific perception; (3) their agenda of problems-to-be-solved; and (4) their criteria of adequacy for scientific explanation.[2] These various grounds of incommensurability are neither incompatible nor unrelated but they do reveal genuine ambiguities and tensions within Kuhn's case for incommensurability. To put the matter succinctly, Kuhn variously argues in different contexts that rival paradigms are incommensurable (1) because they do not speak the same scientific language,[3] (2) because they do not address, acknowledge, or perceive the same observational data,[4] (3) because they are not concerned to answer the same questions, or resolve the same problems,[5] and (4) because they do not construe what counts as an adequate, or even legitimate, explanation in the same way.[6] In any case, the basic point is the absence of *shared* scientific concepts, observational data, theoretical problems, and criteria of explanatory adequacy which stand independently of rival paradigms and in whose terms they can be commonly assessed. Without these common desiderata shared by the rival theories that punctuate scientific development, judgments of progress toward the truth, rationally compelling argument between rivals, and the existence of sufficient reasons for transferring theoretical allegiance from one to another also seem to go by the wayside. While this much is clear, the problem of interpreting Kuhn is motivated by two questions: first, the question of which of these four alleged grounds of incommensurability is most basic to explicating and justifying the others, and thus the relativism argument taken as a whole; secondly, the question of how radical the discontinuities between rival paradigms are, on Kuhn's analysis and must be, in order to justify the relativism essential to Kuhn's intention. The line of critical argument which I will reconstruct from the work of Scheffler and Shapere rests on an interpretation which makes the incommensurability of rival scientific concepts or languages the key pillar of Kuhn's relativism. Secondly, their interpretation attributes to Kuhn an absolute and extreme discontinuity between rival paradigms that effectively precludes any logical contact whatsoever between them. In brief, I will dispute this interpretation—despite the fact that it does capture some strains in Kuhn's complicated argument; I will argue that the incommensurability of scientific problems provides the central basis for explicating and justifying the relativism argument as a whole. Furthermore, on my interpretation Kuhn's argument involves a far less radical discontinuity between rival paradigms but nonetheless sufficient to justify the relativism Kuhn intends.

According to Scheffler and Shapere's line of interpretation, which I will dispute (call it the 'neo-positivist' interpretation), Kuhn's relativism depends on his key claim that every scientific paradigm is essentially imprisoned within (1) its own unique and untranslatable language, or conceptual framework; and it is for *this* reason that rival paradigms cannot, thus do not, share commonly formulatable (2) observational data, (3) theoretical problems, and (4) criteria of explanatory adequacy. On this reading, Kuhn must assume that the whole observational language employed by a paradigm to characterize its data is thoroughly, inextricably, and necessarily infected in its meaning by the paradigm's unique theoretical concepts and meanings.[7] Either the paradigm's theoretical language is its observational language (i.e. the key terms are literally identical), or superficially distinct observational terms have their meaning wholly determined by their context, their relation to the paradigm's theoretical terms. In either case rival paradigms, each with their own unique theoretical concepts, are equally imprisoned within their own observational languages and thus within their own observational data. Furthermore if competing theories do not share sufficient language for commonly formulatable data, then surely they also lack the common resources for sharing questions concerning the data, or anything else, for that matter.

Thus, on the neo-positivist interpretation, Kuhn's relativism hinges on a thoroughgoing conceptual relativism and related holistic doctrine of scientific meaning; according to the relativism so construed, everything a paradigm does—what it sees, the data it recognizes, the questions it poses, the explanations it offers all necessarily presuppose in every instance its own special and untranslatable theoretical concepts. As a result, rival paradigms cannot even seek to explain the *same* observational data or answer the *same* questions concerning these data. This becomes Kuhn's most basic point of disagreement with a positivist conception of science. For while a positivist account allows that every new fundamental physical theory exhibits its own special theoretical concepts and assumptions, it nevertheless insists that an independent observational language with some essential residue of autonomous meaning survives every transformation in basic theoretical concepts. And, as against Kuhn's account, positivism maintains that it is precisely *this* continuity in scientific discourse which is presupposed in the very possibility of the validation of one theory as against another ([9], pp. 47–66). Given this reading of Kuhn, it is easy to see how what Shapere and Scheffler take to be the most radical aspects of his view follow, and how their line of criticism persuasively develops.

Because rival paradigms lack any access to a common language, they cannot be meaningfully compared. Thus, according to Scheffler, Kuhn infers that incommensurable theories must also be incomparable. He stresses that on Kuhn's view there can be nothing like genuine communication between rival paradigms, not to speak of rational argument or suasion ([9], pp. 16–17). For this reason, Kuhn is led to characterize the transition from one paradigm to another as a process of 'conversion' or a 'leap of faith'—in which one is mystically converted to a new language-game, rather than won over to rational allegiance to a more sound body of beliefs. In explaining why some scientists embrace the new language-game and others do not, Kuhn must fall back on what from a positivist standpoint are non-scientific or irrational factors—such as the age, professional training, or past career of the scientist in question. When one paradigm finally triumphs over its predecessor, whatever epistemological superiority it may be said to have reduces to the brute fact that it has effectively won a majority of those people identified as scientists over to its new language-game and associated world view; it is not to be found in the fact that it constitutes a better account of the same data and problems than its predecessor. In short, by imprisoning every scientific paradigm in its own world of uncommunicable meanings, Kuhn effectively reduces the logic of scientific development to the psychology and sociology of 'conversion', mystical 'gestalt switches' from one way of 'seeing' the world to another ([9], pp. 18–19, 76–77; [10], pp. 366–8).

This reading of Kuhn provides the basis for the persuasive line of critical argument developed by Scheffler and Shapere. First of all, if rival scientific paradigms are as insular, self-enclosed, and imprisoned within their own language as Kuhn maintains, in what sense can they be rivals or compete? If they cannot communicate or argue, how and on what can they disagree? If each is necessarily focussed on its own data and problems, in what sense do they offer incompatible accounts of the *same* subject-matter or domain? The clear implication is that Kuhn's incommensurability cannot account for the evident facts of theoretical conflict in scientific development ([9], p. 82; [11], p. 391). Secondly, Kuhn's own account of the role of 'anomalies' in scientific development implies a commonly formula-table observational point of contact between rival paradigms. On his view an 'anomaly' is an observed datum which the established paradigm cannot handle but which the new paradigm resolves in a way that lends it some initial credibility. If rival paradigms can thus speak to the same empirical situation, they must share *some* common concepts, data, and problems. How is this possible, given Kuhnian incommensurability? The implication is clearly that Kuhn is inconsistent and must violate his own relativism in developing a half-way plausible account of scientific development. Indeed Scheffler suggests that Kuhn's anomalies are simply the positivist's falsifying or disconfirming evidence in disguise ([9], p. 89).

Finally, Scheffler and Shapere attack the holistic conception of scientific meaning, which, on their interpretation, is the indispensable pillar upon which Kuhn's entire incommensurability argument rests. First of all, they stress the fact that the proponents of rival paradigms do engage in argument, coherent debate, and rational suasion, which establishes a strong prima facie case for some substantial continuity of concept and discourse from one paradigm to the next ([9], pp. 79–80). But, more importantly, they in effect argue that there is no good reason, nor does Kuhn provide any, for maintaining that all of the concepts and language employed by proponents of a particular paradigm necessarily have their meanings wholly determined by its context of distinctive theoretical concepts. In particular, they suggest that Kuhn's view that all scientific language is theory-dependent stems from a confused and ill-worked out conception of meaning. The distinction between the sense or connotation and the reference or application of a concept is neglected by Kuhn and thus he fails to consider that changes which a new paradigm effects in one are compatible with a stability of meaning and commensurability in the other. Shapere argues that in the case of the concept of mass from Newton to Einstein, or that of planet from Ptolemy to Copernicus, it is the reference of the term that changes, while its sense remains stable—which may be sufficient for commensurability ([11], pp. 340-41). Scheffler argues that even when the connotation of observational concepts changes in a new theory, they typically retain a stability of reference which is sufficient to lend experimental laws, data, and meanings an independent status and sustain commensurability between rival theories ([9], pp. 61-62). The fact that Kuhn fails to make such distinctions, to distingush between the different ways meanings may change yet remain constant, undermines his key contention that rival paradigms are imprisoned within their own language. And Scheffler and Shapere assume that once the possibility of such a shared observational language is assured, the commensurability of data, problems, and explanations is also vindicated. The philosophical underpinnings of Kuhn's relativism are thus defeated. Finally, it is clear that, apart from these underpinnings, Scheffler and Shapere both find any relativist conclusion to be philosophically unacceptable and a 'reductio' of the argument for it.[8]

In sum, the neo-positivist critique of Kuhn rests on an interpretation which (1) makes the incommensurability of scientific meanings the most basic premise of the relativism argument and furthermore (2) characterizes the conclusion of this argument in terms of the most absolute epistemological break between the old paradigm and the new one which replaces it. Each fundamental scientific theory constitutes a world unique unto itself and the transition from one theoretical tradition to another can only be represented as an irrational or non-ratinal leap of faith explainable in psychological and sociological terms.

In the following section, I will develop a different reading of Kuhn's relativism argument. Then in later sections I will employ this reading to defend his relativism against the line of criticism advanced by Scheffler and Shapere and finally, to situate it in a more adquate critical perspective.

II

On the interpetation of Kuhn's relativism to be developed here, it is the incommensurability of scientific *problems* between rival paradigms and not that of *meanings* which constitutes the most basic premise of the argument. Secondly, so construed, Kuhnian incommensurability will turn out to be compatible with a considerable overlap between the language, problems, data and standards of rival paradigms; certainly sufficient overlap to account for the shared context of rational debate which Kuhn as well as his critics find to be a pervasive feature of scientific development. Thus his view does not entail the kind of absolute epistemological break between rival paradigms attributed to it by Scheffler and Shapere. Rather he maintains that there is insufficient overlap in the problems and standards of rival paradigms to rank them on the same scale of criteria. Finally, on our reading Kuhn's relativist conclusion entails neither that the transition to a new paradigm is 'irrational' nor that there is no sense of progress at all in the development of science. Rather its thrust, is, first, that the balance of reasons or the demands of scientific rationality never unequivocally favor one paradigm (either the old or the new) over its rival; and secondly, that in consequence, contemporary paradigms do not represent progress over what they replace *in the sense of* progress toward the truth concerning nature. This in a nutshell is the reading of Kuhn which we must now explain and elaborate.

It will be useful to begin by calling our attention to the kinds of formulation in Kuhn which most explicitly articulate the reading I will develop here:

> But paradigms differ in more than substance, for they are directed not only to nature but also back upon the science that produced them.... As a result, the reception of a new paradigm often necessitates a *redefinition of the corresponding science. Some old problems may be relegated to another science, or declared entirely 'unscientific.'* Others that were prevously non-existent or trivial may, with a new paradigm, become the very archetypes of significant achievement. And *as the problems change, so often, does the standard that distinguishes a real scientific solution from a mere metaphysical speculation, word game, or mathematical play.* The normal-scientific tradition that emerges from a scientific revolution is not only incompatible but often actually incommensurable with that which had gone before. ([1], p. 103, my italics)

> *By shifting emphasis from the cognitive to the normative function of paradigms,* the preceding examples enlarge our understanding of the ways in which paradigms give form to the scientific life ... when paradigms change, there are ususally significant shifts in the criteria determining the legitimacy both of problems and of proposed solution....
> That observation returns us to the point from which this section began.... *To the extent ... that two scientific schools disagree about what is a problem and what a solution, they will inevitably talk*

> *through each other when debating the relative merits of their*
> *respective paradigms. In the partially circular arguments that regular-*
> *ly result, each paradigm will be shown to satisfy more or less the*
> *criteria it dictates for itself and to fall short of those dictated by its*
> *opponent . . . since no paradigm ever solves all the problems it defines*
> *and since no two paradigms leave all the same problems unsolved,*
> *paradigm debates always involve the question: which problems is it*
> *more significant to have solved?* ([1], pp. 109–10, my italics)

On the basis of such passages the primary claim advanced by incommensurability in Kuhn is that the *standards* of adequacy each paradigm
implicitly sets for itself are sufficiently disparate from one to the next to
block any uniform basis for a judgment that one is, on balance, more
reasonable to accept than its rival.[9] Furthermore, the main reason in Kuhn
that these standards or critieria of adequacy are disparate in this way is *not*
primarily that each paradigm is imprisoned within its own concepts; but
rather that the rivals do not identify *the* questions or problems that any
adequate paradigm must resolve, in the same way. On this reading the most
revolutionary dimension of a new paradigm is not primarily the fact that it
involves novel theoretical concepts; rather, it is the fact that the new
paradigm implies a shift of commitment to a new set of theoretical
problems as the 'core' of the discipline—substantively different from the
problematic which defined the hard core of science under the old
paradigm.[10] Even though rival paradigms share some of the same
problems, they do not weigh their importance in the same way, assigning
them different orders of significance and priority in the achievement of
what will count as the success of a paradigm, or alternatively, a tolerable
level of failure. Thus, when Kuhn characterizes paradigm debates as
necessarily at 'cross-purposes', he means literally that; it is not that the
rivals lack a sufficient commonalty of language to communicate or argue.
It is rather that they lack a sufficiently common definition of the discipline
and its criteria of explanatory adequacy to allow their discourse to
terminate in rational consensus—even concerning the relative merits and
defects of their paradigms, apart from the key issue of which is superior.[11]
Thus, conflict between scientific theories becomes much more like conflicts
in ethical and political life than the absolute distinction between scientific
and normative discourse advanced by classical positivism allows. In both
cases, the conflicts have an irreducible normative dimension and implicitly—
if not explicitly—embody incompatible answers to the question of which
aims, values, and problems *ought* to dominate and define a certain domain
of activity.

The elaboration of this interpretation of Kuhn requires that we carefully reconstruct the relationship of the incommensurability of scientific problems to that of standards, observational data, and scientific concepts. As the preceding formulations already suggest, what makes the different problems of concern to rival paradigms 'incommensurable' is not their mere difference, but the fact that these differences are incorporated into the standards of explanatory adequacy each paradigm implicitly sets for itself and all theory. It is important to clarify this. Rival scientific theories might focus on different if partially overlapping sets of problems and nonetheless mutually accept the same standards of explanatory adequacy, thus avoiding imcommensurability. For example, though their problematics are different, the rival paradigms might agree that a common subset of problems which they share define the core of the discipline—the most important domain for the establishment of any theory's rational credibility. Both would thus implicitly subscribe to the standard which evaluates the relative success of theory in terms of how well it deals with the privileged core-problems at the heart of the discipline. Yet, it is precisely this kind of agreement which the claim of the incommensurability of scientific problems intends to rule out. For Kuhn the point is not simply that rival paradigms (a) focus on different sets of problems, (b) give these problems different priorities in their respective research programs, and (c) define the most basic problems differently—all of which might simply be a reflection of the pragmatics and strategy of research, the interest, and preferences of particular scientists, etc. Rather, for Kuhn, these differences gain epistemological significance because they are built into the very standards of theoretical adaquacy, the defining aims of the science, in terms of which each paradigm evaluates itself and its rivals. We must keep in mind that for Kuhn every paradigm derives its conceptions of science, its *privileged* problematic and standards from the brilliant scientific achievement with which it is born. Hence the kind of problems whose solutions define the standards of good theory for any given paradigm are generally resolved to a greater or less degree by that paradigm but either unresolved, unrecognized, or consigned to a minor theoretical importance by its rival(s). Thus each paradigm implicitly defines standards of scientific adequacy favoring its achievements and research program and unfavorable with respect to the work of its rivals.[12]

In order to further elaborate our interpretation, we need to explain how the incommensurability of observational data fits into the relativism argument. In many contexts where Kuhn argues that rival paradigms implicitly address different problems, he means quite straightforwardly that they seek to explain different observational data. Hence the capacity of each paradigm to explain the range of data which its problems define as of key importance generates the major type of criterion of explanatory adequacy Kuhn has in mind. The basic point is thus that rival paradigms are incommensurable because they imply different criteria of explanatory adequacy, the major criterion of each being how well it answers its own distinctive questions and explains its own privileged range of data. An example will help bring these points into focus.

      Kuhn considers the transition from the pre-Daltonian to the Daltonian paradigm of chemistry to be among our best examples of scientific revolution ([1], p. 133). His account of this transition stresses the alleged fact that the pre-Daltonian chemistry of the phlogiston theory and the theory of elective affinity achieved reasonable answers to a whole set of questions effectively abandoned by Dalton's new chemistry.[13] The old chemistry was able to explain the observable qualities of chemical substances—e.g. why the metals were so much more alike in their observed metalline qualities than their ores, and also the qualitative changes they undergo during chemical reactions, such as the formation of observed acidic properties. For example it explained the common properties of the metals as due to their possession of phlogiston, lacking in their ores ([1], pp. 99–100). In effect, the new 'quantitative' chemistry of Lavoisier and Dalton abandoned any concern for these questions and these observational data— whose treatment constituted the main achievement of the earlier model of chemistry. Thus, the new paradigm 'ended by depriving chemistry of some actual and much potential explanatory power' ([1], p. 107)—though it brought in its wake the capacity to treat a whole range of data and problems (concerning weight relations and proportions in chemical reactions) only accorded minimal recognition before. Yet, as Kuhn sees the matter, what has occurred in this transition is 'a change of standards'; because 'During much of the nineteenth century failure to explain the qualities of compounds was no indictment of chemical theory' ([1], p. 107)—even though this capacity constituted one of the main criteria of explanatory adequacy within pre-Daltonian chemistry. Thus, to complete the example, Dalton's paradigm *cannot* be characterized as simply offering a better and more rational account of chemical phenomena than its predecessor; for the two paradigms seek to explain different kinds of observational data, in response to different agendas of problems, and in accordance with different standards of success.

      At this point, it will be useful to underscore the main disagreement between Kuhn's relativism and a positivist account concerning the role of observational data, on the interpretation of Kuhn I am developing here. It is clear that an essential feature of positivism is also the insistence on the capacity of a new theory to handle new types of observational data and problems which the old theory did not adequately treat, or treat at all. Indeed, on the positivist account of science, it is precisely the capacity of a new theory to handle more types of data and problems than the old, and to handle the old theory's data and problems more simply, economically, adequately, etc. that makes it superior to its predecessor. This familiar positivist criterion of scientific progress rests on two assumptions which Kuhn's account purports to discredit: (1) first, that every new scientific theory seeks to handle *all* of the genuine data and problems treated by the old, and (2) secondly, that every new theory gives the data and problems adequately handled by the old the same importance in its criteria of success, of explanatory adequacy, as the old theory did. On Kuhn's view, every new paradigm—no matter how successful and well-established it becomes— involves *losses* as well as gains with respect to its predecessor(s) in terms of the kinds of data and problems it is concerned to handle, and can in fact handle.[14] Such a loss is exemplified in the above case of Dalton's new chemistry which effectively abandons the central data and problems of the old 'qualitative' chemistry. Secondly, although the new paradigm handles *some* of the data and problems treated by its predecessor,[15] typically the rival paradigms do not give the same importance or priority to these common elements in defining their respective criteria of success, or theoretical adequacy.

To illustrate this second point, let us briefly return to the Dalton example. The problem of changing weight relations in chemical reactions brilliantly handled by Dalton's paradigm did in fact surface before his work, in the form of certain anomalies for the phlogiston theory of combustion ([1], pp. 71–72). On this theory the combustion of a substance was explained as involving a loss of phlogiston and was thus assumed by most chemist to entail a loss of weight; the fact that certain substances were observed to gain weight in combustion constituted anomalous data for the phlogiston theory which some of its exponents gradually came to regard as serious and tried unsuccessfully to accommodate in various ways.[16] Yet within pre-Daltonian chemistry this problem, though recognized, was not acknowledged as a very important kind of problem and certainly not the most important or 'paradigmatic' kind at the heart of chemistry as it became for Dalton; for the latter but not the former it was the observational problem and data of weight relations which constituted the epistemological crux of chemical theory, upon which its very success or failure wholly depends. Thus it is clear that for Kuhn rival paradigms do share some empirical point(s) of contact—some common observational data and problems (e.g. weight-gain in combustion between the pre-Daltonian and Daltonian paradigms of chemistry). Yet this commonalty is entirely compatible with the incommensurability of observational data in Kuhn's sense, on our interpretation, for two reasons. First of all, the shared data which are 'anomalous' for the old paradigm but successfully explained by the new enjoy a far greater epistemological importance relative to the standards implicit in the new paradigm that they enjoy relative to those implicit in the old paradigm. Hence the capacity to explain these data does *not* constitute a unitary criterion of theoretical adequacy or explanatory power accepted by both paradigms. Secondly, quite apart from the shared data, the observational data (and problems) which the rival paradigms do *not* share are sufficient to generate incommensurability. For the very substance of these differences in data and observational concerns is incorporated into the standards of good theory implicit in the rival paradigms. The core observational data which each paradigm can effectively explain but which are unacknowledged (or declared 'unscientific') by the rival paradigm constitute from the former's standpoint *essential* explicanda with which *any adequate* theory *must* deal; and by this standard, each paradigm is rationally and scientifically superior to its rival—regardless of how well its rival handles anomalous data and its own privileged range of data.

In sum, on our reconstruction of Kuhn's position rival paradigms can and do exhibit some continuity of common observational data and concerns; and at the same time they also exhibit incommensurability with respect to their criteria of observational adequacy, or, i.e., of fidelity to data. This incommensurability of data thus provides Kuhn's main source of the incommensurable problems and standards of rival paradigms.[17]

* * * * *

III

At this point it can easily be explained how Kuhn's relativism argument, on our interpretation, circumvents the most straightforward and damaging criticisms leveled against it by Shapere and Scheffler. On our view, this argument does not depend on the sort of holistic doctrine of scientific meaning attributed to it by the latter authors;[18] hence the persuasive criticisms they advance against this doctrine[19] do not provide cogent reasons for rejecting Kuhn's incommensurability thesis. Furthermore, this thesis does not imply an absolute epistemological break between mutually 'incommensurable' paradigms which *a priori* imprison themselves within their respective language, data, problems, and standards of science, and blocks the possibility of any coherent debate or comparison between them.[20] Hence Kuhn's position does not exhibit the prima facie implausibility which accrues to it on the Scheffler-Shapere reading.

On our view, incommensurable paradigms can and do share *some* observational data, problems, and language; the crux of the thesis of incommensurability is Kuhn's claim that there are basic, non-cumulative differences in the observational data and problems of concern to rival paradigms which are incorporated into their respective standards of theoretical adequacy. Hence on our reading, the role of anomalies in Kuhn's theory does not create any inconsistency, as is the case according to the Scheffler-Shapere reading.[21] Kuhn makes it clear that in scientific revolution, a new paradigm only prevails if (1) it resolves data and problems ('anomalies') which have come to be regarded as important but irresolvable on the old paradigm, and (2) it also effectively deals with *some* of the old paradigm's other problems (and data) as well as posing and resolving wholly new problems.[22] There is *this* much continuity in data, problems, and discourse from one paradigm to the next; but *this* much is not sufficient for commensurability, and is thus not inconsistent with the relativism (as it is, on the neo-positivist interpretation). Rival paradigms can share this much and nonetheless exhibit fundamental disagreements irresolvable by scientific argument concerning the set of problems and data that any adequate theory must treat (only some of which they share); and the order or priority among these problems in determining what is to count as scientific success, or a *tolerable* level of failure (the minimal achievement presupposed by the continuing plausibility of a theory).

Likewise, incommensurability is not inconsistent with the fact that rival paradigms are rivals and as such must disagree about something.[23] On our view, incommensurable paradigms can and do disagree with respect to the data and problems they share, including the 'anomalies'. For example, the old and new chemistry disagree concerning how to explain the phenomenon of weight-gain in combustion: what really occurs in combustion, the nature of the substance essentially involved in it, etc. Thus this criticism of Scheffler and Shapere's is not telling.

But an adequate defense of Kuhn concerning the possibility of disagreement must also assume the offensive, because his theory of science rejects a fundamental, positivist assumption which underlines the Scheffler-Shapere argument concerning disagreement. This assumption is that physical theories can only be incompatible (or disagree) to the extent that they share an empirical subject-matter and offer logically incompatible answers to the same questions of fact concerning this subject-matter. Kuhn's philosophy of science maintains that this is neither the only nor the most basic respect in which rival theories are incompatible. On his view the most basic level of disagreement concerns the normative question of how the subject-matter as a whole ought to be defined. What is the empirical subject-matter of their discipline, properly construed; which data and problems constitute the essential explicanda of science, how important is the subject-matter which rival paradigms share, as against what they do not share, etc.? Yet our above question may be raised anew: is it not the case that rival paradigms must share a subject-matter in order to disagree over how the subject-matter as a whole ought to be defined? Certainly Aristotle and Galileo have rival paradigms of terrestrial motion; and the pre- and post-Daltonians had rival paradigms concerning the chemical behavior of substances undergoing changes of physical properties. Nonetheless, Kuhn's theory holds that a continuous subject-matter (e.g. terrestrial dynamics) shared at *this* level of abstraction is compatible with radical shifts in the problems or observational aspects of the domain held to be essential to the discipline, and to the essence of the domain itself. Aristotelians had a theory of terrestrial motion, yet this theory did not embrace the problems or aspects of motion brought to the fore by Galileo's theory of pendulum motion. Thus rival paradigms can disagree with respect to the explanation of a common subject-matter or domain abstractly conceived (e.g. terrestrial motion), and nonetheless disagree at an even more fundamental methodological level concerning how this subject-matter should be defined, what problems and phenomena within it are essential or most important to explain, what it excludes, etc.

In sum, neither the role of anomalies nor the fact of disagreement is inconsistent with Kuhn's incommensurability thesis. Thus on our reading, Kuhn's relativist position is far more plausible and coherent than it appears on the Scheffler-Shapere view. The crux of this position does not deny that rival paradigms can disagree over a shared empirical subject-matter; rather, it denies in principle that disagreements can be rationally resolved at *this* level. For, the question of which paradigm better explains that data they share, like the question of how serious the failure of one or the other is with respect to these data, essentially raises a more basic normative question: with respect to the data and problems they do not share, which are more essential or important for an adequate theory to explain? The force of Kuhn's thesis that this is an irreducibly normative disagreement is that it cannot be rationally resolved by standards acceptable to rival paradigms.

* * * * *

VI

In this section, we begin by arguing that a fair evaluation of Kuhn's epistemological position requires that we distingush (1) a 'long-run' relativism from (2) a 'short-run' relativism, concerning the development of scientific knowledge. This section then focuses on the analysis and critique of (1) the 'long-run' relativism; in particular, we present separate evaluations of *two* independent arguments implicit in Kuhn for this 'long-run' relativism—(a) the 'loss-of-data' argument and (b) the 'shift-in-standards' argument. The next and final section takes up the 'short-run' relativism and seeks to evaluate the challenge it poses to positivism.

The need to distinguish between a 'long-run' and 'short-run' relativism emerges when we attempt to evaluate Kuhn's relativism in the context of the very scientific examples he employs to defend it. We have seen that his most straightforward challenge to the positivist view of progress in scientific knowledge turns on the claim that due to losses in observational explicanda in scientific development, it does not satisfy the positivist criterion of progress—increasing and *cumulative* empirical adequacy. Do Kuhn's own scientific examples support this 'loss-of-data' thesis? Unfortunately these examples—while brilliant and profoundly suggestive—are not developed in a direction which speaks unambiguously to this thesis. The clearest and most persuasive example developed in his discussion is that of the chemical revolution to which we have repeatedly returned in order to illustrate the loss-of-data thesis. However, even this example has an equivocal aspect. While it convincingly supports this thesis with respect to the transition from the pre-Daltonian to Daltonian chemistry, Kuhn himself suggests that twentieth-century chemistry has taken up and explained many of the qualitative data and problems abandoned in the Daltonian program ([1], pp. 148-49). Similarly, his example of the transition from pre-Newtonian to Newtonian dynamics nicely illustrates his related thesis concerning loss of problem-solving-ability (in this example the capacity to explain gravitational forces); but Kuhn himself points out that Einstein's relativity theory subsequently reintroduces this problem into physics and succeeds in explaining gravitational forces, thus incorporating a standard and capacity implicit in pre-Newtonian dynamics but lost in Newtonian physics ([1], pp. 148-49).

In sum, Kuhn's actual treatment of these cases suggest the need to distinguish between a relativism of the short run and a relativism of the long run, both of which pose significant but independent challenges to positivism in their own right. In the long run, scientific development *as a whole* may or may not recoup all of its 'temporary' losses in observational explicanda, and thus exhibit cumulative progress; even so, it is a separate question whether in the short run *every* major period of theoretical revolution also constitutes a cumulative progress in scientific knowledge and rationality (i.e. whether scientific development exhibits an unbroken, gradual, continuous, cumulative progress). Thus we need to advance separate evaluations for these two relativisms in Kuhn. The remainder of this section focuses on the long-run relativism. There are two arguments in Kuhn's work for this long-run relativism, which have not been sharply distingushed up to now; let us call them (a) the 'loss-of-data' argument and (b) the 'shift-in-standards' argument, and treat them in that order.

(a) The 'Loss-of-Data' Argument

This argument is by now familiar. It depends on the loss-of-data thesis which we have seen is not unequivocally supported by Kuhn's own scientific examples. Yet this is not the most serious problem with this first argument against the positivist model of scientific progress. Even assuming other scientific examples more favorable to Kuhn's position, in the nature of the case this first argument *at its best* is inductive and cannot philosophically establish the *impossibility* that 'in the long run' science will recoup all of its 'temporary' losses in observational explicanda and thus achieve cumulative progress. Why not? In accordance with Kuhn's own historical approach, every view of scientific development 'as a whole' always assumes the standpoint of contemporary physical theory. Thus the most a loss-of-data thesis could plausibly establish is that *contemporary* physical theory at *this* point in its development exhibits losses with respect to the genuine observational data and problems explained by *its* predecessors. There is nothing in Kuhn's argumentation or examples which would establish that future science in principle cannot explain all of the genuine observational explicanda of other historical theories; at best he offers an inductive argument against the likelihood of this prospect relative to the losses in data characteristic of scientific development up to the present. Hence Kuhn's long-run relativism argument really reduces to an interesting short-run relativism issue: Is *contemporary* physical theory cumulative with respect to the observational explicanda of its predecessors, or not? While none of Kuhn's examples (to my knowledge) establish the negative answer his position argues, it should provoke exponents of a positivist position explicitly to meet this challenge.

Why is this a serious challenge to positivism if, as we have argued, it does not refute the possibility of progress in science? The positivist mode of scientific progress is typically coupled with the secure assumption that contempoary physical theory indisputably satisfies the criterion of increasing and cumulative empirical adequacy with respect to its predecessors. That is, this model maintains that scientific progress as an increasing and cumulative body of knowledge is not merely 'the' regulative standard of science which it 'can' fulfil, but is in fact the standard actually fulfilled by contemporary physical theory. Against this secure assumption, Kuhn urges that scientists (and by implication philosophers of science) characteristically tend to (mis)represent past theories and scientific development from the exclusive vantage point of contemporary physical theory. Those aspects of past theory which can be viewed as contributions to contemporary physical theory are elevated into the center postition of scientific development. Aspects of past theory (e.g. certain observational explicanda, concerns and problems), which may no longer be considered as part of physical theory on the contemporary paradigms, are forgotten, suppressed, or obscured. As a result, the claim of contemporary physical theory to be 'cumulative' with respect to its predecessors (to explain all of the genuine observational explicanda they explained) may rest on a prejudicial, distorted, or incomplete representation of the world of observational explicanda actually at the heart of past theories. A closely related issue concerns how Kuhn and positivists identify the class of predecessor 'scientific' theories with respect to which contemporary physical theory is to be evaluated as cumulative or non-cumulative. Positivist accounts typically seek to demonstrate the cumulative progress represented by contemporary physical theory (Einstein) relative to theoretical developments beginning with Galileo and Kepler (to Newton, etc.), which they see as marking the birth of science, properly understood. Kuhn insists that Aristotelian and medieval paradigms of motion also constitute scientific theories (they explained large classes of genuine observational explicanda simply, etc.) and must be taken into account when considering the respects in which contemporary scientific development is or is not cumulative.

   To summarize, Kuhn's loss-of-data examples cannot establish a 'long-run' loss-of-data thesis and thus the impossibility of cumulative progress in scientific knowledge (long-run relativism). But his short-run loss-of-data thesis concerning contemporary physical theory (it does not explain all of the genuine observational explicanda of all of its predecessors)—if true—will unsettle the positivist assumption that scientific progress is unambiguously actualized in contemporary physical theory. Defenders of a positivist account will want to reply to this Kuhnian challenge, and to do so they will undoubtedly have to reconstruct the worlds of observational explicanda central to past theories more sympathetically and in greater detail than they have yet done. This brings us to the second argument for long-run relativism in Kuhn's work.

(b) The 'Shift-in-Standards' Argument

Unlike the 'loss-of-data' argument, the 'shift-in-standards' argument directly rejects the positivist criterion of scientific progress as increasing and cumulative empirical adequacy. Rather it advances a relativist criterion of scientific knowledge—one which relativizes scientific evaluation to the standards internal and specific to particular physical theories in the history of science. Furthermore, the argument also depends on Kuhn's claim that a study of this history reveals shifts in the standards by which theories evaluate themselves and their rivals. In sum, this argument maintains (1) that any physical theory can only be evaluated relative to its own standards of adequacy, and (2) that in fact successive physical theories in the development of science embody different, indeed *incompatible* standards of scientific valuation. On this view, every historical system of scientific theory turns out to satisfy its own standards of knowledge more adequately than rival or alternate systems of theory. Each theory is thus 'best' in its own terms, and there are no other terms by which theories can be evaluated (hence, relativism). Notice that on the present argument, even if, e.g., contemporary physical theory satisfies the positivist criterion—i.e. explains all of the genuine observational explicanda of its predecessors and more (no loss of data), it would not thereby represent progress in scientific knowledge. Why not? Because (so the argument claims) past physical theories have implicitly maintained standards of scientific knowledge incompatible with the positivist criterion of increasing, cumulative empirical adequacy. Indeed, even if this criterion is the one implicit in contemporary physical theory, Kuhn's argument here rejects the privileged epistemological status of contemporary theory relative to its predecessors.

Furthermore, the shift in standards asserted by this argument need not necessarily involve loss of data. Though there is no loss of data in a new paradigm, the rival paradigms may still exhibit incompatible criteria of theoretical adequacy, e.g. concerning the non-observational problems to be solved or concerning what counts as a sufficiently 'simple' or 'accurate' explanation of (shared) observational data.[24] Suppose Newtonian dynamics explains all the observational data explained by Aristotle's dynamics and more; nonetheless, the necessity of explaining (non-observational) gravitational forces constituted both a standard and an achievement of Aristotelian dynamics, relative to which Newtonian dynamics fails (though it was to reject this standard). Or, to cite another favorite Kuhnian illustration, rival paradigms sometimes maintain incommensurable standards because these standards implicitly justify incompatible trade-offs between 'simplicity', 'accuracy', 'breadth of observational explicanda', etc. ([2], pp. 199-200; [4], p. 262). Of course, from the fact that historical paradigms exhibit incompatible criteria of theoretical adequacy, we can derive the long-run relativism *only* if we accept a radically relativist criterion of scientific knowledge. But the relativist argument under discussion advances such a criterion—which denies the existence or relevance of 'external' standards of scientific evaluation, and *requires* that theories be evaluated by their *own* internal standards.

We may now proceed to the evaluation of this second argument for long-run relativism implicit in Kuhn. The plausibility of this argument depends on two basic issues: (1) Do physical theories in the history of science in fact exhibit 'incompatible' standards of theoretical adequacy? and (2) Is Kuhn's implicit relativistic criterion of scientific knowledge and progress philosophically acceptable? Let us begin with the first issue, the shift-in-standards thesis.

It is noteworthy that this thesis is even more methodologically problematic to establish or discredit than the loss-of-data thesis. To defend it, it would not suffice to establish that rival historical paradigms depend on different problems, observational explicanda, ranges of conceptual possibility; it must *also* be established that these differences were incorporated into the very criteria of theoretical adequacy dominant in the scientific communities in question. This latter thesis requires a kind of historical scholarship into the development of science which goes well beyond standard accounts and is reminiscent of idealist historiography. It would not suffice to explore past physical theories 'from the outside', so to speak; rather, it would also be imperative to reconstruct the subjective understanding of these theories and indeed of science itself (its criteria of adequacy) implicit in the scientific communities involved in their development. Similarly, Kuhn's shift-of-standards thesis cannot be refuted by 'external' historical studies which succeed in establishing *some* cumulative element in concepts, observational data, or problems through scientific revolution; for, the crucial question concerns how these elements entered into past scientists' criteria of theory and alleged revolutions at this level of their subjective understanding of science itself.[25]

Kuhn's own treatment of scientific development makes genuine contributions to our understanding of the standards internal to past scientific tradition, from within their own standpoint. However his treatment does not provide unambiguous support for the long-run shift-of-standards thesis which the relativism argument (as presently construed) requires. The problem here concerns the sense in which the different standards of historical paradigms are 'incompatible' and do or do not allow the possibility of 'cumulative' development. Consider Kuhn's treatment of the Aristotle-Newton-Einstein case (see Note 16). On his account, it appears that a standard of theoretical adequacy (the need to explain gravitational forces) implicit in and satisfied by Aristotelian physics is (1) not satisfied by and is finally abandoned in Newtonian dynamics but (2) is reintroduced and fulfilled in Einstein's theory. In keeping with this account, we may also assume that Aristotelian and Newtonian physics each respectively maintains and fulfils some standard(s) of theoretical adequacy absent in and unsatisfied by the other. The standards of these rival paradigms are 'incompatible' in a weak sense, but not in a strong sense which would rule out 'cumulative' progress. They are incompatible in the weak sense that, taken together with the achievements of each theory, they justify incompatible judgments concerning which is the better theory. But they are not necessarily incompatible in the strong sense that the satisfaction of the standards of the one implies the violation of the standards of the other. Hence, on Kuhn's account, Einstein's physical theory reintroduces and satisfies an Aristotelian standard (the need to explain gravitational forces) abandoned by Newtonian physics, *without* thereby necessarily violating Newtonian standards of theoretical adequacy. If a new theory can thus define and satisfy standards which incorporate the different (and 'incompatible' in the weak case) standards of preceding paradigms, the possibility of a 'cumulative' shift of standards obtains and the present relativism argument is weakened. After all, why should a theory be evaluated exclusively on its own standards *if* another theory satisfies these standards plus other additional ones as well? As far as I know, Kuhn's scientific examples do not exclude this possibility and in some cases appear to support it.

Nevertheless, Kuhn's shift-of-standards thesis remains quite challenging to a positivist conception of scientific progress. If, as it claims, past physical theories did not and would not have accepted the positivist criterion of increasing, cumulative, empirical adequacy, what is this criterion's epistemological status? If they did accept it, positivists will want to show this, against Kuhn's examples. If we grant that scientific development does exhibit shifts in standards, are the standards of contemporary physical theory cumulative or non-cumulative with respect to its predecessors? Defenders of a positivist account of science will undoubtedly want either to deny the existence of such shifts in standards or argue that they have been 'cumulative' in the above sense. While Kuhn's treatment of scientific development does not establish his long-run shift-in-standards thesis, it certainly generates a new philosophical context for the defense or critique of positivist accounts.

Let us now return to the second issue underlying shift-in-standards argument—the philosophical acceptability of its relativistic criterion of scientific knowledge. Even if we were to grant that there are non-cumulative shifts-in-standards in scientific knowledge which is relative to these allegedly shifting standards of scientific practice? Must we evaluate every scientific theory in terms of standards *it* accepts? In dealing with this issue, we will present our most fundamental criticism of Kuhn's long-run relativism concerning scientific knowledge. To put the matter succinctly, Kuhn does not develop any independent philosophical discussion of the nature of scientific knowledge, and thus fails to explore the possibility that positivism and his own historical relativism do not exhaust the episte-mological alternatives. As his position stands, the various criticisms of the positivist criterion of scientific knowledge lead rather naturally to a relativistic criterion of scientific knowledge. But this move is gratuitous because it uncritically dismisses the possibility of a theory of science which rejects positivism while avoiding the turn to relativism and historicism.

* * * * *

(c) A Non-Relativist Alternative to Positivism

Some writers ([6], [14]) have employed Kuhn's work to suggest a criterion of scientific progress which would avoid positivism and relativism in far too facile and superficial a manner; in effect, they have argued that all of Kuhn's long-run relativism arguments can be made compatible with the existence of progress in science, if we simply adopt as its criterion 'maximal problem-solving ability' (which does not require 'cumulative' problems or data). As we pointed out in the previous section, Kuhn himself employs such a criterion to formulate the sense in which he is 'a convinced believer in scientific progress' ([2], p. 206). Nonetheless, he refuses to take such a criterion as 'the' criterion of scientific knowledge and truth. In our view, the reasons for this implicit in his position are instructive and indirectly reveal the difficulty in elaborating a *plausible* epistemological alternative to postitivism and relativism. First of all, contrary to what the writers who employ the criterion of maximal problem-solving ability assume, Kuhn argues that this criterion cannot be grounded in scientific practice itself. Of course, every theory seeks to maximize its capacity to resolve its own privileged problems—those it takes to define the discipline and to be especially revealing of the way the world is. But, according to Kuhn, no theory is willing to evaluate itself and its rivals according to a criterion of problem-solving ability which abstract from the identification of the problems at issue. Besides different theories do not necessarily agree on a shared way of individuating and counting problems, of ranking their relative importance, or even of judging the relevant measure of 'accuracy' in solutions. Thus because there is no universal concept of problem-solving ability, such a philosophical criterion of scientific knowledge is not grounded in scientific practice.

Suppose, as philosophers, we construct such a criterion and treat it as external to the self-understanding of science; how is it to be philosophically justified as 'the' criterion of scientific knowledge? Surely, Kuhn is right in his implicit denial that any and every criterion we might construct relative to which science has progressed is therefore an adequate criterion of scientific *knowledge* and *its* progress. At the very least, writers who favor such an approach would need to elaborate some philosophical theory of knowledge which would justify the unique epistemological status they grant to one particular dimension of science as 'the' mark of scientific knowledge, as against others. Such a theory would seek to ground its standard of scientific progress in the very nature of empirical knowledge itself. Furthermore, Kuhn's resistance to *this* criterion ('maximal problem-solving ability') stems from his firm intuition that the progress of science as knowledge of the world presupposes *some* essentially 'cumulative' dimension at the level of its content. The march of technique does not mark advance in knowledge. The latter, unlike the former, seems to assume some common world which can be known in a 'cumulatively' adequate way. To many of us, even if it can be shown that on some 'neutral' concept of 'more' one physical theory solves more of 'its' problems than its historical predecessors solved of 'theirs', this formulation already smacks of a relativism concerning scientific knowledge which cannot be defined away by means of choosing an appropriate measure of 'progress'.

What plausible epistemological alternatives are there, then, to positivism and relativism, if we grant the force of the 'cumulativist assumption' implicit in Kuhn, positivism, and common sense? It may still be possible to elaborate a theory of scientific knowledge which adheres to this assumption while rejecting its standard philosophical intepretation in positivism and Kuhn. Both assume that relativism can only be avoided by 'cumulativity' at the level of the problems, observational explicanda, and standards internal to scientific practice *itself*. The philosophical traditions mentioned above (American pragmatism, Hegel, and Marx) implicitly define scientific knowledge in terms of the larger goals and problems of human civilization itself; the way is then open to represent progress in scientific knowledge by means of its essential role in mankind's 'cumulative' progress in the struggle with the perennial problems of human life and survival. Depending on how these problems are defined (e.g. are they ultimately problems of the spirit as in Hegel, or problems of social and technological oraganization, as in Marx), and how scientific culture is related to their cumulative resolution in history, different philosophical models of science result. Needless to say such models must themselves survive relativist challenges and indicate the sense in which human civilization itself exhibits progress. Furthermore, many will undoubtedly reject any such theory of scientific knowledge which sacrifices its alleged autonomy. We cannot take these issues up here. Our point is only this: even remaining within Kuhn's 'cumulativity' assumption, there are philosophical models of scientific knowledge and progress which reject positivism and relativism.

* * * * *

VII

In this final section of our discussion, we will argue that Kuhn's 'short-run' relativism presents a well-grounded and formidable challenge to several aspects of the positivist conception of science; in particular (a) its gradualist view of scientific progress, (b) its image of scientific rationality (or methodology), and (c) its very construal of philosophy of science itself. A distinction will be drawn between a short-run relativism concerning scientific knowledge and one concerning scientific rationality. In order to keep the distinct 'relativisms' which our argument has uncovered in Kuhn clearly before us, it will be useful at this point to provide succinct formulations of the claims each involves:

Long-run Relativism Concerning Scientific Knowledge:—It is not the case that scientific development *as a whole* can constitute a progress in scientific knowledge and truth.

Short-run Relativism Concerning Scientific Knowledge:—It is not the case that every major *stage* of scientific development (in which one theoretical tradition is supplanted by a rival one) constitutes a progress in scientific knowledge and truth.

Short-run Relativism Concerning Scientific Rationality:—It is not the case within scientific development that new theories are always or even characteristically more rational to accept than their predecessors and come to be accepted by scientists because they are more rational (better supported by evidence, more simple, etc.).

In the remainder of this section, we will try to show that Kuhn's scientific examples and philosophical arguments have their greatest power, originality, and promise in relation to his short-run relativism, and especially the novel conception of scientific rationality and philosophy of science which it suggest. Hence the thrust of this final section is quite different from that of the last: there we found it necessary to focus on criticisms of Kuhn's long-run relativism, here much of the focus will consist in a sympathetic elaboration of the implications of the short-run relativism.

(a) The Gradualist View of Scientific Development

Our examination of long-run relativism in Section VI revealed that there is little systematic or explicit attempt by Kuhn to establish the long-run loss-of-data thesis or to defend the historicist, relativistic criterion of scientific knowledge which his arguments respectively required. On the other hand, his argumentation and examples are explicitly and impressively developed with respect to particular revolutionary periods of scientific development and the epistemological characteristics of the scientific community's transition from one theory to another. His scientific examples convincingly support the conclusion that at least in some cases of scientific revolution (e.g. the Dalton case), the loss-of-data thesis is tenable. Hence, regardless of whether there is cumulative progress of scientific knowledge in the long-run, the fact of short-run loss-of-data poses a powerful challenge to the positivist model of scientific development as a gradual, continuously cumulative progress in scientific knowledge. Some new theories replace old ones and develop to their full explanatory power even though they fail to preserve all of the genuine observational knowledge explained by their predecessors.

Positivist accounts of science typically assume that the philosophical criterion which grounds progress in scientific knowledge in the long run is also satisfied by every major period in its development.[26] Even if Kuhn's long-run relativism is rejected, his short-run argument challenges this positivist assumption: scientific development as a whole may ultimately satisfy a criterion of progress which is not satisfied by its major stages, transitions, or parts (the short-run). In effect, this yields a far more complicated model of progress in scientific knowledge than positivism has provided. Relative to the very criterion which succeeds in grounding such progress in the long run, one theoretical tradition in science may have supplanted another even though it did not constitute a better theory than its predecessor. Each may have contained explanatory capacities absent in the other and only finally unified in a univocally progressive theory centuries later. Kuhn's account of the transition from pre-Daltonian to Daltonian chemistry certainly seems to exhibit this pattern. This, then, is the thrust of Kuhn's short-run relativism concerning scientific knowledge: it is not the case that every major stage of scientific development constitutes a univocal progress in scientific knowledge and truth. While it doesn't imply a philosophical relativism concerning science as a whole, it certainly generates a different approach to the representation of scientific development.

(b) The Image of Scientific Rationality

This short-run relativism concerning scientific knowledge also implies a critique of the positivist model of scientific rationality or methodology. Positivist accounts of science typically assume that the philosophical criteria which ground progress in scientific knowledge in the long run roughly correspond to the actual criteria underlying scientific behavior and methodology, at least in so far as it is rational.[27] Thus the positivist model of the standards by which scientific knowledge is evaluated is also taken to provide an account of actual scientific reasoning, debate, and theoretical choice throughout the development of science. On this account, scientists in the past have transferred their allegiance to a new paradigm because it better satisfies the standard of increasing and cumulative empirical adequacy than its predecessor. However, if this positivist standard is not satisfied in all scientific revolutions, then it cannot capture the actual reasons at work in these transitions or the sense in which they are rational. Thus Kuhn's short-run loss-of-data thesis and the scientific examples which support it also challenge the positivist model of scientific rationality. Short-run relativism concerning scientific knowledge implies a closely related short-run relativism concerning scientific rationality: relative to the positivist criterion of increasing, cumulative empirical adequacy, it is not the case (a) that all new scientific theories are more reasonable to accept than the theories they replace and (b) that they are in fact accepted by scientists on these (positivist) grounds.

If we turn to Kuhn's shift-in-standards thesis, we will find the basis for a far more powerful short-run relativism concerning scientific rationality than that provided by the loss-of-data thesis. Our critical discussion of this relativism will seek to show that it develops a convincing alternative model of philosophy of science at odds with positivism concerning the privileged terrain of problems at the core of epistemology. Thus it has a methodological significance as well as raising issues of substance. Let us explain.

Positivism is often taken to provide a theory concerning the reconstruction, comparison, and evaluation of fully developed theories; the process through which such theories are developed is either relegated to the psychology of discovery or assumed to be governed in its rational aspects by the same criteria which positivist accounts employ to analyze the finished products. Kuhn's theory of science challenges this epistemological approach by treating scientific development in a way which implicitly drives a wedge between the epistemology of (completed) scientific knowledge and that of its rational development. To be sure, his theory challenges positivism at both levels but on somewhat different grounds. We have seen the ways in which his loss-of-data and shift-of-standards arguments challenge the cumulative model of progress in scientific knowledge (short-run and long-run): this challenge is situated on positivism's own privileged terrain of comparing finished theories. However, much of Kuhn's argumentation is focused on the epistemological properties of scientific debates, choices, and conflicts in the development of these theories well before they can be compared as more or less fully developed alternatives. His shift-of-standards thesis exhibits its most forceful and independent challenge to a positivist account of scientific rationality on this terrain.

As we have seen, Kuhn's shift-of-standards thesis denies that rival paradigms share sufficiently overlapping criteria for evaluating evidence to permit either to establish or exhibit rational superiority over the other. A positivist account can certainly grant that in the stages before the rivals are more or less fully developed, the available evidence is typically insufficient to indicate the rational superiority of one or the other.[28] Thus it can allow wide latitude to what scientists reasonably do in these stages and relegate to psychology the task of explaining the different choices they make during them, on the assumption that this issue lacks epistemological significance. In effect, Kuhn offers an alternative epistemological model of scientific development which purports to give a more comprehensive and adequate explanation of the sense in which divergent scientific choices and judgments throughout revolutionary period are 'rational'.[29] His most basic theoretical innovation is to attempt to undercut the positivist emphasis on 'insufficient evidence' as the central epistemological element in these periods; instead his account identifies this element as incompatible principles (i.e. criteria, standards) for weighing the importance of different sorts of evidence (observational explicanda and problems). On this view, there are irreducible normative disagreements concerning how the discipline ought to be defined in these periods; such disagreements underlie the sense in which divergent choices are rational in revolutionary periods and constitute an essential epistemological component in the rationality of the whole process through which these periods end.

Let us compare the two models at a more concrete level. On a positivist account, if available evidence is insufficient to ground rational choice in the early stages of revolutionary debate, there must come a point where the evidence is sufficient, and this must be the point at which the bulk of the scientific community transfers its allegiance to the new paradigm. The implication is that those scientists who cling to the old paradigm at *this* point do so at a price to their scientific rationality. On Kuhn's account, most members of the scientific community transfer their allegiance to a new paradigm well in advance of the point where it can explain more than the old paradigm. Indeed, even in cases where a new paradigm may ultimately explain everything its predecessors did and more (i.e. where the 'loss-of-data' thesis does not hold), most scientists will have switched to the new paradigm well before this point. On the other hand, even at the point where the new paradigm explains far more than the old, some scientists maintain their allegiance to the old paradigm for reasons which are neither less scientific nor credible, according to Kuhn'n model, than those in favor of the new paradigm.[30] The fact that faced with the same bodies of evidence, scientists make these incompatible choices at *every* stage of scientific development, does not reflect an aberration of scientific rationality or a matter of merely psychological import, on Kuhn's model. These choices are rational and develop in a rational way on the assumption that they essentially involve different criteria of science (or, principles of evidence) and an irreducible element of 'conversion' from one to another. This concept of conversion embodies an epistemological claim: namely that new theories cannot develop unless scientists embrace the new criteria implicit in them in the absence of 'compelling' scientific reasons to do so (indeed as we explained above, the good reasons in favor of either paradigm can only become 'compelling' if its own criteria are already accepted). If this claim is accepted, it provides a substantial reason for Kuhn's attempt to incorporate the sociology of the scientific community's conversions into the philosophy of science: for the classical positivist criteria of evidence, while necessary, will not be sufficient to account for the logic of scientific development.

This summarizes the challenge and alternative Kuhn's shift-of-standard thesis poses to a positivist account of scientific rationality. It remains to underscore the fact that this short-run relativism with respect to scientific rationality is independent of the loss-of-data thesis and his relativism concerning scientific knowledge. Let us assume in a given case that a new paradigm at some late stage in its development succeeds in explaining all of the genuine observational explicanda of its predecessors and more; let us assume that we count this as progress in scientific knowledge, in retrospect—using the cumulative criterion. Nevertheless practically all the reasonable choices to resist or switch to this new paradigm (those responsible for its very development) will have occurred before this point and cannot have rested on this cumulative criterion. More importantly, suppose that we in retrospect, as philosophers or contemporary scientists, employ the positivist cumulative criterion, or some other criterion (pragmatic, etc.) to evaluate finished theories and their progress as scientific knowledge; it does not follow that the past scientific communities actually responsible for the development of these theories did employ or even would have accepted this criterion (even at the point where it *is* satisfied). To capture *their* scientific rationality, we need to attend to *their* standards of adequate theory, their conceptions of science. If these undergo transformation, as Kuhn's shift-of-standards thesis claims, his relativism concerning *scientific rationality* and the logic of scientific development is a quite powerful position even if we reject the relevance or decisiveness of this thesis with respect to *scientific knowledge*.

Why is this the case? Why can't a philosophical theory (such as positivism) simply construct an objective and external criterion of scientific rationality, as well as of scientific knowledge, quite *independently* of the shifting standards internal to scientific development itself? In that case, a Kuhnian shift in standards would no more imply a short-run relativism concerning scientific rationality, than it implied a long-run relativism concerning scientific knowledge. There are two points to be made in response to this suggestion.

First, such an objective, external conception of scientific rationality could indeed be constructed, but only at a price. The price is that while it will yield retrospective comparisons of well-developed theories (e.g. $T2$ is more reasonable than $T1$), it gains this by losing any power to explain the actual reasons and rational principles operative in scientific life itself. Secondly, there are good reasons for preserving a relativistic and subjectivist conception of rationality even where we deny the relevance of such reasons to the issue of knowledge and truth. We often assume that what it is reasonable for an agent or community to do and believe is relative to their own ends, norms, and experience in ways which do not affect what is true or what they know. Within a given framework of experience, people may reasonably believe things that are false; within a certain structure of norms and values, people may reasonably do things which, from an objective and external standpoint, are wrong. In sum we often invoke a subjectivist conception of rationality to understand and evaluate an agent's or community's *particular* choices, judgments, conflicts, etc. in the framework of its *own* experience and norms; whereas, we require an 'objective' conception of knowledge (truth, or morality) to develop a larger critique of this very framework itself. This standpoint thus ties the concept of rationality to the basic standards of a subject (e.g. a community) in a way that is far more problematic for the concepts of knowledge and truth. In consequence, Kuhn's shift-in-standards thesis provides more powerful support for a relativism concerning scientific rationality than is the case for scientific knowledge.[31]

NOTES

1. The line of argument which I glean from Scheffler and Shapere is most explicit in [1] but it is also expressed in [9], [10], [11], and [13]. Let me grant at the outset that I do not deal with every criticism Scheffler and Shapere advance against Kuhn. Nonetheless, I do purport to treat what seems to me to be their most powerful critique of his distinctively epistemological arguments.

2. The evidence for my interpretation is scattered throughout [1], [2], [3], and [4]. In documenting it, I content myself with the citation of representative passages, though the reader must evaluate it in the context of the whole of these works. My treatment really offers a 'rational reconstruction' of Kuhn's argument, which purports to expose its strongest elements; nonetheless, I am also concerned to defend my reconstruction as providing the best *over-all* reading of Kuhn's writings.

3. E.g. [1], pp. 98–102 (Newton-Einstein example), 130–5 (Proust-Berthollet example). Kuhn also stresses the role of language in generating incommensurability in [2], pp. 200–5 and [4], pp. 266–77.

4. E.g. [1], pp. 111–35 where Kuhn attacks the concept of 'the given' and develops a theory of scientific perception.

5. E.g. [1], pp. 103–10 (Lavoisier-Dalton and Newton-Einstein examples).

6. E.g. [1], pp. 2–4, 103–10. Kuhn also stresses the incommensurability of standards as central in [2], pp. 185–6, 199–200 and [4], pp. 259–63. However, reading these passages in terms of 'incommensurability of standards' requires my interpretation below.

7. Shapere is most explicit in holding this reading of Kuhn's relativism: 'But this relativism, and the doctrines which eventuate in it, is not the result of an investigation of actual science and its history; rather it is the purely logical consequence of a narrow preconception about what "meaning" is' [12], p. 68. But, the same interpretation of Kuhn is also to be found in Shapere's [11], pp. 389–90 and Scheffler's [9], pp. 15–19, 49. It assimilates Kuhn's epistemological position to that of Feyerabend who makes a relativist-wholistic view concerning meaning central to his theory of science; this assimilation of Kuhn to Feyerabend is argued by [12], pp. 65–68 and strongly suggested by [9], pp. 49–52.

8. Thus Scheffler characterizes relativism as 'a reductio ad absurdum of the resonings from which it flows' ([9], p. 19). And much of Shapere's most recent argument against Kuhn's own latest formulations is that 'It is a viewpoint as relativistic, as antirationalistic, as ever' ([13], p. 708). Below we dispute the equation of 'relativistic' with 'antirationalistic'. In addition, our whole presentation of Kuhn's relativism disputes the assumption that any such relativism is a 'reductio'.

9. The '... issue of paradigm choice can never be unequivocally settled by logic and experiment alone ... ' ([1], p. 94). The arguments one paradigm presents to its rival may be powerful and sound; but they 'cannot be made logically or even probabilistically compelling for those who refuse to step into the circle. The premises and values shared by the two parties to a debate over paradigms are not sufficiently extensive for that' ([1], p. 94).

10. 'A revolution is for me a special sort of change involving a certain sort of reconstruction of group commitments' ([12], pp. 180–1).

11. 'If there were but one set of scientific *problems,* one world within which to work on them, and one set of *standards* for their solution, paradigm competion might be settled more or less routinely by some process like counting the number of problems solved by each. But, in fact, these conditions are never met completely. The proponents of competing paradigms are always at least slightly at *cross purposes* ... the proponents of competing paradigms will often disagree about the list of *problems* that any candidate for paradigm must resolve. Their *standards* or their definitions of science are not the same ... ' ([1], pp. 147–8, my italics).

12. This element of circularity which obtains between a paradigm's criteria of adequacy and its own empirical success may create the impression that for Kuhn paradigms are self-confirming and effectively immune to empirical failure or inadequacy. Thus Scheffler characterizes Kuhn's theory as 'an extravagant idealism' in which 'each viewpoint creates its own reality' and 'reality itself is made by the scientist rather than discovered by him' ([9], p. 19). Yet, Kuhn's entire conception of 'normal science' as a research program of puzzle-solving laced with empirical *failures, set-backs,* and eventual *anomalies* makes it quite clear that

paradigms are *not* self-confirming. The fact that a paradigm's standards privilege its own achievements and research programs does not guarantee that the research program will succeed.

Concerning this issue Meiland in [6] is correct. There he argues that Kuhn's position is perfectly compatible with the 'objectivity' of science in the sense of 'the possiblity of independent checks on the theories and hypotheses of scientists' ([6], p. 180). However, we criticize his final interpretation of Kuhn below.

13. In my estimation, Kuhn's development of this example offers the clearest and most powerful illustrative evidence of his incommensurability thesis. It is given in various places as follows; [1], pp. 69–72, 99–100, 107, (phlogiston theory and Lavoisier); pp. 130–5 (affinity theory and Dalton); p. 139 (remarks on Dalton); and p. 148 (remarks on Lavoisier).

14. 'There are losses as well as gains in scientific revolutions and scientists tend to be peculiarly blind to the former' ([1], p. 167); '. . . new paradigms seldom or never possess all the capabilities of their predecessors . . . ' ([1], p. 169); '. . . a community of scientific specialists will do all it can to ensure the continuing growth of the assembled data that it can treat with precision and detail. In the (revolutionary) process the community will sustain losses. Often some old problems must be banished. Frequently, in addition, revolution narrows the scope of the community's professional concerns . . . ' ([1], p. 169).

15. In order that scientists embrace a new paradigm it 'must seem to resolve some outstanding and generally recognized problems (of the old paradigm) that can be met in no other way', and 'Second, the new paradigm must promise to preserve a relatively large part of the concrete problem-solving ability that has accrued to science through its predecessors' ([1], 169, my addition in parentheses).

Having established this element of preserved continuity from one paradigm to its successor, Kuhn goes on to make his characteristic point: 'To say this much is not to suggest that ability to solve problems is either the unique or unequivocal basis for paradigm choice. We have already noted many reasons why there can be no criterion of that sort' ([1], pp. 169–70).

16. This attempt was unsuccessful not in the sense that no phlogiston chemist could explain the phenomenon of weight gain in combustion; but in the sense that none could explain it in *any one* way which was acceptable to *all* or even *most* practitioners of the phlogiston theory. As many of the latter proliferated different versions of this theory to meet the weight-gain problem, it became 'harder and harder to know what the phlogiston theory was' ([1], p. 72). Cf. the excellent and detailed account of this crisis in [8].

17. In our exposition so far we have treated all incommensurable problems as involving incommensurable data. However we must note that quite apart from the issue of data, Kuhn's text indicates another sort of incommensurability of problems and thus another source of incommensurable standards. The standards in question pertain to the scientific legitimacy of one or another type of ultimate explanation proferred by a theory. On Kuhn's account, seventeenth-century Newtonian science shared the assumptions of the mechanical philosophy and thus rejected as unscientific or tautological the innate, occult forces of scholastic physics (e.g. the natural tendency to fall). In keeping with this standard of mechanico-corpuscular

explanation, Newtonian science repeatedly sought to develop a suitable mechanical explanation for its own gravitational forces, but ultimately did not succeed in this endeavor. By the middle of the eighteenth century, most Newtonians accepted the attraction and repulsion of gravity as innate forces, irreducible properties of matter *neither* needing nor permitting an explanation in terms of more basic, mechanical properties of matter. On the other hand, within Einsteinian physics, these gravitational forces are assumed to admit and thus require explanation: they constitute explicanda with which any 'adequate' physics must deal. Thus the rival paradigms of Einstein and mid-eighteenth-century Newtonian science involve incommensurable standards concerning what sort of entities, properties, and assumptions may legitimately function as 'unexplained explainers' or self-sufficient posits in a theory. Put differently, Einstein's physics insists on the necessity of answering a problem ultimately suppressed in mid-eithteenth-century Newtonian science and defines its criterion of adequacy for all physical explanations in terms of the possession of a resolution of this problem. Furthermore, in this respect, Kuhn suggests that the standards of Einsteinian physics are much closer to Aristotelian physics than to mid-eighteenth-century Newtonian science—for Aristotle also had an answer to the sort of problem ultimately banished from Newtonian science ([1], pp. 105–8; [2], pp. 206–7).

The incommensurability argument here seems stronger in the comparison of Aristotle with Newton than between Newton and Einstein. As Kuhn presents these examples, Newton-to-Einstein appears to be a gain with *no* loss which is hard not to see on a positivist model. If Einsteinian physics added to Newtonian science an explanation of gravity absent in the latter without *any loss* to the data and problems handled by Newton the case for incommensurability would appear weak. How could a Newtonian rationally reject Einsteinian physics on the *sole* ground that it explains something unexplained in the Newtonian scheme? Kuhn's development of this example is not wholly convincing.

On the other hand, Aristotle-to-Newton involves a loss and thus a change of standards supportive of 'incommensurability'. Aristotelian physics insists on and provides an answer to the question of motion at a level absent in Newtonian science altogether. This is a stronger example in the context of Kuhn's general argument.

18. For an exposition of this doctrine see pp. 114–16 above.

19. For these criticisms see pp. 116–18.

20. For this reading of Kuhn see pp. 115–16.

21. See pp. 115–18 above.

22. For the relevant references, see note 15 above.

23. For this criticism, see pp. 116–17 above.

24. For examples of shifts in standards which do not seem to imply loss of data, see the Aristotle-Newton and Newton-Einstein examples ([1], pp. 105–8; [2], pp. 206–7) and my discussion of them in Note 17 above. For another such example, see the Ptolemy-Copernicus example ([1], pp. 149–50).

25. From this standpoint, there is something lacking in Shapere's otherwise illuminating treatment of the transition from Aristotelian to Newtonian dynamics via the mediating 'impetus' theory ([12], pp. 71–81). As we have seen, for Shapere, the challenge of Kuhn's relativism and incommensurability thesis largely focuses on

the question of *conceptual* continuity and discontinuity in scientific development. Hence, Shapere's own historical discussion itself focuses on and clarifies this level of continuity and innovation in the development of Newtonian from Aristotelian dynamics. Indeed, Shapere explicitly acknowledges the Kuhnian insight concerning the ways fundamentally different concepts shape what problems can be raised and what can count as a coherent explanation of them in rival paradigms ([12], pp. 78–79). Nevertheless, what we do *not* learn from Shapere's treatment is how the criteria governing the theory of motion, the conception of what dynamics is, may have altered in this period; similarly, we do not learn whether and in what ways the observational explicanda thought to be essential (or most essential) to dynamics may have shifted (with or without loss of data) in this period. Yet, these are the sorts of things we need to know from a philosophical history of science if Kuhn's relativist theory of scientific development is to be appreciated and ultimately evaluated.

26. In his attempt to reformulate a positivist theory of science in response to Kuhn (and other critics), Scheffler [9] himself makes this assumption.

Furthermore, in this context it is noteworthy that Kuhn's short-run loss-of-data relativism argument poses a direct problem for several other recent attempts to reformulate a positivist theory of science in response to his work. Imre Lakatos has developed what he calls 'sophisticated falsificationism' which concedes Kuhn's criticisms of 'naive falsificationism' and even adopts some of Kuhn's concepts (e.g. 'anomaly' and 'research-program'). Yet Lakatos's position advances an epistemological criterion of 'progressive problem-shifts' which itself rests on the positivist assumption that scientific development is continuously cumulative with respect to its observational explicanda ([5], pp. 116–32, 177–80). While this position purports to refute the relativist aspects of Kuhn's account of science, Lakatos does not even consider Kuhn's loss-of-data argument or examples which apply with equal force to his 'sophisticated falsificationism'. Following Lakatos in some degree, Meynell rests much of his critique of Kuhn's relativism on the same assumption that scientific development is continuously cumulative with respect to its observational explicanda, without even considering Kuhn's arguments against this assumption ([7], pp. 86, 88). On this basis, the following conclusion appears warranted: because they do not appreciate what on our interpretation are Kuhn's strongest relativist arguments (concerning short-run loss of data, and shifts of standards), Scheffler, Meiland, Lakatos, and Meynell develop various responses to Kuhn's critique of positivism which themselves rest on undefended assumptions also challenged by this critique. While this does not prejudge the question of whether these authors' position could not be developed to meet Kuhn's arguments, it does argue that their responses to Kuhn are inadequate or incomplete as they stand.

27. Scheffler [9] explicitly makes this assumption: 'Underlying historical changes of theory, there is, moreover a constancy of logic and method, which unifies each scientific age with that which preceded it and with that which is yet to follow: Such constancy comprises not merely the canons of formal deduction, but also those criteria by which hypotheses are confirmed with the test of experience and subjected to comparative evaluation . . . it is this methodology which makes the cumulative growth of tested scientific knowledge as a public possession' ([9], pp. 9–10.

28. See Scheffler, [9], p. 80: '... the existence of common evaluation criteria is compatible with borderline regions in which these criteria can yield no clear decision.'

29. Kuhn characterizes his theory of science as 'an attempt to show that existing theories of rationality are not quite right and that we must readjust or change them to explain why science works as it does' ([4], p. 264).

30. A case in point is Priestly, who never accepted the oxygen theory of combustion ([1], pp. 156–9).

31. I would like to express my gratitude to the National Endowment for the Humanities for supporting much of the research on which this paper is based (Younger Humanist Fellowship 1974–75). The paper has profited from the valuable comments and assistance of Zeno Vendler. In addition, others who have read it and made suggestions incorporated into it are Andrew Feinberg, Arthur Fine, Neal Grossman, Larry Laudan, Fred Olafson, Robert Pippin, Avrum Stroll, and Paul Teller. The author also wishes to express his appreciation to the Editor of *Inquiry* for his editorial criticism and assistance.

REFERENCES

[1] Kuhn, T. 1970. *The Structure of Scientific Revolution* (2nd ed.), University of Chicago Press, Chicago. First published in 1962 (Chicago).

[2] Kuhn, T. 1970. 'Postscript-1969' in [1], pp. 174–210.

[3] Kuhn, T. 1970. 'Logic of Discovery of Psychology of Research?', in I. Lakatos and A. Musgrave (eds.), *Criticism and the Growth of Knowledge*, Cambridge University Press, Cambridge, pp. 1–25.

[4] Kuhn, T. 1970. 'Reflections on my Critics', in *Criticism and the Growth of Knowledge*, op. cit., pp. 231–79.

[5] Lakatos, I. 1970. 'Falsification and the Methodology of Scientific Research Programmes', in *Criticism and the Growth of Knowledge*, op. cit., pp. 91–197.

[6] Meiland, J. 1974. 'Kuhn, Scheffler, and Objectivity in Science', *Philosophy of Science*, vol. 41 (June), pp. 179–87.

[7] Meynell, H. 1975. 'Science, the Truth, and Thomas Kuhn', *Mind*, vol. 84 (January), pp. 79–93.

[8] Partington, J. and McKie, D. 1937. 'Historical Studies on the Phlogiston Theory—I. The Levity of Phlogiston', *Annals of Science*, vol. 2, no. 4, pp. 361–404.

[9] Scheffler, I. 1967. *Science and Subjectivity*, Bobbs-Merrill, Indianapolis.

[10] Scheffler, I. 1972. 'Vision and Revolution: A Postscript on Kuhn', *Philosophy of Science*, vol. 39, pp. 366–74.

[11] Shapere, D. 1964. 'The Structure of Scientific Revolutions', *The Philosophical Review*, vol. 73, pp. 383–94.

[12] Shapere, D. 1966. 'Meaning and Scientific Change', in R. Colodny (ed.), *Mind and Cosmos: Essays in Contemporary Science and Philosophy*, University of Pittsburgh Press, Pittsburgh, pp. 41–85.

[13] Shapere, D. 1971. 'The Paradigm Concept', *Science,* vol. 172 (May), pp. 706–9.

[14] Laudan, L. 1976. 'Two Dogmas of Methodology', *Philosophy of Science,* vol. 43, no. 4, pp. 585–97.

Moral Relativism

INTRODUCTION TO
Moral Relativism

Just as there are many types of cognitive relativism, so there are many doctrines labeled "moral relativism." Philippa Foot identifies the version of moral relativism which she considers important by setting forth several features: (1) There are wide variations in moral judgments between different cultures and different generations. (2) No one set of these opinions appears to have any more claim to truth than any other. (3) The concepts of "objectivity" and "truth" apply to moral judgments only within a community of shared reactions, although these judgments do not report these reactions.

That moral judgments are not reports of individual or group reactions—for example, "I like this" or "most of us approve of that"—is shown by the fact that one can meaningfully accuse both individuals and groups of being mistaken in their moral judgments; if their moral judgments were reports of their own reactions, they would presumably have the last word on this, since they know their own reactions best. Instead of reporting reactions, moral judgments are applications of community or group standards to individual cases. Such judgments are to be evaluated, according to the relativist, only according to the standards of the group or society of which the person making the moral judgments is a member "without the slightest thought that [those] standards are correct." There is no absolutely true set of moral standards against which the standards of a group can be measured and judged correct or incorrect. In fact, as Foot points out, a moral relativist can even hold that moral judgments should be evaluated relative to the standards of the individual making the judgment, whether or not that individual's standards are identical with those of the individual's group.

Thus, the idea of relative truth finds a place in the doctrine of moral relativism, just as it does in the doctrines of some cognitive relativists. We are speaking here of what Foot calls "substantial truth." There are various

149

uses of the word 'true'. For example, a person may say of a judgment of taste "That's very true" merely to indicate the speaker's agreement with the judgment and nothing beyond that. But this is not substantial truth. The relativistic doctrine of substantial truth is that "truth is relative to one or another of a set of possible standards." In moral relativism the standards are moral principles; in cognitive relativism the standards are those embedded in a conceptual framework. Nothing is true *simpliciter* but instead is true relative to this or that set of standards.

Foot gives particular attention to replying to some common objections to moral relativism in order to establish relativism as a position to be taken seriously. The first objection is that the relativist is committed to believing that an action can be right in one country or period and wrong in another. The idea here is that since an action might be right by the standards of one country or period and wrong by the standards of another, the relativist must regard the action as both right and wrong, which seems paradoxical and is perhaps even contradictory. A stock relativist reply, not mentioned by Foot, to this kind of objection goes like this: This is certainly not what the relativist believes; instead, the relativist believes that there is no absolute right and wrong; right and wrong must be relativized to standards, with the result that what the relativist believes is that the action is right-by-standards-S1 and wrong-by-standards-S2. Now there is no contradiction since the predicate "right-by-standards-S1" and the predicate "wrong-by-standards-S2" do not contradict each other. (Note the parallel here between relative right and relative truth.) Foot gives a different reply to the objection. What the relativist believes will depend on what the relativist judges. And a relativist's judgment about a judgment is always made relative to a particular set of standards. The relativist, like the rest of us, can only use one set of standards at a time. And an action will be either right or wrong relative to the set of standards used, not both right and wrong. Hence the relativist is absolved of contradiction.

A second common objection to moral relativism is that it is a totally subjectivist doctrine. For it holds that "if a man thinks something right, it is right for him." This clearly does not apply to the version of moral relativism developed by Foot in this paper. Moral right and wrong are determined by a set of standards. A person might believe that an action is right while the relevant set of standards yields the conclusion that the action is wrong. In this case the person wrongly believes that the action is right. Thus, an action is not right for a person just because he thinks it is.

Finally, she deals with the objection that a moral relativist can have no moral beliefs of his own. Why might anyone think this is so? Perhaps it is because relativists allegedly believe that no moral judgment is true. We might fill out this argument in the following way: to believe a proposition is to believe that it is true; consequently, a relativist who believes that no moral judgment is true cannot consistently believe any moral judgment. Foot's reply to this is that moral relativists do believe that moral judgments can be true, but that this truth is "local truth," that is, truth relative either to local standards or to individual standards. Hence relativists can have their own moral beliefs.

Having answered common objections in order to show that moral relativism must be taken seriously, Foot asks whether moral relativism of the type under discussion is correct. In other writings she has argued that there are constraints on what can count as a moral code. Nevertheless these constraints allow the existence of more than one moral code, and it is still an open question as to whether one such code is correct and the rest mistaken. Foot believes that the resolution of this issue must begin from what all human beings have in common and that, to ascertain this, moral philosophers must talk, much more than they now do, about "the human heart and the life of men in society."

Moral Relativism*

Philippa Foot

Some philosophical questions interest only philosophers: they would never occur to the plain man, and if he hears of them he may very well think that those who spend their time on philosophy must be a trifle mad. There are, however, other problems, no less philosophical and just as important, that are apt to present themselves to any enquiring mind. One does not have to be a philosopher by trade or training to have doubts, for instance, about freewill; and it has even struck many innocent of philosophy that perhaps the world looks undetectably different to different persons, one man systematically seeing as red what the other sees as green. The thesis of moral relativism is one of these natural philosophical thoughts. Very many students, beginning philosophy, are sure that relativism is true; and although they are often taken aback when reminded that it is, for example, common for members of our materialistic society to criticise this society for its materialism they usually think that some adjustments will save the theory. One might therefore expect that moral relativism would be a central topic among those discussed in classes and in the journals. Surprisingly, however, the truth has for long been quite otherwise. Many recent books on moral philosophy ignore the problem or give it perfunctory treatment, and it is only in the last two or three years that strong, interesting, articles have begun to appear in print.[1]

Why was the subject so long neglected? Probably it was because few of those teaching, and writing, philosophy believed moral relativism to be anything they need worry about: some thought they knew how to discredit it in a few easy moves, and others supposed vaguely that it had been done.

*Reprinted with permission of the author; The Lindley Lecture at the University of Kansas (1978), pp. 3-19.

In fact, as we shall see, there were elements in the prevailing theories of ethics—in emotivism for instance—that made it seem difficult even to formulate relativism except in a version that was indeed easy to refute.

C.L. Stevenson is one of the few influential moral philosophers of the past thirty or forty years to have treated the subject of relativism at any length. He argued, in an essay called 'Relativism' printed in *Facts and Values* in 1963, that his own 'emotivist' theory of moral judgment gave a basis for the refutation of moral relativism. Now what Stevenson actually says about relativism, what he takes it to be, is rather odder than most people remember if they have not been reading him lately: he says, for instance, that an account of moral judgment taking 'X is good' to mean the same as 'I approve of X' is not relativistic, whereas the same theory would be relativistic if requiring the speaker's name to be inserted instead of 'I'. The interest of Stevenson's discussion is not, however, in these details but rather in a certain assumption; namely the assumption that a relativistic theory identifies a moral utterance with an assertion of psychological or sociological fact. The relativist is supposed to identify the thought that a given action is morally good or bad with some proposition about the reactions that people have to it; and it is on this that Stevenson's 'refutation' depends. He points out that the identification must be mistaken because the two types of propositions are backed up in different ways. If someone is asked why he thinks certain things morally good or bad he does not set out to show that some individual or group really does have this or that reaction to it, but tries to bring forward facts about the action itself. Moreover, in putting forward his moral views he expresses feelings or attitudes and tries to change the feelings and attitudes of others, whereas a statement of psychological or sociological fact lacks this dynamic aspect.

One does not have to share Stevenson's emotivism to agree that moral judgments are not descriptions of reactions, since his first argument seems sufficient for the proof. Stevenson will, however, have refuted moral relativism only if his assumption is true of all its versions. And it seems implausible to deny that other models are possible. For outside ethics we actually find judgments that do appear to be relativistic but not in Stevenson's sense.

It will be worth spending a little time considering what might be meant by calling certain types of judgments relativistic: and what relativism amounts to in those areas in which it seems to belong. I am thinking, for instance, of certain judgments of 'taste,' such as those asserting that some people but not others are goodlooking, that some food or drink is appetising or delicious, or that certain colours go well together for furnishings or clothes. Here, it seems, we find wide variations in judgments between different cultures and different generations. One does not have to go as far as ancient Mexico to find a set of faces that we find ugly while supposing that they were once admired, and while we think Nureyev's a better looking face than Valentino's there was a time when the verdict would probably have gone the other way. It is obvious that there is the same kind of disagreement about the palatability of food and drink; and combinations of colors once declared deplorable are now thought particularly good. The old rhyme said that 'blue and green should never be seen', and black and brown were once seen as colours that killed each other as we should say that navy blue kills black.

The reason why such judgments seem undoubtedly relativistic is not, of course, that a wide variety of opinions exist, but rather that no one set of these opinions appears to have any more claim to truth than any other. But there is a problem here. For if the differences in the application of concepts such as 'good-looking' are as great as this, why are we so confident that at different times or in different places the judgments are *about the same thing?* This difficulty must be taken seriously, and may lead us to cut down the number of judgments that we would count as certainly relativistic, even in the area of 'taste'. Perhaps some kind of relativism is true of many other judgments, but relativism is most obviously true where we need set no limit to the variations in the application of an expression, or rather no limits to its application within a given domain. This condition seems to be fulfilled for our examples, but it would not have been fulfilled had we been operating with concepts such as *prettiness,* or even *handsomeness.* It makes sense to speak of another society as thinking good-looking just the faces we think not good-looking, but not as thinking pretty just the faces we think not pretty. The examples most suitable for the present purposes are those that are rather general, and this is why I suggested considering the good-looking, the good-tasting, and the good combinations of colours.

Let us suppose then that there are in different communities divergent sets of such judgments which we have no hope of reconciling, and that in this area we also have no thought of distinguishing the opinions of one group of people as right and those of the others as wrong. Shall we say that this is because the judgments describe reactions such as admiration and liking, and that reactions vary from place to place and time to time? This, which fits Stevenson's version of relativism, is not, in the area we are now discussing, the truth. To say that someone is good-looking is not to say that his looks are admired, any more than to say that someone is likeable is to say that he is well-liked. No doubt it is true that the concept *likeable* depends on reactions of liking. And no doubt it can operate as it does only on account of shared reactions of liking. Shared reactions are also necessary if the language of a particular community is to contain a word like 'elegant', or if it is to be possible to say in it that certain colours go well together. But there is no reason to think that the judgments describe the reactions. One might as well think that 'is red' means the same as 'seems red to most people', forgetting that when asked if an object is red we look at it to see if it is red, and not in order to estimate the reaction that others will have to it. That one does not describe one's own reaction of admiration in saying that someone is good-looking is shown by the fact that one may admit a mistake. That one does not describe the reactions of others in one's community is shown by the fact that one may accuse them of mistake. Nor is this kind of language empty, the mere reiteration of the expression of one's own reaction. There is room here for the idea of showing, even if not of proving or demonstrating. An individual who makes some very idiosyncratic judgment may simply be ignored or told that he is out of his mind. But he may say something that his fellows find instructive, either with an explanation or without it. I do not want to attribute to any particular type of judgment one jot of (local) objectivity that does not really belong to it, or any method for bringing agreement that does not really go along with it. But distinctions are there to be made. It will not do for one of us to say that Charles Laughton got up as the Hunchback of Notre Dame presented the appearance of a good-looking man; but Laughton's brother's suggestion that he was, in his own person, good-looking was a surprising but possible corrective idea.

What this discussion shows is that if a relativistic thesis is true of the judgments under scrutiny it does not assert relativism as understood by Stevenson. And yet it is certainly relativism. For the key concepts will work as they do work—with a kind of objectivity and the attribution of truth—only where there are shared reactions. Once this background is left behind it is impossible to speak of 'right' and 'wrong', 'mistaken' and 'correct', as we commonly do. And therefore it is empty to say of the judgments of another group whose reactions are very different from ours that their opinions are wrong. Our own discussions of these matters of 'taste' implicitly invoke the standards set by our paradigms and our way of going on from them, and here we can speak of right and wrong. But if we are talking of the views of another society we shall speak of what is true by their standards and by our standards, without the slightest thought that our standards are 'correct'. If the ancient Mexicans admired the looks of someone whose head had been flattened, a proposition not *about* this admiration may have been true as spoken by them, though it is false as spoken by us.

We have, then, a version of relativism true of some judgments and not vulnerable to a Stevensonian type of refutation. The question is whether moral assertions might similarly admit only of relative truth. It will probably be objected that this is impossible because moral judgments do not depend on local moral standards as our judgments of taste were thought to depend on local standards of taste. The thought behind this objection is that a challenge to a moral judgment or moral system can be made 'out in the open' as it were, with no agreed method, formal or informal, for showing that the challenge is justified. The idea is that there can be disagreement, with each party thinking the other mistaken, even if there is in principle no way of settling the 'dispute'. It is therefore supposed that an individual can challenge the views of his own society not just in the way that we think it possible for someone to query some judgment of taste, but more radically. He is to be able to say anything he likes about what is morally good and bad, so long as he is consistent, and is to be taken seriously as a man of very eccentric taste would not be. It follows also that the members of one society may similarly challenge the moral view of another society. No common starting point is necessary, and nothing to back up an accusation of falsity or mistake.

Anyone taking this position will insist that moral assertions do not have merely relative truth. Local standards are supposed to be irrelevant, and there is to be no point at which a set of moral opinions inconsistent with one's own are to be admitted to have just as much truth. This is an argument that we should examine carefully; it is perhaps not as powerful as it looks.

The case against construing moral judgments as relativistic along the lines that fit judgments of taste has been made to depend, it seems, on some points of linguistic usage. It was thought crucial that we can say of the moral opinions of our own society, or of some other society, that they are 'mistaken' or 'false', and this was described in terms of a 'challenge' to moral views that differ from our own. The question is whether 'challenge' is the right description if words such as 'true' and 'false' are used as they are supposed to be used here; and in general whether it is important that these words are or are not so employed. It will be remembered that by our hypothesis talk of truth and falsity was to go on even in the absence of any kind of proving or showing, or any *possibility* of proving or showing, that one view rather than the other was in fact true. And this is, of course, a situation very different from that in which the vocabulary of 'true' and 'false' is used in discussing ordinary matters of fact, in everyday life or in science or history, or even literary criticism. Using Bernard Williams' terminology one might say that words such as 'true' and 'false' are not used 'substantially' when used like this.[2] This is not, of course, to say that there is something wrong with the usage, but it does raise doubts about the weight that can be placed on it in discussions of relativism. The linguistic facts were appealed to in the attempt to show that moral judgments could not be relativistic as some judgments of taste seem to be. Yet if we suppose, as a kind of thought experiment, that the same linguistic possibilities exist in the case of these other judgments we see that their relativism is left unchanged. In this new situation it would be possible for an individual to reject as 'false' everything that other members of his society said about good-looking faces, and such things, and it would be possible for one society so to describe the views of another society however far apart their judgments. The important point is that substantial truth would still belong only where common standards were in some sense presupposed; it would still be right to deny that there was any substantial truth belonging to the standards of any particular community.

According to the argument just presented relativism is true in a given area if in that area all *substantial* truth is truth relative to one or other of a set of possible standards. And it is now possible to see that individualistic subjectivism may itself be a form of moral relativism. (Perhaps we would call it a limiting case.) For even if the truth of moral judgments is not relative to local community standards it (the substantial truth) could still be relative to the standards of the individual. This is how it is, in effect, in emotivist and prescriptivist theories, since these theories deny the presence of objective criteria, or any objective method by which differences between individuals with radically different basic moral principles could in principle be resolved. If these theories are correct, anyone who queries the truth of a moral judgment, and still possesses the resource of testing it by his more basic moral principles, uses 'true' substantially; but beyond this point he does not. It follows that the emotivist or prescriptivist is committed to a form of relativism, however little he may like the label. Stevenson, who claimed to have refuted moral relativism, turns out to be himself a kind of moral relativist.

This account of relativism is gravely deficient in so far as it depends on the idea of substantial truth, and gives only merest indication of what this is. Nevertheless there is enough in what has been said about that, and in the comparison with judgments of taste, to make it possible to enquire further into the implications of moral relativism; and at this point I want to refer to a discussion of the topic appearing in Walter Stace's book *The Concept of Morals* in 1937.

Stace takes the relativist to be one who denies that there is any single objective standard of morals, and this is, of course, in line with what we have just been saying. But he also attributes to him two other beliefs: firstly that the very same action that is right in one country or at one period may be wrong in another and secondly that if a man thinks something right it is right for him.

Let us consider the first proposition, once more thinking about the analogy provided by our relativistic judgments of taste. It was seen that such assertions may be true by the standards in operation in one social context and false by those equally well established in another; but it would be wrong to infer, for example, that some men are good-looking in a certain place but not elsewhere, as if their complexions suffered when they moved. And it would be similarly misleading to say that a man might become less good-looking as time went on not because he got older but because standards changed. Nor could two sets of standards be employed simultaneously, to make the same man at the same time both good-looking and ugly. This would be no better than declaring in mid Atlantic, half way between Southern Italy and the U.S., that a man of a certain height was both tall and short. If, for a certain type of judgment, a local standard automatically comes into force, every proposition of this form will presuppose one rather than another. Even with the limiting case of relativism, where the reference is supposed to be only to the standards of the speaker, it will be impossible to employ two sets of standards at once.

Stace is wrong, then, in thinking that the moral relativist is committed to the first of the two propositions listed above. But is he wrong also about the second? This is much more interesting, and more debatable, but we have first to try to get clear about what it means to say that if a man thinks something right it is right for him. It could, I suppose, be taken as denying any distinction between 'A thinks it right to do X' and 'It is right for A to do X', rather as we might deny the distinction between 'A thinks the temperature in the room pleasant' and 'The temperature in the room is pleasant for A'. So interpreted the proposition would deny the possibility of error about matters of right and wrong, and this would seem to make it obviously false. For even on subjectivist theories a man may apply his own standards wrongly, and hence there is a possibility of 'correction' that is not simply a change of mind. There is, however, another interpretation, starting from the thought that if we say 'X is right for A' we are committed to a favorable judgment on the doing of X by A, and going on to assert that this is the judgment to be made wherever A is following his conscience in doing X. It is usually supposed, I think, that it is absurd to think this implied by moral relativism as we have so far discussed it, but I am inclined to believe that something like it is true.

Let us consider the thought that if a man follows his conscience he will act well, and first its relation to the proposition that if he goes against his conscience he will act badly. It seems to be taken for granted by contemporary moralists that the two propositions are on the same footing, and do not need to be considered separately, but this is curious given that Aquinas, who would strenuously have disagreed, wrote powerfully against this view.[3] Aquinas argues that a man acts badly if he goes against his conscience, whatever it may be that his conscience tells him to do, so that even the erring conscience 'binds'. It does not follow, however, that anyone who follows his conscience necessarily acts well: he will also act badly when he intentionally does the things that are evil, even if he thinks them good. Of a man such as Himmler, who seems to have believed that he *should* gas Jewish men, women and children (and therefore indisputably innocent human beings), Aquinas would have said that so long as he thought as he did he could not but act badly. For either he would spare the lives of those in the concentration camps, and so go against his conscience or else he would kill them and so do an evil deed. To the suggestion that a parallel argument could be used to show that whatever Himmler did he would act well, since either he would follow his conscience or else do something good, Aquinas would have replied that good and evil are not symmetrical, as the argument requires. If a man's action is bad in that he is going against his conscience, and good in that he is sparing or saving lives, he acts badly. And he also acts badly if he follows his conscience and does something that is bad. For a single defect is enough to make anything defective whereas a single merit does not suffice to make it good. This surprising principle turns out to be one with which we must agree, and agree quite generally. A house is a bad house if it is either badly designed or badly built; it is a good house only if good in both ways. An apple is bad if it is either worm-ridden or tasteless, and good only if free from either defect. This is not to say that any small defect is enough to make us call something bad: the point is that there is substantial asymmetry of the kind that Aquinas requires.

It is possible, therefore, to maintain with Aquinas that although the erring conscience binds it does not excuse. One may consistently say that if a man thinks he is doing wrong he is doing wrong, but that he may also be doing wrong when he thinks he is doing right. The case is parallel to that of any judge, who has two ways of giving an unjust judgment, firstly by giving one that he believes to be unjust, and secondly by giving one that really is. And similarly anyone has two ways of demeaning himself: he can do what he sees as low or unworthy or demeaning, or he can do something to which these terms do, though he does not see it, apply.

It follows that in discussing the implications of relativism one must deal separately with the two propositions 'If he thinks he is acting badly he is acting badly' and 'if he thinks he is acting well he is acting well'.

That someone who goes against his conscience *ipso facto* acts badly cannot, I think, be denied. One might say that there could not be a more radical moral defect than that of being prepared to do what one believes to be wrong. A man of whom this is true is like an archer who does not even aim at the target, it will be the merest chance if he does what *is* good when he is doing what he *sees* as bad. His will is following evil and is therefore an evil will. This thesis has, however, nothing to do with relativism: it must be accepted by non-relativist and relativist alike.

Can a relativist also agree with a non-relativist in thinking that a man may act badly when he believes he is acting well? This is more doubtful. He can, of course, allow the case of one who misapplies his own principles, so that there is no question of adopting the slogan 'What he thinks is right is right'. But let us put this aside, and ask what the relativist can consistently say about one who reasons correctly from his own moral principles, and does what his conscience tells him to do. If our relativist (B) has moral principles telling him that it is wrong to do action X, but X is what is required by the morality of another man (A), what will B be able to say about the doing of X by A? We will suppose that there are no circumstances other than the fact that A thinks X required of him that could make B say that X *as done by* A was right rather than wrong, or good rather than bad. How will A's conscience affect B's judgment in such a case? Aquinas would be free to say that A acted badly because of the action A was doing; but could a relativist say this too?

The issue hangs, I think, on the question of the innocence or culpability of a man who holds particular moral views. Aquinas, like Aristotle, makes a distinction between ignorance of matters of fact, which is often not culpable, and ignorance of the moral law, which always is.[4] It is within anyone's power to put aside his erring conscience, and if he continues in it this is because he does not want to follow the truth. He can therefore be blamed even when he follows his conscience, because he is at fault in having this conscience. But now consider our relativist. Unlike Aquinas he cannot say that the truth is there to be seen by anyone who wants to see it, because as a relativist he has denied the existence of objective universal criteria of moral truth. So if he says that A will act badly in doing X, after already agreeing that A will act badly if he goes against his conscience and does not do X, he must think that although A can only act badly he is in this moral trap through no fault of his own. A could, we may suppose, have changed his moral opinions, and perhaps he could still change them but B cannot say that he should change them or should have changed them. Unlike Aquinas he cannot insist that someone with these opinions must have wanted not to know the truth, or not wanted to know it enough to discover it. Therefore A was not morally at fault in holding his opinions, and it is for this reason that he is in the moral trap through no fault of his own.

It is the objection to the idea that a man can be in this kind of situation that seems to me to tell against the possiblity that a relativist can judge him adversely when he follows his conscience. Nor am I impressed by the suggestion that the innocent man who can only act badly is a figure with whom we are familiar from the consideration of the (quite different) case of conflicting duties. The arguments supposed to show that someone breaking a promise to avert some great evil does what he 'ought not' to do in spite of doing the best he can in the circumstances seem to me specious, relying on a somewhat romantic admiration for one who is ready to turn regret into the semblance of remorse. This must, of course, be shown, not here, but elsewhere; I mention it only because otherwise I shall probably be accused of forgetting it. Meanwhile the objection stands to the idea that one way may be bad whatever one does, though through no fault of one's own.

It has been argued in the preceding paragraphs that relativism as a theory of the logical status of moral judgment does not leave the practice of making moral judgments unaffected. In terms of the usual jargon, metaethical relativism may be said to imply some measure of normative relativism. This thesis must not, however, be confused with the proposition that no one who holds a relativist moral theory can consistently make moral judgments at all. This quite different idea comes from the thought that a moral relativist is one who denies that any one moral assertion is any truer than any others, and who therefore can *have no moral opinions of his own.* Is this a consequence of relativism? It seems that it is not. For looking to our old model we observe that opinions about matters of taste are not disturbed by the belief that judgments of taste (or the particular judgments of taste that we considered) have only relative truth. We say the Nureyev is good-looking, that oysters are delicious, and that blue and green go well together, without worrying about the fact that by the standards of some other society these things might be false, and that our standards are not better than theirs. Local truth is the only substantive truth that we have, and it is this truth that we tacitly claim for our opinions when we express them. If there is something that makes this kind of accommodation impossible in the case of moral opinions it must be brought to light. Why is it not enough that we should claim relative truth for our moral judgments, taking it as truth relative either to local standards or to individual standards, according to our theory of moral judgment?

Some will no doubt argue that moral judgments are different from judgments of taste in so far as we must wish to see others adopt our own moral system, whereas we do not mind what they think about good looking faces and other matters of 'taste'. Everyone must necessarily preach his own moral opinions, refusing to live and let live, and he therefore cannot say that opposing views are as good as his own. That this is an invalid argument can be seen, I think, by considering the case of imperatives. If two men give opposite instructions each will, in general, want his own order obeyed and the other disregarded. This does not, however, mean that the other order must be seen as in some way invalid or defective: it can be allowed to have equal status even while one urges that one's own should be obeyed. It might be considered a linguistic accident that we do not use 'true' of the imperatives we issue or support and 'false' of those we oppose: if we did do so it would leave the differences between imperatives and assertions as they are, and it would be quite wrong to think that we should be supporting some imperatives *as* we support some propositions in the empirical sciences or in everyday matters of fact because we supported them and used the word 'true'. If we wanted to say in these circumstances that no one imperative was any truer than any other this would make a valid point, and be perfectly consistent with our wish to see our own imperatives carried out. We could also, if we liked, go on calling some imperatives and not others 'true'. With moral judgments it is the same. If there are good reasons for accepting moral relativism (and we have yet to ask about that) then we have to admit that moral judgments opposed to our own are true by some other peoples' standards as ours are true by ours, and that there is no choosing between them on objective grounds. If we believed this we could with perfect consistency put our weight behind our own moral directives, but would have to recognize that if we called them 'truer' than some judgments from another system this truth would not be substantial truth.

So much for the implications of moral relativism. I must now approach, with some trepidation, the extremely difficult question whether relativism is a correct theory of moral judgment.

Let me ask, first, whether we have the same reason to accept moral relativism as we had to accept relativism for our handpicked bunch of judgments of taste? This, is seems to me, we do not. For our starting point there was the thought that some rather general judgments of taste could be identified through any amount of variation in the application of the key concepts through the relevant domain. I myself have frequently argued that such variation cannot be postulated in the case of moral judgment, because the thought of moral goodness and badness cannot be held steady through any and every change in the codes of behaviour taught, and in their grounds.[5] From this it follows that not everything that anyone might want to call a 'moral code' should properly be so described. And this shows, incidentally, that hypotheses about 'cultural relativism' are not toally independent of moral theory. Even if an anthropologist is inclined to call a certain code a moral code, and to go on to talk about a morality radically different from our own, it does not follow that we should accept this way of describing the phenomena. An anthropologist may be as confused or prejudiced as anyone else in applying words such as 'morality' to the teaching of an alien culture.

I shall assume that even general moral terms such as 'right' or 'ought' are restricted, to a certain degree, in their extension, at least at the level of basic principles. It is not possible that there should be two moral codes the mirror images of each other, so that what was considered fundamentally right in one community would be considered wrong at the same level in the other. It seems that some considerations simply are and some are not evidence for particular moral assertions. Nevertheless it does not look as if a correct account of what it is to have a moral thought, or a moral attitude, or to teach a moral code, will suffice to dismiss relativism out of hand. Even if some moral judgments are perfectly objective, there may be others whose truth or falsity is not easily decidable by criteria internal to the subject of morality. We may suppose, I think, that it is clearly an objective moral fact that the Nazi treatment of the Jews was morally indefensible, given the facts and their knowledge of the facts. The Nazis' moral opinions had to be held on grounds either false or irrelevant or both, as on considerations about Germany's 'historic mission', or on the thought that genocide could be a necessary form of self-defence. It was impossible, logically speaking, for them to argue that the killing of millions of innocent people did not need any moral justification, or that the extension of the German Reich was in itself a morally desirable end. Yet after such things have been said the problem of moral relativism is still with us.[6] Even if the fact that it is morality that is in question gives us some guaranteed starting points for arguments about moral right or wrong, how much is this going to settle? Are there not some moral matters on which, even within our own society, disagreement may be irreducible? And is it not possible that some alien moral systems cannot be faulted by us on any objective principles, while our moral beliefs can also not be faulted by theirs? May there not be places where societies simply confront each other, with no rational method for settling their differences?

In the most penetrating critique of relativism that has appeared for many years[7] Bernard Williams has recently argued that this is so, and he bases his belief in moral relativism on this possibility. He thinks that although the vocabulary of appraisal can be used 'substantially' in the consideration of the moral beliefs of some alien cultures, this is not always the case. Is he right about this? He supposes the 'substantial' employment of terms such as 'true' or 'false' can occur only where a system is in 'real confrontation' with our own; and real confrontation turns out to be given by the fact that we could, without suffering hallucination or otherwise losing our grip on reality and rationality, come to hold those beliefs. What is puzzling is why he thinks this relationship to be either necessary or sufficient to give substance (he says, perhaps significantly, 'point or substance') to the vocabulary of appraisal. If we think back to the judgments of taste discussed earlier in this lecture we see that anything of this kind would be irrelevant there. By some process of acculturation we could, no doubt, come to hold quite different opinions about good-looking faces, delicious foods, and combinations of colors. But this does not mean that we can *criticise* the systems which are a real option for us. 'True' and 'false' get a substantial use where there are objective criteria, or at least methods of some kind for settling disputes, and this seems to have nothing to do with 'real confrontation' as defined by Williams.

Nevertheless Williams is surely right in thinking that if some societies with divergent moral systems merely confront each other, having no use for the assertion that their own systems are true and the others false except to mark the system to which they adhere, then relativism is a true theory of morality. Yet at this point one may become uneasy about his reasons for saying that relativism is true. For it seems strange to suggest that there is any society whose values we can identify without being able to set them critically beside our own, and our own beside theirs. Some parts of the moral vocabulary do indeed seem unusable when we are considering very alien and distant communities. For instance it would be odd then to talk in terms of the permissible and the impermissible, simply because language of this kind cannot venture very far from actual sets of permissions and prohibitions. But this does not mean that we cannot in any way judge the moral rules and values of societies very different in this respect from our own. Granted that it is wrong to assume identity of aim between peoples of different cultures; nevertheless there is a great deal that all men have in common. All need affection, the cooperation of others, a place in a community, and help in trouble. It isn't true to suppose that human beings can flourish without these things—being isolated, despised or embattled, or without courage or hope. We are not, therefore, simply expressing values that we happen to have if we think of some moral systems as good moral systems and others as bad. Communities as well as individuals can live wisely or unwisely, and this is largely the result of their values and the codes of behavior that they teach. Looking at these societies, and critically also at our own, we surely have some idea of how things work out and why they work out as they do. We do not have to suppose it is just as good to promote pride of place and the desire to get an advantage over other men as it is to have an ideal of affection and respect. These things have different harvests, and unmistakably different connexions with human good.

No doubt it will be argued that even if all this is true it leaves moral relativism substantially intact, since objective evaluation of moral systems can go only a little way, and will come to an end before all the radical disagreements are resolved. One wonders, however, why people who say this kind of thing are so sure that they know where discussions will lead and therefore where they will end. It is, I think, a fault on the part of relativists, and subjectivists generally, that they are ready to make pronouncements about the later part of moral arguments, and moral reviews, without being able to trace the intermediate steps. Nor is it that they just do not bother to take the whole journey; for there are reasons why they are not able to. One of these has to do with conventions about moral philosophy, conventions that forbid the philosopher to fill chapters with descriptive material about human nature and human life. It isn't supposed to be part of his work to think in the somewhat discursive way that is suitable to reflections about the human heart, and the life of men in society. It is, of course, a kind of decency that keeps moral philosophers in the analytic tradition away from the pseudo-profundity that is found in some philosophies as well as in vulgar preachers. Yet it may be that they have to do this work, and do it properly, before they will know the truth about divergent moralities and values. And we have, after all, a right tradition of history and literature on which to draw.

There is, however, another reason why moral philosophers tend to give only a sketch of the beginning and end of discussions of the values of different societies; and this has to do with a gap in our philosophical understanding. Perhaps it would be better to speak of a series of gaps, of which I shall give instances in the next few paragraphs. My thought is that there are some concepts which we do not understand well, and cannot employ competently in an argument, that are, unfortunately, essential to genuine discussions of the merits of different moral systems.

Let me give some examples of the kind of thing that I have in mind. I would suppose, for instance, that in some fundamental moral enquiries we might find ourselves appealing to the fact that human life is of value. But do we really understand this thought? Do we know what we mean by saying that *anything* has value, or even that we value it, as opposed to wanting it or being prepared to go to trouble to get it? I do not know of any philosopher living or dead who has been able to explain this idea. And then again we are likely to find ourselves talking about happiness, which is a most intractable concept. To realize that one does not understand it one has only to try to explain why, for instance, the contented life of someone on whom a pre-frontal lobotomy has been performed is not the happy life, or why we would count someone as unfortunate rather than endowed with happiness if he were tricked into thinking he was successfully spending his life on important work when he was really just messing around. That we do not understand the concept of happiness is shown, once more, by the fact that we are inclined to think stupid thoughts about the idea of great happiness, as if it were simply extreme and prolonged euphoria. That great happiness depends on its objects is a surprising idea once we understand this, as it should be understood, as a conceptual not a causal matter. It seems that great happiness, unlike euphoria or even great pleasure, must come from something related to what is deep in human nature, and fundamental in human life, such as affection for children and friends, and the desire to work, and love of freedom and truth. But what do we mean by calling some things in human nature deep, and some things in life fundamental? In one way we know this, because we are able, for instance, to understand a man who says at the end of his life that he has wasted his time on 'things that don't matter'. But what are things that 'matter' if they are not the trivial things on which we spend so much time? Clearly such questions are relevant to fundamental discussions of the moralities of other societies and our own. It is impossible to judge a society's morality if we cannot talk about its values, and we must be able to handle the thought of false values if we are to say what is wrong with a materialistic society such as ours. But what is it to have false values if it is not to think too highly of things that do not matter very much?

It seems, then, that we are all at sea with some of the ideas that we are bound to employ in any real discussion of divergent moralities. What we tend to do is to ignore these ideas, and pretend that the debate can be carried on in other terms. But why should this be supposed possible? With other, more jejune, concepts we shall get another discussion, and from it we cannot draw conclusions about how the first would end. Moving from one to the other we are merely guessing at results, and this is, I think, exactly what happens in many arguments about moral relativism. Personally I feel uncomfortable in these arguments, and perhaps this is because I am advancing opinions on the basis of a guess. The practical conclusion may be that we should not at the moment try to say whether moral relativism is true or false, but should start the work farther back.

NOTES

1. See, for instance, Bernard Williams, 'The Truth in Relativism', *Proceedings of the Aristotelian Society* (1974–75) (this volume, pp. 175–85); Gilbert Harman, 'Moral Relativism Defended', *Philosophical Review* (1975) (this volume, pp. 189–204) and remarks in David Wiggins, 'Truth, Invention, and the Meaning of Life', *Proceedings of the British Academy* (1976).

2. 'Consistency and Realism', *Aristotelian Society Supplementary Volume* (1966). Also 'The Truth in Relativism'.

3. *Summa Theologica* la 2ae. Q.19 a 5 and 6.

4. Ibid, la 2ae Q6, a 8, and Q.19, a 6.

5. See, e.g., P.R. Foot, 'Moral Arguments', *Mind* 1958, and 'Moral Beliefs', *Proceedings of the Aristotelian Society* 1958–59.

6. Compare P.R. Foot 'Morality and Art', *Proceedings of the British Academy* 1970.

7. 'The Truth in Relativism'.

An Inconsistent Form of Relativism

AND

The Truth in Relativism

Many writers on relativism, cognitive as well as moral, are content to point out the alleged inconsistencies and "absurdities" of the position and then move immediately on to other subjects. In the preceding paper Philippa Foot takes a much more serious attitude, closely examining the usual objections to moral relativism and finding them hasty and unconvincing. Bernard Williams has also taken a more serious attitude toward moral relativism: while fully recognizing that some versions of relativism are obviously fallacious, he has tried to formulate a position which preserves the truth in relativism.

The type of relativism which is capable of definitive refutation is that which maintains each of these two propositions: (1) the term 'right' means "right for a given society" and (2) it is wrong for people in one society to condemn or interfere with the values and moral behavior of another society. This version—which Williams calls "vulgar relativism"—contradicts itself by asserting in the first proposition that all uses of 'right' and 'wrong' are relative to a society and then in the second proposition employing the term 'wrong' in a nonrelative way.

Williams develops another type of relativism which we may call "appraisal relativism" and which is not contradictory in the same way: For a person whose own system of moral beliefs $S1$ does not stand in real confrontation with another system of beliefs $S2$, questions of appraisal of $S2$ do not genuinely arise. Questions of appraisal do genuinely arise, according to Williams, when $S2$ is a "real option" for holders of $S1$ in the sense that it is possible for holders of $S1$ to "go over" to $S2$. "Going over" to $S2$ means living within $S2$ while still maintaining their hold on reality and acknowledging their transition to $S2$ in the light of rational comparison between $S1$ and $S2$. Notice that while vulgar relativism appraises actions, appraisal relativism appraises appraisals, some as genuine appraisals and others as not genuine. Moreover, while vulgar relativism relativizes terms such as 'right' and 'wrong', appraisal relativism uses such appraisal terms as 'genuine' in an unabashedly absolute sense. Thus, appraisal relativism does not mix absolute and relative meanings together in one doctrine and avoids self-contradiction.

But now an important question arises. If appraisal relativism does not hold the meanings of appraisal words to be relative, then in what way is it a form of *relativism*? Well, what makes any doctrine a form of relativism? One feature which makes a doctrine a form of relativism is that it alleges something to be relative to something else. We have seen that this is so in the case of vulgar relativism, where meanings of terms are relativized to societal codes. Appraisal relativism fulfils this requirement too. Specifically, it makes the activity of genuinely appraising an S relative to (dependent upon) various sorts of conditions—for example, the nature of one's own moral code and (as we shall see) one's own concerns. Appraisal relativism holds that not every S can be genuinely appraised in just any situation whatever and lays down some of the conditions of genuine appraisal to which genuine appraisal is then relative.

It should be noticed that appraisal relativism would lead to something of the same results as does vulgar relativism. One purpose of vulgar relativism is to serve as an argument against interfering in other societies. Appraisal relativism has a somewhat parallel use for some cases. Suppose that Sk is a belief system which Jones cannot genuinely appraise. Then Sk is not a system which Jones can be justified in judging to be defective or inferior to his own. And hence Sk is not a system which Jones could be justified in interfering with on the basis of such judgments. Of course, this is not to say that Jones could not interfere with that society; it is only to say that Jones would lack a rational basis for doing so.

Foot calls Williams' article "the most penetrating critique of relativism that has appeared for many years." But she objects to his condition that $S2$ be a real option for holders of $S1$ in order for the latter to be able to give a genuine appraisal of the former. She is puzzled as to why Williams believes this to be either a necessary or a sufficient condition of genuine appraisal and argues against its being a sufficient condition: "But this does not mean that we can criticise the systems which are a real option for us. 'True' and 'false' get a substantial use where there are objective criteria, or at least methods of some kind for settling disputes, and this seems to have nothing to do with 'real confrontation' as defined by Williams."

Nevertheless, even if Foot's objection is correct, Williams' real-option condition may express a necessary condition of genuine appraisal. In explaining the real-option condition Williams tells us that a "relation to our concerns . . . alone gives any point of substance to appraisal." There certainly is a difference between an appraisal idly made with nothing at stake and an appraisal made in response to genuine concerns. Our concerns usually lead us to make appraisals in the first place; after all, we do not appraise every conceivable moral system. And these concerns provide some of the criteria— especially criteria of importance—on which appraisal is based. When we encounter another moral system, it is natural to think that this is an alternative to our own, one which we could easily adopt and in fact which we are morally required to adopt if it is superior to our own system. But if the alternative moral system does not respond to our concerns, we cannot judge it as better than ours, and consequently it is not an alternative for us. And the alternative cannot respond to our concerns if we cannot adopt it. Perhaps this is Williams' reason for limiting genuine appraisal to systems which we could adopt. Perhaps this is why the real-option condition is taken by Williams to be a necessary condition of genuine appraisal.

But is the real-option condition even a necessary condition of genuine appraisal? Consider the moral code of a medieval Samurai. It is certainly true that the life of a medieval Samurai is not one that could be lived today, since it can be lived only within a society having certain institutions and values that are lacking today. But we still might be able to genuinely appraise the belief-system of a Samurai. Imagine a businessman whose ideal is to contribute to the economic and material development of his society. Various inventors, explorers, and entrepreneurs are his heroes. Upon reading James Clavell's novel *Shogun,* which gives a superbly sympathetic portrait of Japanese Samurai life and ideals,[1] our businessman condemns the Samurai for concerning himself solely with duty, loyalty, and honor, thus making no contribution whatsoever to the economic development of Japan. The businessman feels that the Samurai is a parasite whose domination of Japanese medieval society blocks efforts toward improvement of the material situation. (This is a judgment which our businessman might well share with a Communist.) This seems to be a case in which the S being evaluated does have a relation to the evaluator's concerns, even though that S cannot be adopted by the evaluator. And because the S is related to the evaluator's concerns, the businessman's appraisal seems genuine rather than idle. The real-option requirement thus seems too strong to serve as a necessary condition of genuine appraisal. We can genuinely appraise systems of belief which we cannot adopt.

Williams is right in pointing out and emphasizing the difference between genuine and notional appraisal. A fuller exploration of the conditions of genuine appraisal might well lead, as Williams believes, to a strong and important form of moral relativism.

NOTE

1. New York: Atheneum, 1975.

An Inconsistent Form of Relativism*

Bernard Williams

Let us at this stage of the argument about subjectivism take a brief rest and look round a special view or assemblage of views which has been built on the site of moral disagreements between societies. This is *relativism,* the anthropologist's heresy, possibly the most absurd view to have been advanced even in moral philosophy. In its vulgar and unregenerate form (which I shall consider, since it is both the most distinctive and the most influential form) it consists of three propositions: that 'right' means (can only be coherently understood as meaning) 'right for a given society'; that 'right for a given society' is to be understood in a functionalist sense; and that (therefore) it is wrong for people in one society to condemn, interfere with, etc., the values of another society. A view with a long history, it was popular with some liberal colonialists, notably British administrators in places (such as West Africa) in which white men held no land. In that historical role, it may have had, like some other muddled doctrines, a beneficent influence, though modern African nationalism may well deplore its tribalist and conservative implications.

Whatever its results, the view is clearly inconsistent, since it makes a claim in its third proposition, about what is right and wrong in one's dealings with other societies, which uses a *nonrelative* sense of 'right' not allowed for in the first proposition. The claim that human sacrifice, for instance, was 'right for' the Ashanti comes to be taken as saying that human sacrifice was right among the Ashanti, and this in turn as saying that human sacrifice among the

*Reprinted with permission of the author and publisher from Bernard Williams, *Morality: An Introduction to Ethics* (New York: Harper & Row, 1972), pp. 22–26. Copyright © 1972 by Bernard Williams.

Ashanti was right; i.e., we have no business to interfere with it. But this last is certainly not the sort of claim allowed by the theory. The most the theory can allow is the claim that it is right for (i.e., functionally valuable for) our society not to interfere with Ashanti society, and, first, this is certainly not all that was meant, and, second, is very dubiously true.

Apart from its logically unhappy attachment of a nonrelative morality of toleration or noninterference to a view of morality as relative, the theory suffers in its functionalist aspects from some notorious weaknesses of functionalism in general, notably difficulties that surround the identification of 'a society'. If 'society' is regarded as a cultural unit, identified in part through its values, then many of the functionalist propositions will cease to be empirical propositions and become bare tautologies: it is tediously a necessary condition of the survival of a group-with-certain-values that the group should retain those values. At the other extreme, the survival of a society could be understood as the survival of certain persons and their having descendants, in which case many functionalist propositions about the necessity of cultural survival will be false. When in Great Britain some Welsh nationalists speak of the survival of the Welsh language as a condition of the survival of Welsh society, they manage sometimes to convey an impression that it is a condition of the survival of Welsh people, as though the forgetting of Welsh were literally lethal.

In between these two extremes is the genuinely interesting territory, a province of informative social science, where there is room for such claims as that a given practice or belief is integrally connected with much more of a society's fabric than may appear on the surface, that it is not an excrescence, so that discouragement or modification of this may lead to much larger social change than might have been expected; or, again, that a certain set of values or institutions may be such that if they are lost, or seriously changed, the people in the society, while they may physically survive, will do so only in a deracinated and hopeless condition. Such propositions, if established, would of course be of first importance in deciding what to do; but they cannot take over the work of deciding what to do.

Here, and throughout the questions of conflict of values between societies, we need (and rarely get) some mildly realistic picture of what decisions might be being made by whom, of situations to which the considerations might be practically relevant. Of various paradigms that come to mind, one is that of conflict, such as the confrontation of other societies with Nazi Germany. Another is that of control, where (to eliminate further complications of the most obvious case, colonialism) one might take such a case as that of the relations of the central government of Ghana to residual elements of traditional Ashanti society. In neither case would functionalist propositions in themselves provide any answers at all. Still less will they where a major issue is whether a given group should be realistically or desirably regarded as 'a society' in a relevant sense, or whether its values and its future are to be integrally related to those of a larger group—as with the case of blacks in the United States.

The central confusion of relativism is to try to conjure out of the fact that societies have differing attitudes and values an *a priori* nonrelative principle to determine the attitude of one society to another; this is impossible. If we are going to say that there are ultimate moral disagreements between societies, we must include, in the matters they can disagree about, their attitudes to other moral outlooks. It is also true, however, that there are inherent features of morality that tend to make it difficult to regard a morality as applying only to a group. The element of universalization which is present in any morality, but which applies under tribal morality perhaps only to members of the tribe, progressively comes to range over persons as such. Less formally, it is essential (as was remarked earlier) to morality and its role in any society that certain sorts of reactions and motivations should be strongly internalized, and these cannot merely evaporate because one is confronted with human beings in another society. Just as *de gustibus non disputandum* is not a maxim which applies to morality, neither is 'when in Rome do as the Romans do', which is at best a principle of etiquette.

Nor is it just a case of doing as the Romans do, but of putting up with it. Here it would be a platitude to point out that of course someone who gains wider experience of the world may rightly come to regard some moral reaction of his to unfamiliar conduct as parochial and will seek to modify or discount it. There are many important distinctions to be made here between the kinds of thoughts appropriate to such a process in different cases: sometimes he may cease to regard a certain issue as a moral matter at all, sometimes he may come to see that what abroad looked the same as something he would have deplored at home was actually, in morally relevant respects, a very different thing. (Perhaps—though one can scarcely believe it—there were some missionaries or others who saw the men in a polygamous society in the light of seedy bigamists at home.) But it would be a particular moral view, and one both psychologically and morally implausible, to insist that these adaptive reactions were the only correct ones, that confronted with practices which are found and felt as inhuman, for instance, there is an *a priori* demand of acceptance. In the fascinating book by Bernal de Diaz, who went with Cortez to Mexico, there is an account of what they all felt when they came upon the sacrificial temples. This morally unpretentious collection of bravos was genuinely horrified by the Aztec practices. It would surely be absurd to regard this reaction as merely parochial or self-righteous. It rather indicated something which their conduct did not indicate, that they regarded the Indians as men rather than as wild animals.

It is fair to press this sort of case, and in general the cases of actual confrontation. 'Every society has its own standards' may be, even if confused, a sometimes useful maxim of social study; as a maxim of social study it is also painless. But what, after all, is one supposed to do if confronted with a human sacrifice?—not a real question for many of us, perhaps, but a real question for Cortez. "It wasn't their business," it may be said; "they had no right to be there anyway." Perhaps—though this, once more, is necessarily a nonrelative moral judgment itself. But even if they had no right to be there, it is a matter for real moral argument what would *follow* from that. For if a burglar comes across the owner of the house trying to murder somebody, is he morally obliged not to interfere because he is trespassing?

None of this is to deny the obvious facts that many have interfered with other societies when they should not have done; have interfered without understanding; and have interfered often with a brutality greater than that of anything they were trying to stop. I am saying only that it cannot be a consequence of the nature of morality itself that no society ought ever to interfere with another, or that individuals from one society confronted with the practices of another ought, if rational, to react with acceptance. To draw these consequences is the characteristic (and inconsistent) step of vulgar relativism.

The Truth in Relativism*

Bernard Williams

This paper tries to place certain issues in the discussion of relativism, not to deal with any one of them thoroughly. It is concerned with any kind of relativism, in the sense that the questions raised are ones that should be asked with regard to relativistic views in any area, whether it be the world-views of different cultures, shifts in scientific paradigms, or differences of ethical outlook. A machinery is introduced which is intended to apply quite generally. But the only area in which I want to claim that there is truth in relativism is the area of ethical relativism. This does not mean that I here try to argue against its truth in any other area, nor do I try to pursue any of the numerous issues involved in delimiting the ethical from other areas.

1. CONDITIONS OF THE PROBLEM

(a) There have to be two or more *systems of belief* (Ss) which are to some extent self-contained. No very heavy weight is put on the propositional implications of the term 'belief', nor, still less, is it implied that all relevant differences between such systems (let '$S1$', '$S2$', stand for examples from now on) can be adequately expressed in propositional differences: the extent to which this is so will differ with different sorts of examples. Any application of this structure will involve some degree of idealization, with regard to the coherence and homogeneity of an S. There is more than one way in which these characteristics may be imposed, however, and difference in these affects the way (perhaps, the sense) in which the resultant S is an idealization.

*Reprinted with permission of the author and the Editor of The Aristotelian Society from *Proceedings of The Aristotelian Society* 75 (1974–75): 215–28. Copyright © 1975 The Aristotelian Society.

The characteristics may be involved in the very identification of the Ss: thus two synchronously competing scientific theories may be picked out in part in terms of what bodies of beliefs hang together. But even in this case the Ss will not just be intellectual items constructed from the outside on the basis of the harmony of their content: there will in fact be bodies of scientists working within these theories (research programmes *etc.*) and seeking to impose coherence on them. If failures in imposing coherence were to be regarded as *a priori* impossible, the structure of description in terms of various Ss would lose a great deal of explanatory value.

In the case of alien cultures, the identification of an S may be effected initially through other features (geographical isolation and internal inter-action of a group of persons), and the coherence of the S operate rather as an ideal limit for the understanding of the group's beliefs. This idea is in fact problematical, at least if taken as indicative of understanding in any objective sense: one comprehensible, and surely plausible, hypothesis is that no group of human beings will have a belief system which is fully coherent. The demand operates, nevertheless, as a constraint on theory-construction about the group, since the data will even more radically underdetermine theory if room is left for indeterminate amounts of incoherence within the S which theory constructs.

The problems of relativism concern communication between $S1$ and $S2$, or between them and some third party, and in particular issues of preference between them. It is worth noticing that quite a lot is taken for granted in the construction of the problem-situation already, in the application of the idea of there being a plurality of different Ss. Thus it is presupposed that persons within each S can understand other persons within that S; also that persons receive information in certain ways and not others, are acculturated in certain ways, *etc.* It may be that some forms of relativism can be shown to be false by reference to these presuppositions themselves: not on the ground (which would prove nothing) tht the *genesis* of the ideas such as 'a culture', like that of 'relativism' itself, lies in a certain sort of culture, but on the ground that the *application* of a notion such as 'a culture' presupposes the instantiation in the subject-matter of a whole set of relations which can be adequately expressed at all only via the concepts of one culture rather than another (*e.g.*, certain notions of causality). Any relativism which denied the non-relative validity of concepts involved in setting up its problem at all, would be refuted. This aspect of the matter has received some attention;[1] I shall not try to take it further here.

(b) $S1$ and $S2$ have to be *exclusive of one another*. That this should in some sense be so is a necessary condition of the problems arising to which relativism is supposed to provide an answer; indeed, it can itself be seen as a condition of identifying $S1$ and $S2$, in any sense relevant to those problems.

Suppose for example that two putative *S*s constituted merely the history or geography of two different times or places: then evidently they are not *S*s in the sense of the problem, because they can merely be conjoined.

A much harder question, however, is raised by asking what are the (most general) conditions of two *S*s excluding one another. The most straightforward case is that in which *S*1 and *S*2 have conflicting consequences, a condition which I shall first take in the form of requiring that there be some yes/no question to which consequence *C*1 of *S*1 answers 'yes' and consequence *C*2 of *S*2 answers 'no'. Under this condition *S*1 and *S*2 have to be (at least in the respect in question) *comparable*.

The questions to which relativism is supposed to give an answer may be raised by the case of conflicting consequences, but relativism will not stay around as an answer to them unless something else is also true, namely that the answering of a yes/no question of this sort in one way rather than the other does not constrain either the holder of *S*1 or the holder of *S*2 to abandon respectively the positions characteristic of *S*1 and *S*2 (and of the difference between them). If this further condition does not hold, there will be a straightforward decision procedure between *S*1 and *S*2, and relativism will have been banished. In the scientific case, the possiblity of this condition holding, granted that *C*1 and *C*2 are consequences of *S*1 and *S*2, lies in the possibility that the consequence follows from the system only using material peripheral to the system and to its most characteristic positions: the situation is the much-discussed one in which theory is underdetermined by observation.

However, if theory is radically underdetermined by observation, can it be required that *S*s are even to this modest degree comparable? Thus, in the spirit of one fashionable line of argument, if every observation statement is theory-laden and all theory-ladenness displays meaning-variance, then it is unclear how there can be one yes/no question which stands in the required relation to *S*1 and *S*2. Here it is important to see how little is implied by there being conflicting consequences of *S*1 and *S*2. All that is required is that there be *some* description of a possible outcome, which description is acceptable to both *S*1 and *S*2, and in terms of which a univocal yes/no question can be formed: it may well be that there are other descriptions of what is (in some sense) the same event which are noncomparable. If this minimal requirement is not satisfied, severe problems are likely to follow, particularly in the case of scientific theories, for the original description of the *S*s. We lose control on the notion of observation, concerning which it is said that it underdetermines theory; and we lose the descriptions of certain passages in the history of science which are the subject and in some part the motivation of these accounts (roughly it looks as though not only the choice of a replacement paradigm, but the occasion of the choice, might emerge as entirely socially determined, as though a chief determinant of the alteration of scientific theory were boredom.)

However it may be with scientific theories, it would perhaps be unwise to exclude, at least at the beginning of the argument, the possibility of systems so disparate that they were not, in terms of conflicting consequences, comparable at all: some social anthropologists have given accounts of the Ss of traditional (pre-scientific) societies in terms which seem to imply that they are quite incommensurable with the Ss of modern, scientific, societies. I shall not go into the question of whether such accounts could be true.[2] The issue is rather, if such accounts were true, what content could be left to the idea that the traditional and the scientific Ss were exclusive of one another—as surely everyone, including these social anthropologists, would say that they were. Here it looks as though the only thing to be said is that, in ways which need to be analysed, it is impossible to live within both Ss. Accepting this vague idea, we can indeed continue to use, at a different level, the language of conflicting consequences, since if it is impossible to live within both $S1$ and $S2$, then the consequences of (holding) $S1$ include actions, practices, *etc.* which are incompatible with those which are consequences of (holding) $S2$.

I do not take this to be a very illuminating assimilation, since the variation required in the interpretation of 'consequence' remains unexplained. But it does harmlessly help to handle a wider range of cases without constant qualification; and it does, more than that, positively bring out one thing—that even in this limiting case (which I shall call that of *incommensurable exclusivity*), there has to be something which can be identified as the *locus* of exclusivity, and hence is not from every point of view incommensurable. This *locus* will be that of the actions or practices which are the consequences of living within $S1$ or $S2$. Another light will be shed on them when we turn, next, to broadly ethical cases.

In ethical cases (taken in a broad sense), the conditions of conflict come out, obviously enough, differently from the form they take with, for instance, scientific theories. The simplest case is that of conflict between answers which are given to yes/no questions which are practical questions, questions about whether to do a certain thing. Now such a question might be a general, or type, action question, asking whether a certain type of thing was to be done in a certain type of situation. In this case, the relevant formulation is that it is possible for $S1$ to answer 'yes' to such a question while $S2$ answers 'no' to it; this is parallel to two theories yielding conflicting predictions, but without the question yet being raised of one or the other actually being borne out in fact. We get a structure resembling the occurrence of an actual observation only when we move to an idea of a particular token action question, as asked by a particular agent in a particular situation. Here the practical question *gets answered* in actual fact; and this occurrence of course trivially satisfies the conditions: the fact that a given question gets answered in this sense in a way which conflicts with, say, the consequence of *S*1 does not constrain a holder of *S*1 to abandon his position (he may say that the agent was wrong so to decide). What actually is done trivially underdetermines systems of belief about what ought to be done.

Action decisions are not the only possible site of conflicting consequences in the ethical case: various forms of approval, sentiment, *etc.* can equally come into it. With these, but also with action-descriptions, difficulties can, once more, arise about the satisfaction of the comparability condition. This condition is easily satisfied under *e.g.,* Hare's theory, which is strongly analogous to a positivist philosophy of science, in regarding an ethical outlook or value system (theory) as consisting of a set of principles (laws) whose content is totally characterised by what imperatives (predictions) they generate. But on any more complex view, very severe problems of comparability arise. Here again, we can appeal to the weak requirement which was made in the theory case: that there be some description of the action (say) in terms of which a univocal yes/no question can be formulated. Thus it is certainly true and important that marriage to two persons in a polygamous society is not the same state or action as bigamy in a monogamous society, nor is human sacrifice the same action as murder in the course of armed robbery. But there may well be descriptions such that a univocal yes/no question can be formed for each of these examples, and *S*1 and *S*2 differ in their answers. There can be, that is to say, system-based conflict: two persons can be in a conflict situation, which can be characterised as their giving opposed answers to the same question of action, approval *etc.,* and be motivated to this by their value system (this is to exclude quarrels inspired by motivations themselves not sanctioned by the value system).

The line I have sketched for describing cases (if there are any) of incommensurable exclusivity implies that for every pair of *S*s which are incommensurably exclusive, there must be some action, practice, *etc.,* which under some agreed description will be a locus of disagreement between the holders of the *S*s. If this condition is not met, it is unclear what room is left for the notion of exclusivity at all, and hence for the problems of relativism.

2. VARIATION AND CONFRONTATION

With regard to a given kind of *S*, there can be both diachronic and synchronic variation. In the history and philosophy of science, anthropology, *etc.,* there is room for a great deal of discussion about the interrelations of and the limitations to these kinds of variation. There is for instance the question whether certain synchronic variations represent certain diachronic ones, *i.e.,* whether certain cultural variations in one place are survivals of what was an earlier culture elsewhere (do the Hottentots have a Stone Age culture?). Again, the definition of a certain class of *S*s can limit variation: thus the range within which something can count as a *scientific theory* is a well-known matter of dispute, as is the question whether the use of such restrictions to delimit what is counted as diachronic variation (to constitute, that is, a history *of science*) is merely a matter of *ex post facto* evaluation. (The matter takes on a different aspect with respect to synchronic variation at the present time, in view of the existence of a unified and institutionalized international scientific culture.)

In many, if not all, cases of diachronic variation, it is an important fact that a later *S* involves consciousness of at least its neighbouring predecessor (though not necessarily, of course, in terms which the predecessor, or again *S*'s successors, would assent to). There are very important issues at this point about the writing of 'objective' cultural history, but I do not intend to take them on. In fact, I propose from this point on to ignore cases in which *S*2 arises in a way which involves some conscious relation with *S*1, and to consider only those in which mutual awareness can be regarded as, in principle, a development independent of the existence of *S*1 and *S*2. While this simplification is a drastic one, it will do for present purposes.

Under this simplification, let us now consider some possible relations, or lack of them, between *S*1 and *S*2. There is, first, the primitive situation in which *S*1 and *S*2 exist in ignorance of one another. After that, there are cases in which at least one of *S*1 and *S*2 encounters the other: either directly, in the case in which persons who hold one of the *S*s encounter persons who hold the other, or indirectly, when persons holding one merely learn of the other.

Some such encounters, I shall call *real confrontations* (the term 'confrontation' is not meant to carry all the implications it has in contemporary politics). For any *S*, there has to be something which counts as assenting to that *S*, fully accepting it, living within it *etc.*—whatever it is, in each sort of case, for an *S* of that sort to be *somebody's S*: I shall call this relation in general 'holding'. There is a real confrontation between *S*1 and *S*2 at a given time if there is a group at that time for whom each of *S*1 and *S*2 is a real option; this includes, but is not confined to, the case of a group which already holds *S*1 or *S*2, for whom the question is one of whether to *go over* to the other *S*. *We shall come back shortly to the question of what a 'real option' is.*

Contrasted with this situation is that of notional confrontation.[3] Notional confrontation resembles real confrontation in that there are persons who are aware of *S*1 and *S*2, and aware of their differences; it differs from it in that at least one of *S*1 and *S*2 do not present a real option to them. *S*1 and *S*2 can of course be in both real and notional confrontation, but not with respect to the same persons at the same time. *S*1 and *S*2 can be in notional confrontation without ever having been in real confrontation: *e.g.,* if no-one comes to know of both *S*1 and *S*2 until at least one of them has ceased to represent real options. Again, *S*1 and *S*2 can be in real confrontation without ever being in notional confrontation: *e.g.,* if no-one ever thinks of one of them after the hour of its struggle (presumably unsuccessful) with the other.

What is it for an *S* to be a real option? In accordance with the starting-point that *S*s belongs to groups (which is not to deny that they are held by individuals, but to assert that they are held by individuals in ways which require description and explanation by reference to the group), the idea of a real option is meant to be a social notion. *S*2 is a real option for a group if either it is their *S* or it is possible for them to go over to *S*2; where going over to *S*2 involves, first, that it is possible for them to live within, or hold, *S*2 and retain their hold on reality, and, second, to the extent that rational comparison between *S*2 and their present outlook is possible, they could acknowledge their transition to *S*2 in the light of such comparison.[4] Both these conditions use concepts which imply that whether a given *S* is a real option to a given group at a given time is, to some extent at least, a matter of degree: this consequence is not unwelcome.

Something must be said in explanation of each of these conditions: let me take the second first. The purpose of this is to ensure that the question of whether an *S* is a real option is not just (granted the satisfaction of the first condition) a matter of such things as the state of psychological technology: we do not want to say that an eccentric scientific theory is a real option for a group of scientists because they could be drugged or operated upon in such a way that they emerged believing it. To the extent that *S*1 and *S*2 are comparable, do expose themselves to experiment which can tend to favour one over the other, *etc.,* these methods of assessment are what are to count in the consideration of the accessibility of *S*2 from S1. Whether something is a real option is a social question, but one rooted in as much rationality as is available on the given type of issue.

In the limiting case of incommensurable exclusivity, this condition will have virtually no effect: there will be little room in such a case for anything except conversion. But even conversion had better be something which can be lived sanely: and this is the force of the first condition. To speak of people who have accepted *S*2 "retaining their hold on reality" is to imply such things as that it is possible for *S*2 to become their *S*, and for them to live within *S*2, without their engaging in extensive self-deception, falling into paranoia, and such things. The extent to which that is so depends in turn, to some degree, on what features of their existing social situation are held constant under the assumption of their going over to *S*2. Thus *S*2 may not be realistically possible for a group granted features of their present social situation, but it might be if those features were changed. The question of whether $S2$ is, after all, a real option for them then involves the question of whether those features could be changed.

It is neither a necessary nor a sufficient condition of an S's being a real option for a group that they think that it is a real option. It is not a sufficient condition, because they may be ill-informed, unimaginative, un-self-aware, optimistic, *etc.,* about what it would be like for them to try to live within that S (and this may not be just a personal, but a social or political mistake). It is not a necessary condition, because they may not have realised what possibilities going over to that S would offer them: the psychology of conversion of course relates to this matter. I regard the question of whether a given S is a real option for a given group at a given time as basically an objective question. Of course, people may differ about such questions as what is included under "a hold on reality," and also, notoriously, about what degree of rational comparability can be displayed by Ss of a given kind. In terms of the present structure, such disagreements may well affect what range of Ss those people will regard as real options, for themselves or others.

In this sense many Ss which have been held are not real options now. The life of a Greek Bronze Age chief, or a mediaeval Samurai, and the outlooks that go with those, are not real options for us: there is no way of living them. This is not to say that reflection on those value-systems may not provide inspiration for thoughts about elements missing from modern life, but there is no way of taking on those Ss. Even Utopian projects among a small band of enthusiasts could not reproduce *that* life: still more, the project of re-enacting it on a societal scale in the context of actual modern industrial life would involve one of those social or political mistakes, in fact a vast illusion. The prospect of removing the conditions of modern industrial life altogether is something else again—another, though different, impossibility.

In this connexion it is important that there are asymmetrically related options. Some version of modern technological life and its outlooks has become a real option for members of some traditional societies, but their life is not, despite the passionate nostalgia of many, a real option for us. The theories one has about the nature and extent of such asymmetries (which Hegelians would ground in asymmetries of both history and consciousness) affect the views one takes of the objective possibilities of radical social and political action.

3. RELATIVISM

Suppose that we are in real confrontation with some S. Then there will be some vocabulary of appraisal—'true-false', 'right-wrong', 'acceptable-unacceptable' *etc.*—which will be deployed, and essentially deployed, in thought and speech about this confrontation. The ways in which it is deployed, and the considerations it is geared into, will of course differ with the type of *S* in question—for instance, with the degree of comparability that obtains between *S*s of this type; but whatever these differences, in speaking of a 'vocabulary of appraisal', I refer only to those expressions which can *at least* be used to express one's own acceptance or rejection of an *S* or an element of an *S*. Such a vocabulary is essentially deployed in reflective thought within situations of real confrontation, since in reflection one has to be able to think, and articulate one's feelings, about the different *S*s which are a real option for one, and to organise what is to be said in favour or against a given *S* becoming one's own; and since *S*s are things held or accepted, not just conformed to, what has to be said in favour of or against a given *S* must have some footing in the appraisal of its content.

We can also use this vocabulary about *S*s which stand in merely notional confrontation with our own. For some types of *S*, however, the life of the vocabulary is largely confined to cases of real confrontation, and the more remote a given *S* is from being a real option for us, the less substantial seems the question of whether it is 'true', 'right', *etc.* While the vocabulary can no doubt be applied without linguistic impropriety, there is so little to this use, so little of what gives content to the appraisals in the context of real confrontation, that we can say that for a reflective person the appraisal questions do not, for such a type of *S*, and when it is standing in purely notional confrontation, genuinely arise.

We can register that the *S* in question is not ours, and that it is not a real option for us; there is indeed quite a lot we can say about it, and relevantly to our concerns—thus certain features of an alien way of life, for instance, can stand to us symbolically as emblems of conduct and character to which we have certain attitudes in our own society: in much the same way, indeed, as we can treat works of fiction. The socially and historically remote has always been an important object of self-critical and self-encouraging fantasy. But from the standpoint I am now considering, to raise seriously questions in the vocabulary of appraisal about this culture considered as a concrete historical reality will not be possible for a reflective person. In the case of such *S*s, to stand in merely notional confrontation is to lack the relation to our concerns which alone gives any point or substance to appraisal: the only real questions of appraisal are about real options.

To think that the standpoint I have just sketched is the appropriate standpoint towards a given type of *S*s is, in a recognizable sense, to hold a relativistic view of such *S*s; relativism, with regard to a given type of *S*, is the view that for one whose *S* stands in purely notional confrontation with such an *S*, questions of appraisal of it do not genuinely arise. This form of relativism, unlike most others,[5] is coherent. The truth in relativsm—which I shall state, not argue for —is that for ethical outlooks at least this standpoint is correct.

This form of relativism (as a structure—its application to any particular type of S will always of course be a further question) is coherent because unlike most other forms it manages, in the distinction between real and notional confrontation, to cohere with two propositions both of which are true: first, that we must have a form of thought not relativized to our own existing S for thinking about other Ss which may be of concern to us, and to express those concerns; but, second, we can nevertheless recognize that there can be many Ss which have insufficient relation to our concerns for our judgments to have any grip on them, while admitting that other persons' judgment could get a grip on them, namely, those for whom they were a real option.

Most traditional forms of relativism have paid insufficient respect to the first of these propositions. The simplest form merely seeks to relativize the vocabulary of appraisal, into such phrases as 'true for us', 'true for them'. It is well known that these formulations do not work, and in particular cannot represent the basic use of the vocabulary in real confrontations. This view could be said to reduce the entire vocabulary of appraisal to expressions for the description of confrontation. Related to this is the view in ethics which I have elsewhere[6] called 'vulgar relativism', the view which combines a relativistic account of the meaning or content of ethical terms with a non-relativistic principle of toleration. This view is not hard to refute; it was perhaps worth discussing, since it is widely held, but to dispose of it certainly does not take us very far. We can perhaps now see that view more clearly. What vulgar relativism tries to do is to treat real confrontations like notional confrontations, with the result that it either denies that there are any real confrontations at all, or else brings to bear on them a principle which is inadequate to solve them, and is so because while it looks like a principle for deciding between real options, it is really an expression of the impossibility or pointlessness of choosing between unreal options.

Opposed to these kinds of views is that which represents the use of the vocabulary of appraisal as solely that of expressing (not stating) that an S is or is not the speaker's own. For such a view (consider for example the pure redundancy or 'speech-act' view of 'true') the issues which have concerned relativists evaporate—there is no way of expressing them. But equally, what has rightly concerned relativists evaporates, and we lose hold on the second truth which the present account is designed to accommodate. The distinction among Ss, between that which is and those which are not the speaker's own, is by no means the most significant in this area. The assumption that it is, is something that the discarded forms of relativism, and the evaporating view which apparently stands opposed to them, seem to have in common.

With those types of *S* for which relativism is not true, it is not that there is no distinction between real and notional confrontations, but that questions of appraisal genuinely arise for *S*s in notional confrontation. But if that is so, then the status of those *S*s will reveal itself also in the relevant criteria for distinguishing real and notional confrontations, the considerations that go into determining that a given *S* is or is not a real option for a given group at a given time. This is important for the case of scientific theories. Phlogiston theory is, I take it, not now a real option; but I doubt that that just means that to try to live the life of a convinced phlogiston theorist in the contemporary Royal Society is as incoherent an enterprise as to try to live the life of a Teutonic knight in 1930's Nuremburg. One reason that phlogiston theory is not a real option is that it cannot be squared with a lot that we know to be true.

These considerations, if pursued, would lead us to the subject of realism. One necessary (but not sufficient) condition of there being the kind of truth I have tried to explain in relativism as applied to ethics, is that ethical realism is false, and there is nothing for ethical *S*s to be true of—though there are things for them to be true to, which is why many options are unreal. But scientific realism could be true, and if it is, relativism for scientific theories must be false.

NOTES

1. See *e.g.,* Steven Lukes, "Some Problems about Rationality," *European Journal of Sociology* 8 (1967), reprinted in B.R. Wilson, ed., *Rationality* (Oxford, 1970); and "On the Social Determination of Truth," in R. Horton and R. Finnegan, ed., *Modes of Thought* (London, 1973).

2. For an illuminating discussion, see Robin Horton, "Levy-Bruhl, Durkheim and the Scientific Revolution," in Horton and Finnegan, ed., *op. cit.*

3. The terminology of 'real' and 'notional' was suggested by Newman's *Grammar of Assent.*

4. 'They' does not mean 'each and every one of them': the problem is a familiar one in the description of social phenomena. There are other difficulties which will have to be overlooked, connected with the very simple use made of the notion of a group—*e.g.,* that it ignores the case of persons who could adopt a different *S* if they belonged to a different group.

5. For a different kind of relativist view which avoids the standard errors, see Gilbert Harman, "Moral Relativism Defended," *Philosophical Review* 84 (1975): 3-22; reprinted in this volume, pp. 189-204.

6. *Morality* (Harmondsworth, 1972), ch. 3; reprinted in this volume, pp. 171-74.

INTRODUCTION TO
Moral Relativism Defended

Gilbert Harman recognizes that the problems of inconsistency and incoherence sketched by Bernard Williams and elaborated more fully by David Lyons are serious objections to moral relativism. But he believes that these problems afflict only some forms of moral relativism (a point also made by Lyons), and, like Williams, he attempts to develop a version which avoids these difficulties.

Harman's version of relativism focuses on just one type of moral judgment, which he calls "inner judgments," and he takes no position one way or the other on other types of moral judgments. Inner judgments are moral judgments which imply that the agent whose action is being judged has reasons to do or to avoid that which the judgment asserts that the agent ought to do or to avoid. As Harman puts it, "If S says that (morally) A ought to do D, S implies that A has reasons to do D which S endorses." Not every use of the term 'ought' expresses an inner judgment. To say that murders ought not to take place is not to make an inner judgment since this does not imply that anyone has reasons or motives not to murder others. But surely, it will be replied, if Jones judges that murders ought not to take place, it follows logically from this that Jones is also committed to judging that Smith ought not to murder Green. This latter judgment seems to be a mere substitution instance of the more general judgment. Harman would disagree with this. He believes that Jones' judgment "Smith ought not to murder Green" would be odd—that is, logically inappropriate—unless there is an implicit or tacit agreement about murder to which Jones and Smith both subscribe. Perhaps a parallel to cases involving ability would help to clarify this point. When we say to someone "You ought to do X," we imply that the person being addressed is able to do X. For example, if we said to a prisoner "You ought to escape from this prison which everyone knows to be absolutely escape-proof," we would say something extremely odd. The oddity here is not logical contradiction in a direct, explicit way, the way in which "Jones is six feet tall and Jones is not six feet tall" is a direct contradiction. If we said "You will escape from this prison which is absolutely escape-proof," we would be contradicting ourselves directly. But to say "You ought to escape from this prison which is absolutely escape-proof" is not a direct contradiction. Instead, its oddity lies in its *implying* that the person can escape when in fact he cannot escape. What would *not* be odd in these situations is to express an *evaluation*. We could say, for example, "It would be a good thing if he were to escape," since this does not imply that he can escape. In the same way, Harman feels that to say "Jones ought to do X" of someone who has no reason to do X is logically odd because it implies that Jones has a reason to do X. But again, we can still evaluate in this situation without logical oddity by saying "It would be good if Jones were to do X".

Under what conditions, in a moral situation, does an agent have a reason to perform a certain action? The condition on which Harman focuses is that produced when the agent is a party to an agreement with others. "There is an agreement, in the relevant sense, if each of a number of people intends to adhere to some schedule, plan, or set of principles, intending to do this on the understanding that the others similarly intend." A person who participates in such an agreement is motivated to behave in a certain way. Harman says that such a person has a certain "motivating attitude." Inner judgments make sense only in relation to some agreement of this type, so that the required motivating attitude is present. To put this in another way, since these motivating attitudes are generated by agreements, inner judgments are *relative* to (make sense only in relation to) such agreements. So Harman is maintaining two theses: (1) there is a type of moral judgment which implies that the speaker and agent share certain motivating attitudes and (2) these motivating attitudes arise from agreements. We have already looked at the argument for the first of these theses, namely, that inner judgments about agents who do not have the motivating attitude in question are logically odd. The argument for the second thesis arises from the observation that we feel that a duty not to harm people has greater weight than the duty to help others. According to Harman, this is due to the fact that people who are well-off would not enter an agreement which made the duty to help others primary since they would have to spend all of their resources helping others. This tends to show that moral duties spring from agreements.

Harman's version of moral relativism is relativistic in several respects. First, it is relativistic in the same way in which most versions are relativistic, namely, in holding that an action may be right according to one set of principles and wrong according to another set. But while most versions go one step further and say that there is no way to determine which set of principles is objectively correct, Harman takes no position on this question. Nevertheless, in claiming that inner judgments make no sense apart from an agreement, he strongly implies that there is no absolutely true moral code, existing apart from human agreement, which renders inner judgments correct. The agent himself decides, in part, which set of principles his actions are to be judged by; the agent does this by entering into an agreement with others. Absolutists in moral theory believe that what persons ought to do is independent of anything they might or might not have agreed to. Harman's view, and many other versions of relativism, deny this. It should be noted that Harman's position is not just a restatement of the well-known view (which Lyons calls "agent's-group relativism") that one ought to judge the agent in terms of the moral principles of the agent and/or the agent's group. Lyons himself believes that Harman's theory "amounts, in effect, to an agent theory." But this is to ignore Harman's requirement that the person making the judgment be a party to the same agreement as is the agent.

Lyons finds Harman's version of relativism unconvincing because he believes that Harman's evidence could be accounted for equally well by other theories. For example, Lyons suspects that the oddity of passing an inner judgment on someone who has no motive to perform the action in question is a practical oddity rather than a logical oddity; it is pointless to tell someone who has no motive to perform an action that he or she ought to perform it. Perhaps Harman could reply by distinguishing between communicating the inner judgment to the agent on the one hand and simply making the judgment without communicating it to the agent on the other hand. Lyons' alternative explanation will fit the former case. But in the latter case we are not telling the agent anything and hence not telling the agent to do something he or she has no motivation to do; hence the oddity in this case cannot be explained in Lyons' way. And if Harman is right that the oddity connected with inner judgments is logical and that this oddity stems from the lack of an agreement between speaker and agent, then the oddity will exist even if the inner judgment is not communicated to the agent. Thus, if this oddity does exist when the judgment is not communicated to the agent, this would support Harman's idea that the oddity is logical and would militate against practical explanations of the oddity.

Moral Relativism Defended*

Gilbert Harman

My thesis is that morality arises when a group of people reach an implicit agreement or come to a tacit understanding about their relations with one another. Part of what I mean by this is that moral judgments—or, rather, an important class of them—make sense only in relation to and with reference to one or another such agreement or understanding. This is vague, and I shall try to make it more precise in what follows. But it should be clear that I intend to argue for a version of what has been called moral relativism.

In doing so, I am taking sides in an ancient controversy. Many people have supposed that the sort of view which I am going to defend is obviously correct—indeed, that it is the only sort of account that could make sense of the phenomenon or morality. At the same time there have also been many who have supposed that moral relativism is confused, incoherent, and even immoral, at the very least obviously wrong.

Most arguments against relativism make use of a strategy of dissuasive definition; they define moral relativism as an inconsistent thesis. For example, they define it as the assertion that *(a)* there are no universal moral principles and *(b)* one ought to act in accordance with the principles of one's own group, where this latter principle, *(b)*, is supposed to be a universal moral principle.[1] It is easy enough to show that this version of moral relativism will not do, but that is no reason to think that a defender of moral relativism cannot find a better definition.

My moral relativism is a soberly logical thesis—a thesis about logical form, if you like. Just as the judgment that something is large makes sense only in relation to one or another comparison class, so too, I will argue, the

*Reprinted with permission of the author and the publisher from *Philosophical Review* 84 (1975): 3-22.

judgment that it is wrong of someone to do something makes sense only in relation to an agreement or understanding. A dog may be large in relation to chihuahuas but not large in relation to dogs in general. Similarly, I will argue, an action may be wrong in relation to one agreement but not in relation to another. Just as it makes no sense to ask whether a dog is large, period, apart from any relation to a comparison class, so too, I will argue, it makes no sense to ask whether an action is wrong, period, apart from any relation to an agreement.

There is an agreement, in the relevant sense, if each of a number of people intends to adhere to some schedule, plan, or set of principles, intending to do this on the understanding that the others similarly intend. The agreement or understanding need not be conscious or explicit; and I will not here try to say what distinguishes moral agreements from, for example, conventions of the road or conventions of etiquette, since these distinctions will not be important as regards the purely logical thesis that I will be defending.

Although I want to say that certain moral judgments are made in relation to an agreement, I do not want say this about all moral judgments. Perhaps it is true that all moral judgments are made in relation to an agreement; nevertheless, that is not what I will be arguing. For I want to say that there is a way in which certain moral judgments are relative to an agreement but other moral judgments are not. My relativism is a thesis only about what I will call "inner judgments," such as the judgment that someone ought not to have acted in a certain way or the judgment that it was right or wrong of him to have done so. My relativism is not meant to apply, for example, to the judgment that someone is evil or the judgment that a given institution is unjust.

In particular, I am not denying (nor am I asserting) that some moralities are "objectively" better than others or that there are objective standards for assessing moralities. My thesis is a soberly logical thesis about logical form.

I. INNER JUDGMENTS

We make inner judgments about a person only if we suppose that he is capable of being motivated by the relevant moral considerations. We make other sorts of judgment about those who we suppose are not susceptible of such motivation. Inner judgments include judgments in which we say that someone should or ought to have done something or that someone was right or wrong to have done something. Inner judgments do not include judgments in which we call someone (literally) a savage or say that someone is (literally) inhuman, evil, a betrayer, a traitor, or an enemy.

Consider this example. Intelligent beings from outer space land on Earth, beings without the slightest concern for human life and happiness. That a certain course of action on their part might injure one of us means nothing to them; that fact by itself gives them no reason to avoid the action. In such a case it would be odd to say that nevertheless the being ought to avoid injuring us or that it would be wrong for them to attack us. Of course we will want to resist them if they do such things and we will make negative judgments about them; but we will judge that they are dreadful enemies to be repelled and even destroyed, not that they should not act as they do.

Similarly, if we learn that a band of cannibals has captured and eaten the sole survivor of a shipwreck, we will speak of the primitive morality of the cannibals and may call them savages, but we will not say that they ought not to have eaten their captive.

Again, suppose that a contented employee of Murder, Incorporated was raised as a child to honor and respect members of the "family" but to have nothing but contempt for the rest of society. His current assignment, let us suppose, is to kill a certain bank manager, Bernard J. Ortcutt. Since Ortcutt is not a member of the "family," the employee in question has no compunction about carrying out his assignment. In particular, if we were to try to convince him that he should not kill Ortcutt, our argument would merely amuse him. We would not provide him with the slightest reason to desist unless we were to point to practical difficulties, such as the likelihood of his getting caught. Now, in this case it would be a misuse of language to say of him that he ought not to kill Ortcutt or that it would be wrong of him to do so, since that would imply that our own moral considerations carry some weight with him, which they do not. Instead we can only judge that he is a criminal, someone to be hunted down by the police, an enemy of peace-loving citizens, and so forth.

It is true that we can make certain judgments about him using the word "ought." For example, investigators who have been tipped off by an informer and who are waiting for the assassin to appear at the bank can use the "ought" of expectation to say, "He ought to arrive soon," meaning that on the basis of their information one would expect him to arrive soon. And, in thinking over how the assassin might carry out his assignment, we can use the "ought" of rationality to say that he ought to go in by the rear door, meaning that it would be more rational for him to do that than to go in by the front door. In neither of these cases is the moral "ought" in question.

There is another use of "ought" which is normative and in a sense moral but which is distinct from what I am calling the moral "ought." This is the use which occurs when we say that something ought or ought not to be the case. It ought not to be the case that members of Murder, Incorporated go around killing people; in other words, it is a terrible thing that they do so.[2] The same thought can perhaps be expressed as "They ought not to go around killing people," meaning that it ought not to be the case that they do, not that they are wrong to do what they do. The normative "ought to be" is used to assess a situation; the moral "ought to do" is used to describe a relation between an agent and a type of act that he might perform or has performed.

The sentence "They ought not to go around killing people" is therefore multiply ambiguous. It can mean that one would not expect them to do so (the "ought" of expectation), that it is not in their interest to do so (the "ought" of rationality), that it is a bad thing that they do so (the normative "ought to be"), or that they are wrong to do so (the moral "ought to do"). For the most part I am here concerned only with the last of these interpretations.

The word "should" behaves very much like "ought to." There is a "should" of expectation ("They should be here soon"), a "should" of rationality ("He should go in by the back door"), a normative "should be" ("They shouldn't go around killing people like that"), and the moral "should do" ("You should keep that promise"). I am of course concerned mainly with the last sense of "should."

"Right" and "wrong" also have mutiple uses; I will not try to say what all of them are. But I do want to distinguish using the word "wrong" to say that a particular situation or action is wrong from using the word to say that it is wrong *of someone* to do something. In the former case, the word "wrong" is used to assess an act or situation. In the latter case it is used to describe a relation between an agent and an act. Only the latter sort of judgment is an inner judgment. Although we would not say concerning the contented employee of Murder, Incorporated mentioned earlier that it was wrong *of him* to kill Ortcutt, we could say that *his action* was wrong and we could say that it is wrong that there is so much killing.

To take another example, it sounds odd to say that Hitler should not have ordered the extermination of the Jews, that it was wrong of him to have done so. That sounds somehow "too weak" a thing to say. Instead we want to say that Hitler was an evil man. Yet we can properly say, "Hitler ought not to have ordered the extermination of the Jews," if what we mean is that it ought never to have happened; and we can say without oddity that what Hitler did was wrong. Oddity attends only the inner judgment that Hitler was wrong to have acted in that way. That is what sounds "too weak."

It is worth noting that the inner judgments sound too weak not because of the enormity of what Hitler did but because we suppose that in acting as he did he shows that he could not have been susceptible to the moral considerations on the basis of which we make our judgment. He is in the relevant sense beyond the pale and we therefore cannot make inner judgments about him. To see that this is so, consider, say, Stalin, another mass-murderer. We can perhaps imagine someone taking a sympathetic view of Stalin. In such a view, Stalin realized that the course he was going to pursue would mean the murder of millions of people and he dreaded such a prospect; however, the alternative seemed to offer an even greater disaster—so, reluctantly and with great anguish, he went ahead. In relation to such a view of Stalin, inner judgments about Stalin are not as odd as similar judgments about Hitler. For we might easily continue the story by saying that, despite what he hoped to gain, Stalin should not have done so. What makes inner judgments about Hitler odd, "too weak," is not that the acts judged seem too terrible for the words used but rather that the agent judged seems beyond the pale—in other words beyond the motivational reach of the relevant moral considerations.

Of course, I do not want to deny that for various reasons a speaker might pretend that an agent is or is not susceptible to certain moral considerations. For example, a speaker may for rhetorical or political reasons wish to suggest that someone is beyond the pale, that he should not be listened to, that he can be treated as an enemy. On the other hand, a speaker may pretend that someone is susceptible to certain moral considerations in an effort to make that person or others susceptible to those considerations. Inner judgments about one's children sometimes have this function. So do inner judgments made in political speeches that aim at restoring a lapsed sense of morality in government.

II. THE LOGICAL FORM OF INNER JUDGMENTS

Inner judgments have two important characteristics. First, they imply that the agent has reasons to do something. Second, the speaker in some sense endorses these reasons and supposes that the audience also endorses them. Other moral judgments about an agent, on the other hand, do not have such implications; they do not imply that the agent has reasons for acting that are endorsed by the speaker.

If someone S says that A (morally) ought to do D, S implies that A has reasons to do D and S endorses those reasons—whereas if S says that B was evil in what B did, S does not imply that the reasons S would endorse for not doing what B did were reasons for B not to do that thing; in fact, S implies that they were not reasons for B.

Let us examine this more closely. If S says that (morally) A ought to do D, S implies that A has reasons to do D which S endorses. I shall assume that such reasons would have to have their source in goals, desires, or intentions that *S* takes *A* to have and that *S* approves of *A*'s having because *S* shares those goals, desires, or intentions. So, if *S* says that (morally) *A* ought to do *D*, there are certain motivational attitudes *M* which *S* assumes are shared by *S,A,* and *S*'s audience.

Now, in supposing that reasons for action must have their source in goals, desires, or intentions, I am assuming something like an Aristotelian or Humean account of these matters, as opposed, for example, to a Kantian approach which sees a possible source of motivation in reason itself.[3] I must defer a full-scale discussion of the issue to another occasion. Here I simply assume that the Kantian approach is wrong. In particular, I assume that there might be no reasons at all for a being from outer space to avoid harm to us; that, for Hitler, there might have been no reason at all not to order the extermination of the Jews; that the contented employee of Murder, Incorporated might have no reason at all not to kill Ortcutt; that the cannibals might have no reason not to eat their captive. In other words, I assume that the possession of rationality is not sufficient to provide a source for relevant reasons, that certain desires, goals, or intentions are also necessary. Those who accept this assumption will, I think, find that they distinguish inner moral judgments from other moral judgments in the way that I have indicated.

Ultimately, I want to argue that the shared motivational attitudes *M* are intentions to keep an agreement (supposing that others similarly intend). For I want to argue that inner moral judgments are made relative to such an agreement. That is, I want to argue that, when *S* makes the inner judgment that *A* ought to do *D*, *S* assumes that *A* intends to act in accordance with an agreement which *S* and *S*'s audience also intend to observe. In other words, I want to argue that the source of the reasons for doing *D* which *S* ascribes to *A* is *A*'s sincere intention to observe a certain agreement. I have not yet argued for the stronger thesis, however. I have argued only that *S* makes his judgment relative to *some* motivational attitudes *M* which *S* assumes are shared by *S, A,* and *S*'s audience.

Formulating this as a logical thesis, I want to treat the moral "ought" as a four-place predicate (or "operator"), "Ought (*A, D, C, M*)," which relates an agent *A*, a type of act *D*, considerations *C*, and motivating attitudes *M*. The relativity to considerations *C* can be brought out by considering what are sometimes called statements of prima-facie obliga- tion, "Considering that you promised, you ought to go to the board meeting, but considering that you are the sole surviving relative, you ought to go to the funeral; all things considered, it is not clear what you ought to do."[4] The claim that there is *this* relativity, to considerations, is not, of course, what makes my thesis a version of moral relativism, since any theory must acknowledge relativity to considerations. The relativity to considerations does, however, provide a model for a coherent interpretation of moral relativism as a similar kind of relativity.

It is not as easy to exhibit the relativity to motivating attitudes as it is to exhibit the relativity to considerations, since normally a speaker who makes a moral "ought" judgment intends the relevant motivating attitudes to be ones that the speaker shares with the agent and the audience, and normally it will be obvious what attitudes these are. But sometimes a speaker does invoke different attitudes by invoking a morality the speaker does not share. Someone may say, for example, "As a Christian, you ought to turn the other cheek; I, however, propose to strike back." A spy who has been found out by a friend might say, "As a citizen, you ought to turn me in, but I hope that you will not." In these and similar cases a speaker makes a moral "ought" judgment that is explicitly relative to motivating attitudes that the speaker does not share.

In order to be somewhat more precise, then, my thesis is this. "Ought (A, D, C, M)" means roughly that, given that A has motivating attitudes M and given C, D is the course of action for A that is supported by the best reasons. In judgments using this sense of "ought," C and M are often not explicitly mentioned but are indicated by the context of utterance. Normally, when that happens, C will be "all things considered" and M will be attitudes that are shared by the speaker and audience.

I mentioned that inner judgments have two characteristics. First, they imply that the agent has reasons to do something that are capable of motivating the agent. Second, the speaker endorses those reasons and supposes that the audience does too. Now, any "Ought (A, D, C, M)" judgment has the first of these characteristics, but as we have just seen a judgment of this sort will not necessarily have the second characteristic if made with explicit reference to motivating attitudes not shared by the speaker. If reference is made either implicitly or explicitly (for example, through the use of the adverb "morally") to attitudes that are shared by the speaker and audience, the resulting judgment has both characteristics and is an inner judgment. If reference is made to attitudes that are not shared by the speaker, the resulting judgment is not an inner judgment and does not represent a full-fledged moral judgment on the part of the speaker. In such a case we have an example of what has been called an inverted-commas use of "ought."[5]

III. MORAL BARGAINING

I have argued that moral "ought" judgments are relational, "Ought (A, D, C, M)," where M represents certain motivating attitudes. I now want to argue that the attitudes M derive from an agreement. That is, they are intentions to adhere to a particular agreement on the understanding that others also intend to do so. Really, it might be better for me to say that I put this forward as a hypothesis, since I cannot pretend to be able to prove that it is true. I will argue, however, that this hypothesis accounts for an otherwise puzzling aspect of our moral views that, as far as I know, there is no other way to account for.

I will use the word "intention" in a somewhat extended sense to cover certain dispositions or habits. Someone may habitually act in accordance with the relevant understanding and therefore may be disposed to act in that way without having any more or less conscious intention. In such a case it may sound odd to say that he *intends* to act in accordance with the moral understanding. Nevertheless, for present purposes I will count that as his having the relevant intention in a dispositional sense.

I now want to consider the following puzzle about our moral views, a puzzle that has figured in recent philosophical discussion of issues such as abortion. It has been observed that most of us assign greater weight to the duty not to harm others than to the duty to help others. For example, most of us believe that a doctor ought not to save five of his patients who would otherwise die by cutting up a sixth patient and distributing his healthy organs where needed to the others, even though we do think that the doctor has a duty to try to help as many of his patients as he can. For we also think that he has a stronger duty to try not to harm any of his patients (or anyone else) even if by so doing he could help five others.[6]

This aspect of our moral views can seem very puzzling, especially if one supposes that moral feelings derive from sympathy and concern for others. But the hypothesis that morality derives from an agreement among people of varying powers and resources provides a plausible explanation. The rich, the poor, the strong, and the weak would all benefit if all were to try to avoid harming one another. So everyone could agree to that arrangement. But the rich and the strong would not benefit from an arrangement whereby everyone would try to do as much as possible to help those in need. The poor and weak would get all of the benefit of this latter arrangement. Since the rich and the strong could foresee that they would be required to do most of the helping and that they would receive little in return, they would be reluctant to agree to a strong principle of mutual aid. A compromise would be likely and a weaker principle would probably be accepted. In other words, although everyone could agree to a strong principle concerning the avoidance of harm, it would not be true that everyone would favor an equally strong principle of mutual aid. It is likely that only a weaker principle of the latter sort would gain general acceptance. So the hypothesis that morality derives from an understanding among people of different powers and resources can explain (and, according to me, does explain) why in our morality avoiding harm to others is taken to be more important than helping those who need help.

By the way, I am here only trying to *explain* an aspect of our moral views. I am not therefore *endorsing* that aspect. And I defer until later a relativistic account of the way in which aspects of our moral view can be criticized "from within."

Now we need not suppose that the agreement or understanding in question is explicit. It is enough if various members of society knowingly reach an agreement in intentions—each intending to act in certain ways on the understanding that the others have similar intentions. Such an implicit agreement is reached through a process of mutual adjustment and implicit bargaining.

Indeed, it is essential to the proposed explanation of this aspect of our moral views to suppose that the relevant moral understanding is thus the result of *bargaining*. It is necessary to suppose that, in order to further our interests, we form certain conditional intentions, hoping that others will do the same. The others, who have different interests, will form somewhat different conditional intentions. After implicit bargaining, some sort of compromise is reached.

Seeing morality in this way as a compromise based on implicit bargaining helps to explain why our morality takes it to be worse to harm someone than to refuse to help someone. The explanation requires that we view our morality as an implicit agreement about what to do. This sort of explanation could not be given if we were to suppose, say, that our morality represented an agreement only about the facts (naturalism). Nor is it enough simply to suppose that our morality represents an agreement in attitude, if we forget that such agreement can be reached, not only by way of such principles as are mentioned, for example, in Hare's "logic of imperatives,"[7] but also through bargaining. According to Hare, to accept a general moral principle is to intend to do something.[8] If we add to his theory that the relevant intentions can be reached through implicit bargaining, the resulting theory begins to look like the one that I am defending.

Many aspects of our moral views can be given a utilitarian explanation. We could account for these aspects, using the logical analysis I presented in the previous section of this paper, by supposing that the relevant "ought" judgments presuppose shared attitudes of sympathy and benevolence. We can equally well explain them by supposing that considerations of utility have influenced our implicit agreements, so that the appeal is to a shared intention to adhere to those agreements. Any aspect of morality that is susceptible of a utilitarian explanation can also be explained by an implicit agreement, but not conversely. There are aspects of our moral views that seem to be explicable only in the second way, on the assumption that morality derives from an agreement. One example, already cited, is the distinction we make between harming and not helping. Another is our feeling that each person has an inalienable right of self-defense and self-preservation. Philosophers have not been able to come up with a really satisfactory utilitarian justification of such a right, but it is easily intelligible on our present hypothesis, as Hobbes observed many years ago. You cannot, except in very special circumstances, rationally form the intention not to try to preserve your life if it should ever be threatened, say, by society or the state, since you know that you cannot now control what you would do in such a situation. No matter what you now decided to do, when the time came, you would ignore your prior decision and try to save your life. Since you cannot now intend to do something later which you now know that you would not do, you cannot now intend to keep an agreement not to preserve your life if it is threatened by others in your society.[9]

This concludes the positive side of my argument that what I have called inner moral judgments are made in relation to an implicit agreement. I now want to argue that this theory avoids difficulties traditionally associated with implicit agreement theories of morality.

IV. OBJECTIONS AND REPLIES

One traditional difficulty for implicit agreement theories concerns what motivates us to do what we have agreed to do. It will, obviously, not be enough to say that we have implicitly agreed to keep agreements, since the issue would then be why we keep *that* agreement. And this suggests an objection to implicit agreement theories. But the apparent force of the objection derives entirely from taking an agreement to be a kind of ritual. To agree in the relevant sense is not just to say something; it is to intend to do something—namely, to intend to carry out one's part of the agreement on the condition that others do their parts. If we agree in this sense to do something, we intend to do it and intending to do it is already to be motivated to do it. So there is no problem as to why we are motivated to keep our agreements in this sense.

We do believe that in general you ought not to pretend to agree in this sense in order to trick someone else into agreeing. But that suggests no objection to the present view. All that it indicates is that *our* moral understanding contains or implies an agreement to be open and honest with others. If it is supposed that this leaves a problem about someone who has not accepted our agreement—"What reason does *he* have not to pretend to accept our agreement so that he can then trick others into agreeing to various things?"—the answer is that such a person may or may not have such a reason. If someone does not already accept something of our morality it may or may not be possible to find reasons why he should.

A second traditional objection to implicit agreement theories is that there is not a perfect correlation between what is generally believed to be morally right and what actually is morally right. Not everything generally agreed on is right and sometimes courses of action are right that would not be generally agreed to be right. But this is no objection to my thesis. My thesis is not that the implicit agreement from which a morality derives is an agreement in moral judgment; the thesis is rather that moral judgments make reference to and are made in relation to an agreement in intentions. Given that a group of people have agreed in this sense, there can still be disputes as to what the agreement implies for various situations. In my view, many moral disputes are of this sort. they presuppose a basic agreement and they concern what implications that agreement has for particular cases.

There can also be various things wrong with the agreement that a group of people reach, even from the point of view of that agreement, just as there can be defects in an individual's plan of action even from the point of view of that plan. Given what is known about the situation, a plan or agreement can in various ways be inconsistent, incoherent, or self-defeating. In my view, certain moral disputes are concerned with internal defects of the basic moral understanding of a group, and what changes should be made from the perspective of that understanding itself. This is another way in which moral disputes make sense with reference to and in relation to an underlying agreement.

Another objection to implicit agreement theories is that not all agreements are morally binding—for example, those made under compulsion or from a position of unfair disadvantage, which may seem to indicate that there are moral principles prior to those that derive from an implicit agreement. But, again, the force of the objection derives from an equivocation concerning what an agreement is. The principle that compelled agreements do not obligate concerns agreement in the sense of a certain sort of ritual indicating that one agrees. My thesis concerns a kind of agreement in intentions. The principle about compelled agreements is part of, or is implied by, our agreement in intentions. According to me it is only with reference to some such agreement in intentions that a principle of this sort makes sense.

Now it may be true our moral agreement in intentions also implies that it is wrong to compel people who are in a greatly inferior position to accept an agreement in intentions that they would not otherwise accept, and it may even be true that there is in our society at least one class of people in an inferior position who have been compelled thus to settle for accepting a basic moral understanding, aspects of which they would not have accepted had they not been in such an inferior position. In that case there would be an incoherence in our basic moral understanding and various suggestions might be made concerning the ways in which this understanding should be modified. But this moral critique of the understanding can proceed from that understanding itself rather than from "prior" moral principles.

In order to fix ideas, let us consider a society in which there is a well-established and long-standing tradition of hereditary slavery. Let us suppose that everyone accepts this institution, including the slaves. Everyone treats it as in the nature of things that there should be such slavery. Furthermore, let us suppose that there are also aspects of the basic moral agreement which speak against slavery. That is, these aspects together with certain facts about the situation imply that people should not own slaves and that slaves have no obligation to acquiesce in their condition. In such a case, the moral understanding would be defective, although its defectiveness would presumably be hidden in one or another manner, perhaps by means of a myth that slaves are physically and mentally subhuman in a way that makes appropriate the sort of treatment elsewhere reserved for beasts of burden. If this myth were to be exposed, the members of the society would then be faced with an obvious incoherence in their basic moral agreement and might come eventually to modify their agreement so as to eliminate its acceptance of slavery.

In such a case, even relative to the old agreement it might be true that slave owners ought to free their slaves, that slaves need not obey their masters, and that people ought to work to eliminate slavery. For the course supported by the best reasons, given that one starts out with the intention of adhering to a particular agreement, may be that one should stop intending to adhere to certain aspects of that agreement and should try to get others to do the same.

We can also (perhaps—but see below) envision a second society with hereditary slavery whose agreement has no aspects that speak against slavery. In that case, even if the facts of the situation were fully appreciated, no incoherence would appear in the basic moral understanding of the society and it would not be true in relation to that understanding that slave owners ought to free their slaves, that slaves need not obey their masters, and so forth. There might nevertheless come a time when there were reasons of a different sort to modify the basic understanding, either because of an external threat from societies opposed to slavery or because of an internal threat of rebellion by the slaves.

Now it is easier for us to make what I have called inner moral judgments about slave owners in the first society than in the second. For we can with reference to members of the first society invoke principles that they share with us and, with reference to those principles, we can say of them that they ought not to have kept slaves and that they were immoral to have done so. This sort of inner judgment becomes increasingly inappropriate, however, the more distant they are from us and the less easy it is for us to think of our moral understanding as continuous with and perhaps a later development of theirs. Furthermore, it seems appropriate to make only non-inner judgments of the slave owners in the second society. We can say that the second society is unfair and unjust, that the slavery that exists is wrong, that it ought not to exist. But it would be inappropriate in this case to say that it was morally wrong of the slave owners to own slaves. The relevant aspects of our moral understanding, which we would invoke in moral judgments about them, are not aspects of the moral understanding that exists in the second society. (I will come back to the question of slavery below.)

Let me turn now to another objection to implicit agreement theories, an objection which challenges the idea that there is an agreement of the relevant sort. For, if we have agreed, when did we do it? Does anyone really remember having agreed? How did we indicate our agreement? What about those who do not want to agree? How do they indicate that they do not agree and what are the consequences of their not agreeing? Reflection on these and similar questions can make the hypothesis of implicit agreement seem too weak a basis on which to found morality.

But once again there is equivocation about agreements. The objection treats the thesis as the claim that morality is based on some sort of ritual rather than an agreement in intentions. But, as I have said, there is an agreement in the relevant sense when each of a number of people has an intention on the assumption that others have the same intention. In this sense of "agreement," there is no given moment at which one agrees, since one continues to agree in this sense as long as one continues to have the relevant intentions. Someone refuses to agree to the extent that he or she does not share these intentions. Those who do not agree are outside the agreement; in extreme cases they are outlaws or enemies. It does not follow, however, that there are no constraints on how those who agree may act toward those who do not, since for various reasons the agreement itself may contain provisions for dealing with outlaws and enemies.

This brings me to one last objection, which derives from the difficulty people have in trying to give an explicit and systematic account of their moral views. If one actually agrees to something, why is it so hard to say what one has agreed? In response I can say only that many understandings appear to be of this sort. It is often possible to recognize what is in accordance with the understanding and what would violate it without being able to specify the understanding in any general way. Consider, for example, the understanding that exists among the members of a team of acrobats or a symphony orchestra.

Another reason why it is so difficult to give a precise and systematic specification of any actual moral understanding is that such an understanding will not in general be constituted by absolute rules but will take a vaguer form, specifying goals and areas of responsibility. For example, the agreement may indicate that one is to show respect for others by trying where possible to avoid actions that will harm them or interfere with what they are doing; it may indicate the duties and responsibilities of various members of the family, who is to be responsible for bringing up the children, and so forth. Often what will be important will be not so much exactly what actions are done as how willing participants are to do their parts and what attitudes they have—for example, whether they give sufficient weight to the interests of others.

The vague nature of moral understandings is to some extent alleviated in practice. One learns what can and cannot be done in various situations. Expectations are adjusted to other expectations. But moral disputes arise nonetheless. Such disputes may concern what the basic moral agreement implies for particular situations; and, if so, that can happen either because of disputes over the facts or because of a difference in basic understanding. Moral disputes may also arise concerning whether or not changes should be made in the basic agreement. Racial and sexual issues seem often to be of this second sort; but there is no clear line between the two kinds of dispute. When the implications of an agreement for a particular situation are considered, one possible outcome is that it becomes clear that the agreement should be modified.

Moral reasoning is a form of practical reasoning. One begins with certain beliefs and intentions, including intentions that are part of one's acceptance of the moral understanding in a given group. In reasoning, one modifies one's intentions, often by forming new intentions, sometimes by giving up old ones, so that one's plans become more rational and coherent—or, rather, one seeks to make all of one's attitudes coherent with each other.

The relevant sort of coherence is not simply consistency. It is something very like the explanatory coherence which is so important in theoretical reasoning. Coherence involves generality and lack of arbitrariness. Consider our feelings about cruelty to animals. Obviously these do not derive from an agreement that has been reached with animals. Instead it is a matter of coherence. There is a prima-facie arbitrariness and lack of generality in a plan that involves avoiding cruelty to people but not to animals.

On the other hand, coherence in this sense is not the only relevant factor in practical reasoning. Another is conservatism or inertia. A third is an interest in satisfying basic desires or needs. One tries to make the least change that will best satisfy one's desires while maximizing the overall coherence of one's attitudes. Coherence by itself is not an overwhelming force. That is why our attitudes towards animals are weak and wavering, allowing us to use them in ways we would not use people.

Consider again the second hereditary slave society mentioned above. This society was to be one in which no aspects of the moral understanding shared by the masters spoke against slavery. In fact that is unlikely, since there is *some* arbitrariness in the idea that people are to be treated in different ways depending on whether they are born slave or free. Coherence of attitude will no doubt speak at least a little against the system of slavery. The point is that the factors of conservatism and desire might speak more strongly in favor of the *status quo,* so that, all things considered, the slave owners might have no reason to change their understanding.

One thing that distinguishes slaves from animals is that slaves can organize and threaten revolt, whereas animals cannot. Slaves can see to it that both coherence and desire oppose conservatism, so that it becomes rational for the slave owners to arrive at a new, broader, more coherent understanding, one which includes the slaves.

It should be noted that coherence of attitude provides a constant pressure to widen the consensus and eliminate arbitrary distinctions. In this connection it is useful to recall ancient attitudes toward foreigners, and the ways people used to think about "savages," "natives," and "Indians." Also, recall that infanticide used to be considered as acceptable as we consider abortion to be. There has been a change here in our moral attitudes, prompted, I suggest, largely by considerations of coherence of attitude.

Finally, I would like to say a few brief words about the limiting case of group morality, when the group has only one member; then, as it were, a person comes to an understanding with himself. In my view, a person can make inner judgments in relation to such an individual morality only about himself. A familiar form of pacifism is of this sort. Certain pacifists judge that it would be wrong of them to participate in killing, although they are not willing to make a similar judgment about others. Observe that such a pacifist is unwilling only to make *inner* moral judgments about others. Although he is unwilling to judge that those who do participate are wrong to do so, he is perfectly willing to say that it is a bad thing that they participate. There are of course many other examples of individual morality in this sense, when a person imposes standards on himself that he does not apply to others. The existence of such examples is further confirmation of the relativist thesis that I have presented.

My conclusion is that relativism can be formulated as an intelligible thesis, the thesis that morality derives from an implicit agreement and that moral judgments are in a logical sense made in relation to such an agreement. Such a theory helps to explain otherwise puzzling aspects of our own moral views, in particular why we think that it is more important to avoid harm to others than to help others. The theory is also partially confirmed by what is, as far as I can tell, a previously unnoticed distinction between inner and non-inner moral judgments. Furthermore, traditional objections to implicit agreement theories can be met.[10]

NOTES

1. Bernard Williams, *Morality: An Introduction to Ethics* (New York, 1972), pp. 20–21 (this volume, pp. 171–74; Marcus Singer, *Generalization in Ethics* (New York, 1961), p. 332.

2. Thomas Nagel has observed that often, when we use the evaluative "ought to be" to say that something ought to be the case, we imply that someone ought to do something or ought to have done something about it. To take his example, we would not say that a certain hurricane ought not to have killed fifty people just on the ground that it was a terrible thing that the hurricane did so but we might say this if we had in mind that the deaths from the hurricane would not have occurred except for the absence of safety or evacuation procedures which the authorities ought to have provided.

3. For the latter approach, see Thomas Nagel, *The Possibility of Altruism* (Oxford, 1970).

4. See Donald Davidson, "Weakness of Will," in Joel Feinberg, ed. *Moral Concepts* (Oxford, 1969).

5. R.M. Hare, *The Language of Morals* (Oxford, 1952), pp. 164-68.

6. Philippa Foot, "Abortion and the Doctrine of Double Effect," in James Rachels, ed., *Moral Problems* (New York, 1971).

7. R.M. Hare, *The Language of Morals* and *Freedom and Reason* (Oxford, 1963).

8. *The Language of Morals*, pp. 18-20, 168-69.

9. Cf. Thomas Hobbes, *Leviathan* (Oxford, 1957, *inter alia*), pt. I, chap. 14, "Of the First and Second Natural Laws, And of Contracts."

10. Many people have given me good advice about the subjects discussed in this paper, which derives from a larger study of practical reasoning and morality. I am particularly indebted to Donald Davidson, Stephen Schiffer, William Alston, Fredrick Schick, Thomas Nagel, Walter Kaufmann, Peter Singer, Robert Audi, and the editors of the *Philosophical Review*.

INTRODUCTION TO

Ethical Relativism and the Problem of Incoherence

Bernard Williams shows that vulgar relativism is self-contradictory. David Lyons feels that logical incoherence threatens many other types of relativism, too, though he agrees with Williams that certain types of relativism are exempt from this difficulty. His exploration of the issue of logical incompatibility and of the strategies which the relativist might employ to avoid logical incompatibility helps us to understand the alternatives open to the relativist.

The problem of logical incoherence arises when a relativistic theory implies that two conflicting moral judgments are equally valid. (The term 'valid' is often used by relativists without explanation of its precise meaning. But we may take it to mean 'true' in some contexts and 'justified' in other contexts.) What is problematic about regarding two conflicting judgments as equally valid? The answer is that we ordinarily believe that two conflicting judgments cannot both be true and, in the long run, cannot be equally justified. Lyons calls this a "conviction shared by laymen and philosophers." If a relativistic theory implies that two conflicting judgments can be equally valid, that theory collides directly with this "shared conviction." To handle this situation, the relativist has at least two broad strategies available. The first strategy is to try to show that the relativistic theory in question does not in fact collide with this common conviction, and Lyons discusses variants of this general strategy at some length. One variant is to try to show that the judgments do not conflict with one another despite appearances. A second variant is to try to show that the two conflicting judgments are not in fact equally valid. But there is a second type of general strategy open to the relativist which Lyons does not mention. The relativist may argue that this conviction of laymen and philosophers alike is mistaken and hence that a relativistic theory is not to be condemned for colliding with this conviction. There is a strong tradition in moral philosophy of constructing moral

205

theories which do not conflict with the settled convictions we do have on moral questions. The relativist, Lyons implies, is well advised to work within this tradition. But there is another tradition in moral philosophy in which moral theories challenge accepted beliefs. And the relativist might be better regarded as providing such a challenge. In this case one could not discredit the relativist's view by pointing out that this view conflicts with what we ordinarily believe. It will be asked: On what basis do we then appraise and judge a relativistic theory if we do not insist that it be constrained by our settled convictions? This is a difficult question, but the answer may perhaps be found in the direction indicated by Thomas Kuhn's views on theory change and scientific progress. Theory change in science is a matter of "conversion" according to Kuhn. And so it may also be with theories in moral philosophy.

To rebut the charge of incoherence, a relativist may try to show that apparently incompatible judgments are neither true nor false. This, at least, avoids the necessity of saying that two incompatible judgments may both be true and follows the first general strategy of avoiding conflict with the "conviction of laymen and philosophers." The relativist may, for example, regard moral judgments as prescriptions for action, as Richard Hare does. Lyons finds a basic difficulty with this maneuver, namely, that moral judgments might still be true or false even if they are prescriptions for action. At the very least the relativist must show, not merely claim, that prescriptions for action are neither true nor false.

The position that moral judgments are not true or false is, Lyons feels, especially implausible in Hare's case because Hare believes that moral judgments can be justified (by deriving particular judgments from general principles). The trouble is that justification in general seems possible only among items which can be "appraised in objective terms (such as weather predictions)." Lyons is here claiming that if we could not determine whether statements of a certain type were true or false, we also could not determine whether statements of that type were justified. For example, we consider a statement justified when we have good evidence for it. But how do we know what counts as good evidence for a statement of that type? Good evidence for a certain type of statement is that which is correlated to a significant degree with the truth of statements of that type. To ascertain that this correlation exists, we need to be able to determine whether at least some statements of that type are true or false. Therefore, to know that something is good evidence for statements of the type in question, we need to know that some of those statements are true. But if moral judgments are neither true nor false, this cannot be known about moral judgments, and hence the notion of justification does not apply to moral judgments.

Theorists like Hare are obviously using a different sense of 'justification' from the one which Lyons is employing here. For Hare the notion of justification is intended to help make the distinction between judgments made on the basis of principle, which therefore achieve a certain level of consistency and regularity, on the one hand and judgments made whimsically and arbitrarily on the other. The former are said to be justified and the latter are said not to be justified. This seems to be a perfectly respectable sense of 'justification'. It seems that for Lyons to insist on his sense of 'justification' is to beg the question against the relativist.

One of the most important contributions in Lyons' paper is the distinction between the content of a moral judgment on the one hand and the making of that judgment on the other hand. To understand the importance of this distinction, let us first consider the case of factual judgments. A person might be justified in making a false factual judgment in the sense that the person might have a good amount of evidence for that judgment even though it is false. Perhaps people in ancient times who believed that the earth was flat were in this situation; the perceived flatness of the horizon provided them with substantial evidence for this false judgment. Two people might make conflicting factual judgments, and yet each have adquate justification for his or her own judgment, for each might have a reasonable amount of evidence for that judgment. The point here is that we are quite willing to accept this situation in the case of factual judgments. There is nothing paradoxical in a factual judgment's being false and the making of it being justified. Therefore, if all that the moral relativist implied were that different people might be equally justified in making conflicting judgments, moral relativism would not be in difficulty. What does seem incoherent and therefore problematic is the implication of some varieties of moral relativism that a *single* judgment can itself be both valid and invalid simultaneously. Here we are turning from the *making* of judgments and from two conflicting judgments to a situation in which the *content* of a *single* judgment is appraised as both valid and invalid. This can happen when one and the same judgment is appraised by persons using different sets of moral principles. Lyons finds this situation problematic: "But it is difficult to understand what this might mean—that such a judgment (the judgment itself, not someone's making it) is simultaneously both valid and invalid."

As Lyons anticipates, the relativist might try to explain what this might mean by trying to relativize the notion of validity. This is to say that the relativist would claim that to call the judgment valid would be to say that the judgment is supported by (can be derived from) the one set of principles, while to call it invalid would be to say that the judgment is not supported by the other set of principles. But Lyons would reply that this is not validity or invalidity of content but instead justification of the making of the judgment; for this is only to say that one set of principles justifies its holder in *making* that judgment, while the other set of principles does not justify its holder in doing so. And this type of "relativistic" justification has already been shown by Lyons to be innocuous. There is nothing paradoxical in the making of a judgment being justified by one set and not by another.

Lyons believes that a "truly relativistic" moral theory would concern itself with the content of moral judgments, not with one's making them. This distinction between the content of a judgment and the making of that judgment can be clearly made in the case of factual judgments. And this distinction can also be drawn in the case of moral judgments, since we can talk about a person's making different judgments (judgments having different content) on different occasions. But if moral judgments are neither true nor false, it does not follow that we can *appraise* the content of a moral judgment in a different way from that in which we appraise the making of that judgment. In the case of factual judgments we can appraise their content as being true or false, and we can appraise the making of them as either justified or unjustified. But if moral judgments are not true or false, then perhaps the only dimension along which we can appraise them is that the making of them is justified or unjustified. If so, then a "truly relativistic" theory could be concerned, as Hare's is, only with the making of moral judgments and not with their content. In such a case, to justify the making of a moral judgment is to justify its content, particularly if the judgment is construed as a prescription for action.

There is at least one other possible way for the relativist to respond to Lyons' challenge. We could appraise moral judgments as right or wrong relative to a set of principles where this depends solely on logical relationships between that judgment and those principles. This would be an appraisal of the *content* of that judgment. Then we would appraise a person's *making* that judgment by referring to what set of principles that person adhered to. This would perhaps provide enough meaning for the notion of appraising the content of a moral judgment to answer Lyons' question as to how a judgment's content could be both valid and invalid simultaneously, while at the same time distinguishing between the appraisal of content and the appraisal of the making of the judgment. Such a theory would surely have a sound claim to being "truly relativistic."

Ethical Relativism and the Problem of Incoherence*†

David Lyons

It is natural to suppose that "ethical relativism" names a single type of theory that either makes good sense or none at all. Opponents of relativism may therefore be expected to argue that is is an incoherent doctrine. Some have done so, understanding it as the combination of blatantly inconsistent claims. Recently, Gilbert Harman has objected to such a strategy of "dissuasive definition" and has shown its inadequacies by developing a theory that is recognizably relativistic while lacking any obvious inconsistencies.[1] It may therefore seem as if ethical relativism is immune to such charges and can continue to demand our respect.

I agree with Harman that relativistic theories do not uniformly lapse into incoherence, but there nevertheless remain reasons for suspecting many relativistic theories of being untenable—reasons not of accidental formulation but rooted deeply in certain ways of thinking about morality. As a consequence, whole classes of relativistic theories may well prove to be incoherent.

In this paper I shall explore the nature and extent of one important threat of incoherence to ethical relativism. I shall sketch the source of that particular threat, I shall show how relativistic theories differ in their vulnerability to it, and I shall suggest that our fears for relativism may be

* Reprinted with permission of the author and The University of Chicago Press from *Ethics* 86 (1976): 107-21. © 1976 by The University of Chicago.

†I began working on this paper while a Fellow of the Society for the Humanities at Cornell University. I am grateful for that institution's most congenial support as well as for the many helpful comments I have received from many persons when reading drafts at Vassar College, the Creighton Club, and at Brown, Cornell, Michigan, and Utah universities.

tempered slightly. Then I shall consider two ways in which relativists might try to avoid (or might luckily succeed in avoiding) such incoherence—that is, by resorting to "relativistic" notions of justification in ethics and by construing moral judgments as having a hidden relativistic structure.

THE PROBLEM

Suppose that Alice and Barbara have been discussing Claudia's proposed abortion. They know Claudia well, and they agree about the circumstances and the likely consequences of the act. But they disagree in their evaluations, Alice maintaining that it would be wrong and Barbara that it would not be wrong for Claudia to have the abortion.

Now, according to some theories about morality, both Alice and Barbara could be making perfectly valid moral judgments. Some anthropologists have suggested, for example, that one's judgment is valid if, and only if, it agrees with the norms or code of one's social group.[2] These writers evidently think it possible for Alice and Barbara to belong to different groups, their groups to have codes that differ about abortion, and their respective judgments to conform to their respective group codes. They are therefore committed to regarding both judgments as valid in some cases. Some philosophers have held that one's moral judgment is fully justified if it accords with the relevant facts and with principles to which one would freely subscribe on due reflection under ideal conditions.[3] Since it is admittedly possible for different persons to embrace differing principles even under ideal conditions, such theorists are committed to endorsing both judgments—that Claudia's act would be wrong and that Claudia's act would not be wrong—in some possible cases.

This clearly generates a problem which, while tacitly acknowledged in the philosophical literature, has not been discussed directly. The judgments made by Alice and Barbara appear to be logically incompatible. They might be straightforward contradictories—unless "wrong" and "not wrong" have restricted ranges of application, in which cases they would seem to be at least strict logical contraries. Appearances can be misleading, of course, but the relevant considerations are not negligible; they involve not merely surface grammar but also the conviction shared by laymen and philosophers that only one of these judgements could possibly be right and also our ways of discussing such cases, which include advancing reasons that are held to warrant drawing or refusing one judgement or the other.[4] Such theories seem to endorse (at least the possibility of) contradictions. Unless something further can be said, they are incoherent and may be committed to the philosophical scrap heaps.

For this reason, or some other, relativists often claim, in effect, that such judgments are not logically incompatible; so of course we cannot assume the opposite here. For convenience, however, I shall refer to such pairs of judgments as "conflicting," thus reflecting the presumption that they are logically incompatible while leaving open our final judgment on the nature of the conflict between them.

It should also be noted that I shall use the term "incoherence" generally rather than "inconsistency" and shall speak of validity rather than truth, because I wish to include within this survey certain ethical theories which deny that moral judgments are either true or false. Since these theories nevertheless regard moral judgments as subject to significant validation or justification, they too are affected by the same threat of incoherence.

TWO KINDS OF RELATIVISM

Not all relativistic ethical theories flirt with this sort of incoherence. We can see this when we try to disambiguate the anthropologists' suggestions. Generally speaking, the idea they embrace is that the existing norms of a social group are the only valid basis for moral appraisals. Beyond this, their suggestion is not entirely clear. Is it that the norms within each group must be used in judging conduct within that group? Or is it that such norms directly govern all the judgments made by members of the group? (There are other possibilities, but these are the most plausible and will serve our purposes.) It makes a great deal of difference which is meant.

Take the first possibility, the one most strongly suggested by the anthropologists, which I shall call agent's-group relativism. It may be understood as the notion that an act is right if, and only if, it accords with the norms of the agent's group. Now, such writers are anxious to impress on us that there are many different social groups, each group having its own norms which can be different from those of other groups. Against that background it seems reasonable to regard such a theory as relativistic, for it recognizes (or at least countenances) a number of different, independent bases for moral appraisals.[5] Nevertheless, such a theory seems not to validate conflicting moral judgments, because each group is regarded, so to speak, as a separate moral realm. If we wish to judge a given act, such as Claudia's proposed abortion, this theory tells us to apply the norms of her social group. It therefore seems to imply that any single item of conduct can correctly be judged in one and only one way.[6]

The second possible interpretation of the anthropologists' idea can be called appraiser's-group relativism because it says, in effect, that a moral judgment is valid if, and only if, it accords with the norms of the appraiser's social group. Such a theory does seem to validate conflicting moral judgments, for reasons we have already noted. Any single act can be judged by people in different social groups, and so judgments of Claudia's proposed abortion, for example, can be governed by different norms. Both Alice's and Barbara's conflicting judgments might well be validated by this theory.

These two theories give us differing instructions for judging conduct within other groups. Both theories tolerate more than one basis for moral appraisals, but the appraiser theory allows differing standards to have overlapping applications[7] while the agent theory apparently does not.

This contrast has, of course, nothing to do with the rampant conventionalism of such theories; it can be found in other families of relativistic theory too. Consider, for example, the individualistic philosophers' theory that was noted at the outset. This says, in effect, that one's moral judgment is valid if, and only if, one would accept it under certain hypothetical circumstances (such as knowing all the relevant facts) that are conceived of as ideal for deciding upon one's moral principles. Now, there is no guarantee that different individuals will subscribe to the same principles, even under "ideal" conditions, so such a theory is relativistic. This is also an appraiser theory and could well validate conflicting moral judgments. By now we can also see the possibility of a contrasting agent theory, which says that a person's conduct must be judged by the principles to which he himself would subscribe under such ideal conditions. This theory would not seem to validate conflicting moral judgments.[8] These two theories give us differing instructions for judging another person's conduct, and the appraiser version does, while the agent version apparently does not, flirt with incoherence.

What seems to make all these theories qualify as relativistic is their acceptance of more than set of *basic* moral standards (social norms or personal principles, for example). But some allow these standards to have overlapping applications, while others do not, and this determines whether a theory will endorse conflicting moral judgments. The threat of incoherence that we are investigating, therefore, does not affect relativistic theories equally.

I have not said that it does not affect agent theories at all because such theories, despite their apparent intentions, can sometimes countenance conflicting judgments too. Consider agent's-group relativism. It may seem secure, so long as we forget that individuals can belong to more than one social group at any time. While suggesting their group-oriented theories, anthropologists have seemed strangely insensible of the fact that, even within the relatively small societies to which they typically refer, social classes, families, and other real social groups (of the sort social scientists are concerned to investigate) are maintained.[9] And social norms can be ascribed to many such groups. Most important, one can belong to groups that have differing values (as well as be disaffected from values that prevail within a group to which one continues to belong). Claudia, for example, might be in a church that condemns abortion and at the same time in a family, peer group, voluntary organization, social class, or political community that condones it. Now, the basic notion underlying agent's-group relativism seems to be that membership in a group makes its prevailing standards validly applicable to one's conduct. If so, the theory implies that Claudia's proposed abortion should be judged by the norms of all the groups to which she belongs. This would allow it to validate conflicting moral judgments—indeed, to both validate and invalidate a single judgment.

Such complications clearly can afflict other agent theories too. Any theory is vulnerable unless it guarantees that differing standards have no overlapping applications to specific cases. Of course, it is possible to secure this, if one is willing to pay the price of necessary revisions. But it is not always clear how to change a theory so as to avoid such embarrassments, while preserving its original point. Most important, it remains to be seen whether incoherence can be avoided in a truly nonarbitrary manner. If a theory has incoherent implications, it is, presumably, quite strictly untenable. But one that avoids incoherence arbitrarily, through ad hoc revisions lacking any independent rationale, cannot be much more tenable. I shall revert to this point later. Meanwhile, I shall restrict my attention to appraiser theories, since the relevant problem affects them primarily. Agent theorists must be wary, but their difficulties present us with no new problems to consider.

THE CHARGE OF INCOHERENCE QUALIFIED

We may need to temper slightly our ideas about the possible incoherence of relativistic theories. Even when a theory is in the worst straits, and seems to tell us that contradictory judgments are both true, there are reasons for hesitating to call that theory incoherent and hence untenable. Since the present point has more general significance than its bearing upon relativism, it may be best to explain it in relation to another sort of theory that is sometimes suspected of incoherence—ethical egoism.

It may be said that egoism is incoherent because it can be used to generate contradictory judgments about cases in which the interests of different individuals conflict. But consider an egoist who also believes in the natural harmony of human interests—that is, between the overall, long-term interests of differing persons. He denies, in effect, that there ever are any cases of the sort just mentioned, which are responsible for the alleged incoherence of his principle. From his overall position, which includes this belief in the natural harmony of human interests as well as ethical egoism it seems impossible to derive the contradictory judgments in question. If so, his position cannot fairly be charged with incoherence on such grounds. And yet his position includes the egoistic principle. If that were incoherent—if it had literally inconsistent (or otherwise incoherent) implications—then presumably we could still generate contradictions from it, even when it is conjoined with some contingent claim. Since we cannot, it seems to follow that such judgments are not entailed by principles like egoism alone, and thus that the egoistic principle itself cannot fairly be charged with incoherence. The relevant implications derive from more complex positions, including beliefs about the relevant facts; and so it is these positions which may or may not be charged with incoherence.

Now, I do not mean to suggest that the implications of a principle are limited to actual cases. This cannot be right, since they are thought to cover possible cases too, such as Claudia's proposed abortion. But the foregoing argument does not restrict their implications to actual cases. My suggestion is that we must differentiate between what can strictly be ascribed to a principle alone and what can only be ascribed to a larger position. Nor do I mean to suggest that one must positively believe in the divergence of different persons' interests in order to be charged with incoherence for holding such a principle. Perhaps an egoist with an open mind about the relevant facts could fairly be charged with having an incoherent position (assuming the principle does in fact yield inconsistent judgments for such cases), because such a person would accept, in effect, the possibility of contradictions. But there seems to be a significant sense in which an egoist who believes in the natural harmony of human interests is not committed to such judgments. Clearly, I have only scratched the surface of a complex question on which more work is needed. For the sake of argument here, let us suppose my suggestion is correct.

If it is, it would seem to follow that a relativistic theory cannot be regarded as incoherent simply because it can be used to generate logically incompatible judgments in the ways we have considered (supposing for the moment that they are strictly incompatible or that a theory so construes them). For, someone might combine a relativistic theory with certain contingent beliefs which imply that the relevant cases never will occur, thus effectively blocking the offending judgments. For example, an appraiser's-group relativist might conceivably maintain that every social group inevitably shares the same set of basic values; someone endorsing the individualistic analogue of that theory might believe that identical basic values must be ascribed to all persons. Such beliefs would block the validation of conflicting moral judgments by such theories. If so, not only the overall positions but also the principles they contain cannot fairly be charged with incoherence. Strictly speaking, such principles would not be rationally untenable.

But even if we accept this line of reasoning, the resulting concession to relativism would seem minimal. A relativist could not deliberately exploit the point, for he could not save his real views from incoherence by merely mouthing certain saving beliefs. To profit from the point, he must sincerely hold those beliefs. (As I have suggested above, he cannot save himself by having an open mind on the matter, for that would still leave him tolerant of contradictions.) And we are unlikely to find such a relativist, because the required beliefs are not only implausible but would deprive his principle of what he is most likely to regard as part of its point—namely, the basis for recognizing several independent grounds for moral appraisals. Moreover, even if there were such a relativist, the possibility of his holding such a principle would not remove its stigma for anyone who lacked his sort of convictions about the relevant facts. For anyone without his special beliefs, such a principle would be rationally untenable. For these reasons, I shall hereafter ignore this qualification on the charge of incoherence.

RELATIVISTIC JUSTIFICATION

The threat of incoherence arises for the relativist because he seems to endorse logically incompatible judgments as simultaneously true. The possible lines of escape therefore seem obvious; he must either show that he is not endorsing them both as true or else deny that the judgments are truly incompatible. The second approach is the standard maneuver, the first being rarely entertained in such a context. The first deserves some special treatment, to which I now turn.

It might appear obvious that a relativist could avoid incoherence if he embraces a noncognitive conception of moral discourse. For, if moral judgments are neither true nor false, it might seem that they could not possibly contradict one another.

There are two reasons for rejecting this suggestion as it stands. In the first place, a relativist cannot simply deny that moral judgments have truth values. He must also regard them as subject to some significant sort of validation or justification and hold that there is more than one basis for such appraisals. It remains to be seen whether the conflicting judgments that he is then committed to endorsing are related in a coherent manner.

In the second place, I wish to separate the issues as far as possible, and so I do not wish to discuss right now (what will be discussed later) whether relativism can be saved if we suppose that apparently conflicting judgments are not really incompatible in the relevant, troublesome cases. Right now we wish to see what difference it might make for a relativist to deny that the relevant conflicting judgments are true, while he nevertheless regards them as logically incompatible. To put the point another way, we wish to see how relativism can fare when it accepts as far as possible the relevant logical appearances—for example, the apparent incompatibility of certain moral judgments that he may wish simultaneously to endorse.

To see what this possibility amounts to, we must shift our focus slightly. What becomes crucial here is not so much the lack of truth values as the character of the relativist's appraisal of moral judgments. Within a noncognitive moral theory, he refrains from endorsing them as true. Is there then a way of endorsing conflicting moral judgments which maintains the spirit of relativism and yet avoids incoherence? I shall argue to the contrary. I shall show, first, how a clearly coherent position that seems relativistic on the surface forsakes relativism entirely. I shall indicate what must be done to transform such a theory into a form of ethical relativism and suggest why that may be impossible. Finally, I shall show how a clearly relativistic theory developed within the present guidelines generates apparently unintelligible results. I will not show that a coherent form of relativism within the current guidelines is impossible, but I will give reasons for supposing that the prospects are not encouraging.

It would be difficult to imagine how to proceed if we did not have Hare's ethical theory to serve as the basis for discussion. At any rate, it seems at first to meet our requirements. Hare regards moral judgments as "prescriptions" for action[10] and so does not construe them as either true or false. Nevertheless, he takes the apparent logic of moral discourse quite seriously, and he offers an apparently relativistic theory of justification.

It seems fair to say that Hare's analysis of the logic of moral discourse is committed to preserving and explaining most of the logical phenomena, save what seems most intimately connected with the notions of truth and falsity. Hare would seem to regard Alice and Barbara's conflicting judgments about Claudia's proposed abortion as logically incompatible, because he believes that such relations are not restricted to the realm of "factual" assertions. Hare tries to account for these phenomena not despite, but rather by means of, his specific noncognitive theory. Thus, the essential meaning of a moral judgment is alleged to be (something like) its prescriptive force, such as the condemnation of Claudia's proposed abortion (by Alice) or the withholding of such condemnation (by Barbara). The relevant relations between such utterances are held to be substantially the same as the relations between an assertion and its denial. But the details (and of course the soundness) of Hare's theory are not at issue here. The main point is that he wishes to preserve the relevant logical phenomena—to treat such judgments as conflicting in the strictest logical sense.

Hare believes, furthermore, that moral judgments can be justified by subsuming them under general principles from which they can be derived when suitable assumptions are made about the facts. One's judgment can be faulted—shown to be unjustified—if such support is unavailable. But a defense is only as good as the support that is offered. Unless one can show not only that one's factual assumptions are reasonable but also that one's basic moral principles are not arbitrary, it would be implausible to speak of justifying moral judgments. It is therefore important that, on Hare's view, even one's basic principles are subject to a kind of rational criticism. It will suffice for our purposes to note here Hare's original suggestions about such criticism (for his later elaborations do not affect the relevant points).

One must consider the "consequences" of a (basic) principle and the "way of life" it represents and make a "decision of principle" whether to accept or reject it. If one accepts a principle under those conditions, one's decision is justified: it is neither "arbitrary" nor "unfounded," Hare says, because "it would be based upon a consideration of everything upon which it could possibly be founded."[11]

The upshot seems to be a form of appraiser relativism, for moral principles are supposed by Hare to have universal scope, and those emerging from decisions of principle can conceivably diverge. As Hare fully recognizes, whether or not a principle can pass the sort of test he describes is a psychological fact about a given person. The relevant dispositions of individuals can vary, so that two persons might make decisions of principle with differing results (for example, one condemning abortion, the other condoning it); their principles could then be applied most rigorously in conjunction with the same set of true factual beliefs about an action (Claudia's proposed abortion, for example) to obtain what in Hare's view would be fully justified moral judgments, which could not be faulted in any way, though they conflicted.

Does this show that an appraiser theory can endorse logically incompatible judgments without lapsing into incoherence? I believe not. If we interpret Hare's theory of justification in the most natural way, its limited claims hardly deserve to be called "relativistic" (they seem in fact to be perfectly innocuous), while a truly relativistic reinterpretation yields a theory that is difficult to understand, if it is at all intelligible.

Hare's theory of justification seems to concern the conditions under which a person can be justified in making or maintaining a moral judgment. It says nothing whatsoever about the judgment itself (its content). Thus, on Hare's theory, Alice can be justified in judging Claudia's proposed abortion to be wrong, and Barbara can simultaneously be justified in judging Claudia's proposed abortion not to be wrong; but Hare's theory speaks only of their judging, not of the contents of their judgments—that is, that Claudia's abortion would be wrong and that Claudia's abortion would not be wrong.

There is nothing especially "relativistic" about a theory which acknowledges the possibility that two individuals can be justified in making their respective judgments, even when the judgments themselves are (regarded as) logically incompatible. Consider a case outside ethics. Alice might be justified in predicting rain tonight while Barbara is justified in predicting none, because justification here is "relative" (in a perfectly innocuous sense) to such things as evidence and reasons, which two people do not necessarily share. Hare may be understood as claiming that justification in morals is similarly "relative" (so far, in this same perfectly innocuous sense) to individuals' "decisons of principle." But that alone is not ethical relativism, because it is compatible with all that an antirelativist might ever desire. Consider Alice's and Barbara's conflicting weather predictions once more. They may both be justified; but one is correct and the other incorrect, regardless of their justifications; that is to say, either it will or will not rain tonight. The parallel supposition in ethics is perfectly compatible with Hare's theory of justification in morals as we have so far construed it. Hare's theory tells us nothing at all about the validity of the judgments themselves. For all we have said so far, it may be the case that Alice's judgment (that is, that Claudia's proposed abortion would be wrong) is correct and that Barbara's conflicting judgment is consequently incorrect.

Now, it may be observed that Hare seems also to believe that moral judgments cannot be, as it were, "objectively" appraised—that they cannot be correct or incorrect independently of the justification one may have for making them. Indeed, his reasons for this belief seem partly to underlie his theory of justification. Hare maintains that "factual" judgments cannot guide conduct, while moral judgments do. He also maintains that moral judgments here have (something like) an imperatival character or component, and he assumes that factual judgments must be expressed in the indicative mood. He then argues that "imperatives" cannot be deduced from "indicatives" alone, which he therefore takes as implying that moral judgments cannot be deduced from factual considerations. From this he infers that moral judgments are logically independent of the facts. One must take account of the facts when making moral judgments, but one must also appeal to (imperative-like) general principles. When one arrives at basic principles, arbitrariness is avoided by the sort of rational reflection that is involved in making decisions of principle. Thus, Hare seems to say, the most that we can possibly do by way of appraising moral principles is to subject them to such personal criticism. And this, he believes, is not negligible. It entitles us to talk quite seriously of "justification."

I wish to maintain, however, that we are not obliged to accept this more radical position, even if we endorse a noncognitive conception of more discourse like Hare's. In the first place, Hare's line of reasoning to his more radical position is fallacious. Hare begs a crucial question by assuming that "factual" judgments must be understood in the indicative while moral judgments must be assimilated to the imperative. This bias seems based on Hare's unwarranted assumption that "factual" judgments, and generally judgments that are properly expressed in the indicative mood, cannot be guides to action. Most important, Hare fails to consider seriously the possibility of logically sound nondeductive arguments from factual premises to moral conclusions. So, Hare has not shown (or even given us any reason to believe) that moral judgments are independent of the facts and cannot be objectively appraised for that (or some other) reason. I have no idea how that might be shown.

In the second place, Hare's noncognitive conception of moral discourse does not seem to preclude the possibility that moral judgments are "objectively" correct or incorrect. It is clear that both Bentham and J.S. Mill, for example, regarded moral judgments as objectively correct or incorrect. And there are good reasons for ascribing to them a noncognitive theory of moral discourse roughly like Hare's [12] The difference is that they believe what Hare appears to deny—namely, that basic principles are objectively correct or incorrect. The result is not obviously untenable. But perhaps an analogy might help to suggest the possibility of such a position. It is not implausible to regard prudential judgments as objectively correct or incorrect, and this idea would seem to have no bearing on the question of whether prudential judgments require a noncognitive analysis. But if that can be said for prudential judgments, why not for moral judgments too?

In the third place, the idea of combining Hare's innocuously "relativstic" theory of justification with the claim that moral judgments are not themselves objectively correct or incorrect is itself suspect. Consider what the resulting position would be like. One would be maintaining that Alice can be justified in judging that Claudia's proposed abortion would be wrong, but that the judgment itself—that Claudia's proposed abortion would be wrong—can be neither correct nor incorrect. The suggestion is dubious, partly because the very notion of "relative" justification has its home among items which can be appraised in objective terms (such as weather predictions). Indeed, we seem to get an understanding of what is meant by justifying one's judgments in that "relative" sense partly by contrasting it with objective appraisal of the judgment itself. It is unclear whether the idea of "relative" justification has any proper application, any reasonable interpretation, outside such a context.

The usual suggestions that it does are based on the notion that the best we can do always counts as justification. That idea is endorsed by Hare when he says that a "decision of principle" can be regarded as justified "because it would be based upon a consideration of everything upon which it could possibly be founded." This is much too indulgent, for it would oblige us to regard any totally unjustifiable assertion as completely justified! (This is especially embarrassing to Hare, since he recognizes no good, logically respectable arguments from factual premises to moral principles; thus he seems to encourage the endorsement of principles that are not only without foundation but also indistinguishable, on his own account of justification, from totally unjustifiable positions.)

To transform Hare's theory into a truly relativistic position, therefore, one needs a good argument for denying that moral judgments themselves are objectively correct or incorrect plus an account of how the notion of "relative" justification can nevertheless apply. I have never seen a plausible account of this matter, and I am uncertain, for the reasons indicated above, whether any such account is possible. Let us see if others can meet this challenge.

Meanwhile, I suggest that if we wish to see what a truly relativistic theory of justification would be like within the present guidelines, we must build upon Hare's theory quite differently. I shall use the materials provided by Hare, without suggesting that the results would meet with his approval.

Such a theory would concern the judgments themselves, not one's making or maintaining them. And here I am uncertain of what terms of appraisal to use. It seems misleading to adopt the term "justified," since it most naturally applies to the attitude rather than its object. And we cannot here, within the confines of noncognitivism, speak of truth. So I suggest that we use the term most favored by ethical relativists—"valid"—hoping it will have no misleading connotations.

The theory can be sketched as follows. More than one basis for moral appraisals is recognized, and these make it possible to validate conflicting moral judgments. For purposes of illustration, let us suppose that the bases are decisions of principle and that Alice and Barbara subscribe to differing principles, such that the judgment condemning Claudia's act is validated by Alice's principles while the withholding of such condemnation is validated by Barbara's principles. To avoid irrelevant complications, we assume further that Alice and Barbara each have internally consistent moral positions, in the sense that the principles attributable to one of them cannot be used to both validate and invalidate one of these judgments or to validate both of them.

Difficulties arise when we imagine the following sort of case. Suppose that Barbara's actual judgment, on this occasion, conflicts with the principles to which she would subscribe on due reflection. Her actual judgment is therefore held to be invalid. (This must be possible, or the theory would imply that all actual judgments are valid.) It is important now to see that, so far as such a theory is concerned, the actual judgments made by Alice and Barbara are identical in content; they have the same meaning. (On the particular theory we are using for purposes of illustration, they have the same meaning because they both condemn Claudia's abortion.) Now, the theory appraises judgments in respect to their contents and by reference to personal principles. But, since different persons' judgments can be identical in meaning, the standards that are invoked cannot, so to speak, tell the difference between one person's judgments and another's. So, whether the relativist likes it or not, Alice's principles can be used to appraise Barbara's judgments as well as her own, and vice versa. The upshot is that such a theory allows one and the same judgment (in respect of content) to be both valid and invalid. In the case we have just imagined, the judgment that Claudia's proposed abortion would be wrong is held valid because it accords with (or is derivable from) Alice's principles and invalid because it conflicts with Barbara's. But it is difficult to understand what this might mean—that such a judgment (the judgment itself, not someone's making it) is simultaneously both valid and invalid.[13]

One might expect the relativist here to try to relativize the notion of validity. But we are speaking of the contents of judgments, not someone's making them, so it is not clear how that might be done; the innocuously "relative" notion of justification seems out of place, for example. It remains to be seen whether any sensible interpretation can be given to this paradoxical appraisal.

The foregoing arguments do not conclusively show that a truly relativistic theory which accommodates most of the relevant logical phenomena is impossible, but it strongly suggests that conclusion. I therefore tentatively conclude that relativism must reject the apparent logic of moral discourse and resort to more desperate theoretical measures.

RELATIVISTIC ANALYSES

Relativistic theories that are threatened by incoherence might try to avoid it by claiming that the relevant conflicting moral judgments are not really incompatible. This has, in fact, been suggested by anthropologists when they claim that to say that an act is wrong simply means that the act conflicts with certain norms.[14] On this approach, appraiser's-group relativism would be modified so that it understands Alice's utterance, "Claudia's proposed abortion would be wrong," to mean that Claudia's contemplated act conflicts with the norms of Alice's group while construing Barbara's assertion, "Claudia's proposed abortion would not be wrong," to mean that Claudia's act would not conflict with the norms of Barbara's group. Now, Alice and Barbara either belong to the same group or they do not. If they do, then the theory regards their judgments as incompatible, which accords with the logical appearances. The troublesome sort of case arises when Alice and Barbara belong to different groups whose respective norms disagree about abortion. The present theory would allow both Alice's and Barbara's judgments to be true but denies that they are incompatible, since one judgment relates the act to one set of norms while the other judgment relates it to another set. In this way, such a theory can avoid endorsing inconsistencies.

Some of the consequences of such theories should not pass unnoticed. On the surface it appears that Alice and Barbara are disagreeing about Claudia's proposed abortion, saying incompatible things about it. But, according to this sort of theory, they are confused if they believe their judgments to be incompatible. In fact, the theory says, they are actually talking at cross purposes.

And consider what the theory says when Alice and Barbara seem to agree about Claudia's proposed abortion, both saying it would be wrong or both denying that. It implies that Alice and Barbara must be understood as meaning different things, appearances notwithstanding.

An attempt might be made to reconcile such theories with our own views about what goes on in moral discourse by accounting for the perceived agreements and disagreements in terms of shared or conflicting attitudes that are expressed by such judgments. When Alice and Barbara disagree in their judgments, their difference is not propositional but rather attitudinal. They have, and their judgments express, different attitudes toward the act in question, one condemning the act (let us say) and the other refusing to condemn it. When they agree about the act, it is not that they make the same assertion but rather that they share an attitude toward the act, both condemning or both refusing to condemn it.

I do not wish to deny that attitudes are expressed by such judgments. The trouble with the suggestion is that Alice's and Barbara's beliefs may be ignored. But their beliefs are essentially connected with the relevant attitudes, in that the condemnatory attitude expressed by the judgment that Claudia's act would be wrong either is, or is grounded upon, the belief that Claudia's act would be wrong. So we cannot account for agreement or disagreement in such cases without deciding how the relevant beliefs are to be analyzed. Such theories are then committed to analyzing the beliefs relativistically along the lines adopted in construing the corresponding utterances. This simply returns us to the original decision of such theories, to reject clear logical phenomena in favor of preserving relativism.

It seems reasonable to say that such a relativist has incurred a sizable debt of explanation and justification. He must give very good reasons why we should regard apparently conflicting judgments as compatible and apparently identical judgments as different, and he must presumably show that they require analysis in one particular relativistic way rather than another. But what reasons are actually given? So far as I can see, they are not clearly reasons for analyzing moral judgments in a certain way.

The anthopologists who suggest such relativistic analyses seem tacitly to reason as follow: When individuals in a given society judge conduct, they typically invoke prevailing standards. Therefore, what it means to call an act "wrong" is that the act conflicts with the group's norms. This reasoning is painfully fallacious.

Harman suggests a different sort of argument for his relativistic analysis. His theory is limited to what he calls "inner" moral judgments—the ones we make when we judge it right or wrong of a particular person to do something or that some particular person ought or ought not to do something. Harman allows that we might judge a certain type of act nonrelativistically, even when we relativistically judge such conduct as performed by a given person.

The relevant part of Harman's reasoning may be summarized as follows: He give examples to show that, when we judge a person's conduct, we take into account that person's own attitudes. We do not invoke considerations which we believe would not count as reasons for him, would not move him or influence his decision. These considerations are closely connected, in Harman's view, with that person's own moral standards. Thus, we refrain from saying that it is wrong of someone to do a certain thing (or that he ought not to do it) if we believe that he would not be moved by the considerations that concern us, or that his action conforms to his own moral code, even when we are ready to condemn the sort of conduct he practices. Therefore (Harman seems to reason), judgments to the effect that it is wrong of someone to do something (or that he ought not to do it) make essential reference—by their very meaning invoke—that person's own attitudes and moral standards.

This amounts, in effect, to an agent theory, so Harman does not seem (does not perhaps intend) to endorse conflicting moral judgments. Because it is a rare attempt to justify a relativistic analysis, however, it merits our attention.

What concerns me is that the data assumed by Harman could equally well be accounted for in other ways—for example, by reference to our substantive convictions about the pointlessness of advising a person when we think we cannot influence him and, more generally, the unfairness of judging a person for doing something (as opposed to judging the sort of act he performs viewed more abstractly) by standards other than his own. We have no clear reason for rejecting this alternative account in favor of Harman's theory about the meaning of the relevant class of judgments. So we have no good reason to reject the nonrelativistic logical phenomena as illusory.

I mention Harman's case because I believe it typical. Relativistic analyses are not supported in the way they need to be. Now, it may be asked what all this shows. Have I succeeded in suggesting any more than that such theories are unfounded and perhaps implausible? That would be far from showing them untenable because of their incoherence.

But the only clear reason that we seem to have for resorting to relativistic analyses of moral judgments is that this will save the vulnerable forms of relativism from the scrap heaps of incoherence. As I suggested earlier, a theory that avoids incoherence by arbitrary modifications, that lacks independent theoretical justification, cannot command our respect. My suggestion now is that similar considerations apply to theories that avoid incoherence through the same devices, not by deliberate design but, as it were, by luck or accident—for example, by fashionably formulating their claims as analyses of meaning, claims which, if formulated in other ways (which happen to be equally supported by the facts) would be untenable.

It looks as if relativism can be given a coherent gloss, even when it endorses conflicting moral judgments. But theories that avoid incoherence by such unjustified claims are, it seems, much worse than unfounded and implausible.

NOTES

1. Gilbert Harman, "Moral Relativism Defended," *Philosophical Review* 84 (January 1975): 3–22 (this volume, pp. 189–204).

2. See, for example, W.G. Sumner, *Folkways* (Boston: Ginn & Co., 1940); M.J. Herskovits, *Man and His Works* (New York: Alfred A. Knopf, 1948), chap. 5, and *Cultural Anthropology* (New York: Alfred A. Knopf, 1955), chap. 19.

3. See, for example, R.M. Hare, *The Language of Morals* (Oxford: Clarendon Press, 1952) and *Freedom and Reason* (Oxford: Clarendon Press, 1963).

4. For an emphatic presentation of such points in another connection, see Carl Wellman, "Emotivism and Ethical Objectivity," *American Philosophical Quarterly* 5 (April 1968): 90–92.

5. As Sumner makes clear and Herskovits implies, this does not mean that the norms themselves are beyond evaluation. Their approach to the norms is, in fact, broadly utilitarian and thus (in a significant sense) nonrelativistic. (Sumner seems to reason that the function of the norms is adaptation to the circumstances, that

something is good insofar as it performs its function well, and thus that norms are good insofar as they are adapted to circumstances—in which case, he assumes, they serve societal welfare.) But the appraisal of conduct is treated as an independent matter, governed by existing norms. (Sumner seems to struggle with the tension here, tying "immorality" to conformity and yet praising enlightened dissent.)

6. I am here ignoring the possibility that some norms of a group may themselves conflict.

7. One could eliminate this feature of the theory, for example, by invalidating "cross-cultural" judgments. But for our purposes we can ignore this possibility.

8. Harman's theory, so far as it goes (it concerns only one type of judgment about conduct), has the basic features of an agent theory, since it allows no more than one set of values (to which one is a tacit subscriber) to govern one's conduct.

9. And the relations between social groups, such as economic exploitation, suggest how naive is the assumption that prevailing social norms serve "societal welfare."

10. As Hare seems to recognize (*The Language of Morals*, pp. 20–24), this characterization ignores half of our possible judgments of conduct, such as Barbara's judgment that Claudia's proposed abortion would not be wrong, which is by no means a "prescription" or imperatival. But Hare's general idea could be expanded into a more adequate theory, as Bentham, for example, was aware; see my *In the Interest of the Governed* (Oxford: Clarendon Press, 1973), chap. 6.

11. Hare, *The Language of Morals*, p. 69.

12. For Bentham, see *In the Interest of the Governed*, chap. 6; for Mill, one must begin with his *System of Logic*, bk. 6, chap. xii. Neither writer will seem unambiguous to modern readers; there are textual grounds for the standard view of them as ethical "naturalists." I am only suggesting a possible interpretation that seems interestingly compatible with their antirelativism.

13. The foregoing argument does not, in fact, require that the two judgments have precisely the same meaning. It would suffice if they were so related that their respective negations were logical contraries. But to regard them as identical is to respect the logical appearances as fully as possible.

14. See, for example, Summer (sec. 439) and Ruth Benedict ("Anthropology and the Abnormal," reprinted in *Value and Obligation*, ed. R.B. Brandt [New York: Harcourt, Brace & World, 1961], p. 457).

INTRODUCTION TO
Relativism and Tolerance

Moral relativists support and defend their views in a variety of ways. One common way is to point to the diverse moral codes embraced by different human societies and the lack of any independent, objective method for determining which of these codes are valid. In taking this approach the moral relativist is trying to show that moral relativism is true. There is no contradiction in the moral relativist attempting to show that moral relativism is true. A difficulty of this sort might arise if the moral relativist were also a cognitive relativist. For then we would want to know what type of truth this is. Is moral relativism absolutely true or only relatively true? And many of the issues discussed earlier in this volume by Mandelbaum and Swoyer would be raised. But the moral relativist can at the same time be a cognitive absolutist and can claim that moral relativism is absolutely true without even the appearance of contradiction, because moral relativism is itself a factual doctrine rather than a moral doctrine and therefore moral relativism does not apply to itself. Moral relativism differs in this from cognitive relativism, since certain forms of cognitive relativism do apply to themselves.

There is a very different way of providing support for a doctrine—different, that is, from trying to show that the doctrine is true. This alternative method of support consists in trying to show that belief in the doctrine leads to valuable results. Some of the proponents of moral relativism have argued for it on the grounds that belief in moral relativism produces a more tolerant frame of mind. For example, the well-known anthropologist Melville Herskovits characterizes the relativistic point of view as maintaining "the validity of every set of norms for the people who have them and the values these represent" and goes on to say that "in practice, the philosophy of relativism is a philosophy of tolerance" and "that a larger measure of tolerance is needed in this conflict-torn world needs no arguing."[1] Herskovits is saying that the acceptance of moral relativism has valuable social results through encouraging the toleration of values and practices different from one's own.

There are several ways of attacking this type of support for a doctrine. One way is to argue that the only legitimate basis for believing a doctrine to be true is the acquisition of sufficient evidence and that it is irrational to believe a factual doctrine on the basis that doing so will have valuable consequences.[2] A second line of attack is to deny that the acceptance of moral relativism does in fact have the consequence in question. For example, the sociologist Orlando Patterson, in an important article on race relations, denies that relativism produces tolerance: "True enough, [relativism] is often associated with a liberal and tolerant attitude. But it is doubtful whether the association is in any way causal... Relativism, in fact, can be associated just as easily with a reactionary view of the world, and can easily be used to rationalize inaction, complacency, and even the wildest forms of oppression. It is all too easy for the reactionary white South African, or American, to say of the reservation Bantus or Indians, that it is wrong to interfere with their way of life since what might appear to be squalor and backwardness to us, may be matters of great virtue to them."[3]

Geoffrey Harrison carefully examines this important question of the relation (if any) between relativism and tolerance. He first describes a relativistic view in which particular moral judgments are justified. Next he describes what he means by saying that person A has a tolerant attitude: "(1) Another party, B, must behave in a manner which A sincerely regards as wrong, and A must be aware of this; (2) A must be capable of preventing or at least hindering B in this activity." (Perhaps we should modify this second condition slightly by saying that A must *believe* himself to be capable of preventing or at least hindering B in this activity.) Harrison adds a third condition: (3) B's attitude of approving this activity "is enough to tip the scales" in favor of A's not interfering. Notice that Harrison has here specified a particular type of tolerance, a type in which A must believe that B's action is wrong but in which B's favorable attitude toward the action prevents A from interfering. We must contrast this with a different type of tolerance, not mentioned by Harrison but sometimes attributed to relativists, according to which B's approval of the action prevents A from even thinking of B's activity as wrong. This second variety of tolerance is linked with the view (noted earlier in this book and termed "agent relativism" by Lyons) that an action is to be judged in terms of the agent's values, not in terms of the appraiser's values.

Harrison gives several reasons why relativism might tend to promote tolerance. If it is believed that no moral principles can be justified above all others, then the only available alternative to settling disputes by force is to tolerate those who disagree with us. Moreover, it is unfair to force our principles on others if ours cannot be justified above theirs. Finally, we cannot think of those who disagree with us as "willfully wicked" and as needing to see the error of their ways if there is no way to make a rational choice between alternative moral systems.

But Harrison believes that these considerations are insufficient to establish a close connection between relativism and tolerance. Primarily he is concerned that the view that A should be tolerant of B's activity gives unjustified weight to B's opinion on the matter. Why should A defer to B in this way? The only possible reason, it would seem, is that A must think that B is correct. If we were to take relativism seriously, we would expect that B should defer to A's condemnation of the activity just as much as A defers to B's approval of the activity. Harrison is reminded of "two men ushering each other through a doorway. Neither can be so impolite as to go through first."

In discussing this issue there is one reply to Harrison that is exceedingly tempting to relativists and is strongly suggested in relativist literature but which is of dubious cogency. Suppose that A and B belong to different cultures. To interfere with B who is acting within his or her own culture is to interfere, not with a single activity, but with a whole way of life. This is true in many of the cases in which people of another society act in a way abhorrent to ourselves by, for example, killing unwanted babies or old people. And interfering with a whole way of life would have unknown and perhaps undesirable effects. In this type of situation it is perhaps better to leave well enough alone and tolerate B's action. Even if this is a plausible position, it does not seem to establish a special connection between relativism and tolerance because it does not seem to be a specially relativistic position. This position hinges on the possibility of unforeseen and undesirable results, and an absolutist can be as worried about such results as a relativist might be.

NOTES

1. Melville J. Herskovits, *Cultural Relativism* (New York: Random House, 1972), p. 31.

2. For further discussion of these issues, and an argument for the legitimacy of this type of support for a doctrine, see Jack W. Meiland, "What Ought We To Believe? or The Ethics of Belief Revisited," *American Philosophical Quarterly* 17:1 (1980): 15-24.

3. Orlando Patterson, "Guilt, Relativism, and Black-White Relations," *American Scholar* 43:1 (1973-74): 126.

Relativism and Tolerance*

Geoffrey Harrison

I

In this paper I shall first set out a schema for moral systems. No originality is claimed for this structure, and while I believe that there are good reasons for accepting it I shall make little attempt to argue for it here. I shall describe it in order to discuss certain implications which are often held to follow from it.

The schema is concerned with the deductive justification of moral obligation judgments made on particular occasions. The paradigm case of such judgments would take the form "A ought to do X" or "X is the right course of action for A." These two I take to be strictly equivalent. There are other forms which more or less approximate to this model, but for my purpose, and simplicity, they may be ignored. If such judgments, made on particular occasions about individual actions, are to be justified by a deductive argument, then that argument must contain another obligation judgment, presumably a universal, among its premises. If this second judgment is also to be justified, to be the conclusion of a valid argument, then one of its justifying premises must also be an obligation judgment, probably of a more general nature, and so on ad infinitum. Well, not quite ad infinitum. In practice all moral arguments, like all explanations, must stop somewhere . At some point our logical moralist will refuse to answer the question "Why ought one to behave like this?" He will refuse since for him there is no answer. We have reached his ultimate moral principle. By definition no moral justification of this principle is possible. If A can justify P_1, then principle P_1 is not ultimate in the required sense and we must regard

*Reprinted with permission of the author and The University of Chicago Press from *Ethics* 86 (1976): 122-35. © 1976 by The University of Chicago.

P_2, from which P_1 is derived, as being the ultimate for A. I can see nothing especially sinister in this. At the purely commonsense level it seems nonsensical to ask a utilitarian why we ought to maximize happiness or a believer why we ought to obey God's commands.

If these ultimate principles are to be justified at all, there are two possibilities. Either they are to be justified by something beyond themselves or they are in some way self-justifying. And if they are justified by something "beyond," then that something must be nonmoral, since moral justifications are ruled out by definition. I said in my opening paragraph that I was going to describe my metaethical position rather than argue for it, and now I am going to be what may be regarded as dogmatic in the extreme. I shall simply reject these alternatives out of hand. I would reject the self-justifying view since I would claim that any principle which was self-justifying must be analytic and that no analytic proposition could function as a substantive moral principle. I accept the well-known view that moral principles do not simply record our determination to use symbols in a certain fashion. Equally, I am not impressed with the chances of a nonmoral justification—the repeal of Hume's law. In recent years numerous attempts have been made to bridge the logical stream between 'is' and 'ought'. I cannot recall a would-be builder who did not get his feet wet.

These possible forms of justification would appear to be exhaustive. If, as I think, none is acceptable, then ultimate principles have no justification. In this they may be contrasted with particular obligation judgments or the more specific rules which are classifiable as right or wrong in terms of some ultimate principle, or set of principles, and the system which it generates. The phrase "some ultimate principle" brings us toward our central problem. Clearly there will be more than one possible candidate for the role of first principle. Indeed I see no reason to doubt that logically there coud be an infinite number of candidates or at least as many as language could make meaningful.

Faced with the daunting prospect of this massive proliferation of principles and their attendant systems, moral philosophers will attempt to cut down the problem to manageable proportions by introducing criteria by which to decide what is acceptable as a moral system. It goes without saying that the assessment made at this point is a nonmoral one. While it is no part of this article to establish and defend any given set of criteria—a task which would occupy many conscientious moral philosophers for several decades—I shall present a specimen group by way of illustration.

1. As already mentioned, no ultimate moral principle shall be analytic, since such a principle could not yield substantive moral judgments without the introduction of another, nonanalytic moral premise.

2. A moral system should be internally consistent. That is, it should be

impossible to prove that, for example, A ought to do X and A ought not to do X by using the same system on the same occasion. This is likely to occur in those systems which have more than one ultimate principle.

3. The system should be applicable to all men, or with Kant, to all rational beings.

4. Given two rival moral systems, the one which is applicable to a greater area of human choice and action is to be preferred. If the purpose of having a moral system is to make it possible for us to take decisions on a consistent and rational basis, then the wider the field of application the better.

5. As moralities are for human purposes, it should be the case either that it is physically and psychologically possible for men to live up to their demands or, if an ideal is set up, that it would be possible for men to approach that ideal to a greater or lesser degree, and that any step toward it, however small, would be of value. It is in this last condition that the most severe pruning of logically possible systems would take place.

Let us suppose that a test like the above in spirit, if not in actual content, can be applied to any moral system anyone cares to propose. While many will fail, it is too much to hope that only one candidate will pass the test. Any system which does pass may be called a "well-established moral system." We may then find ourselves with a number of these well-established systems on our hands. Due to the ruling about psychological possibility, it is likely that these systems will have a great deal in common, for they will tend to recommend and prohibit the same sort of thing. But equally, despite the overlap, one could not reasonably expect that all well-established moral systems would turn out to be extensionally equivalent. There will almost certainly be times at which system A proves X to be obligatory and system B does the same for not-X and both A and B are well established.

The above is a metaethical schema of a possible world. I shall now make a claim that will strike some readers as wildly implausible. I shall claim that, allowing for the fact that it is schematic, it is not too distorted a reflection of the world that we have actually got. It is inaccurate in that no one could seriously believe that any individual ever had such clear-cut moral views logically deducible from one all-embracing first principle (plus some descriptive propositions), as I have suggested. Most moral perspectives are riddled with inconsistences and irrelevancies. They have never been subject to critical examination. But if they were, and if the faults could be ironed out without totally destroying the agent's moral attitudes, then one of my well-established systems would emerge. In this way my picture bears a similar sort of relationship to reality as does Kant's idea of the Kingdom of Ends. It is inaccurate, too simple, but, I hope, illuminating. And it shares another prominent feature with the Kantian ideal. It pictures the moral scene as it would be if men were completely rational. But here the similarity ends. In the

Kantian Kingdom all would be harmony. Men would all recognize the same Good and pursue it. My state, on the other hand, would always be on the verge of a moral civil war.

The metaethical theory I have described I will call "relativism," and those who, like myself, accept it I will call "relativists." We can now discuss a moral attitude commonly believed to follow from the acceptance of relativism. Suppose A and B are disputing what action ought to be taken on a given occasion. Being both fair-minded and rational they listen attentively to each other's arguments and discover that their disagreement does not rest on any factual dispute and that neither has produced an invalid argument. Their dispute can be traced directly to differing moral premises and eventually to differing ultimate principles. They then nonmorally assess their respective systems on the basis of mutually accepted criteria. Both have well-established moral systems. *Ex hypothesi* all rational argument has come to an end. (I realize that there are those following R.M. Hare who will say that a compelling argument can still take place between those who have no moral principles in common. I am disinclined to accept this, but for those who do we could have a dispute between what Hare would term "fanatics.") The alternatives are now to settle the dispute by some nonrational means— persuasive appeals à la Stevenson, threats, bribery, violence—or to agree to differ. For quite good reasons philosophers dislike nonrational solutions. Such settlements do not prove anything about what is right. They merely provide evidence that one party in the dispute is physically or psychologically or economically stronger than the other.

Given a relativist metaethic, must one then always agree to differ? It would seem so. No one, of course, would suggest that relativism entails, in a strict logical sense, that one should agree to differ. Such crude exceptions to Hume's law are not envisaged. But some would say that if you accept relativism, agreeing to differ is the only sensible and fair course. Sensible, since the alternative suggests a Hobbes-like state of moral nature, with moral interest taking over the role traditionally filled by self-interest. Fair, because neither side can conclusively prove his case, or refute the other, and he has no right to impose his own views. Looked at objectively, one moral system is as good as another.

If this argument does not seem sufficient to establish that the only rational course for a relativist is to agree to differ, it may be supported by a second—the argument from determining factors. One of the problems of relativism is to find an answer to the charge that the choice of one ultimate principle rather than another is necessarily an arbitrary one. The natural answer to the question "Why do you accept A?" will be "I prefer it to the others." But at most this is a holding operation. If one is asked for the grounds of this preference, there can be no answer. So to the parody of relativism—"Heads I'll be a utilitarian, tails I'll be an egoist, and if it stands on its edge I'll be a Kantian." To avoid the charge of the arbitrary and irrelevant choice, some relativists will defend themselves by virtually denying that we make any choice at all. The adoption of a moral system is the uncritical acceptance of standards already held by others. The moral stance we adopt is a function of our general personality and circumstance and, like our personality, is the result of certain causal factors. Certain characters will tend toward certain values and moral perspectives. While there are no reasons for choosing one system against another, there will be causes for our choosing the way we do. Some empirical evidence can be produced for this. In the case of moralities it is difficult, due to the problem of establishing just what morality a given person accepts, but in the allied cases of religion and politics where a man's allegiances are more clearly visible one can produce significant correlations between, say, occupation and voting habits or the faith of parents and the faith of their children. There seems no theoretical reason why this kind of investigation should not reveal something of interest in the moral field also. One could accept this type of explanation without being committed to a full-blooded determinism.

Thus we can no longer even afford the luxury of considering our moral opponents as willfully wicked. We are all in similar boats. They, like us, have been unable to make a rational choice between alternative moral systems. Those who do not realize this have been swept along by circumstances into the blind and uncritical acceptance of one morality as objectively correct. The relativists, who do realize this, so it is argued, have liberated themselves, but only at the price of being unable to take any moral decision seriously. In the face of this, agreeing to differ—tolerance of those who by one's own standards are morally wrong, a kind of moral passiveness—is the only answer. To insist on backing your own moral belief, ultimately unfounded, is to be insensitive, self-righteous, and arrogant.

These two arguments are in combination superficially quite persuasive. They are also, I think, quite mistaken.

II

In the last section we looked at the moral dispute between two irreconcilable parties through the eyes of an outside observer, who was assumed to see more of the game. Let us now look at similar disputes through the eyes of one of those taking part.

Suppose that a man claims to believe that a state of affairs X would be undesirable in a nonmoral sense and that anyone who would allow X to occur when he could prevent it would be morally wrong. If this situation does arise for him and he fails to prevent X, what explanation could we give? Four answers would cover the possibilities. (1) When he claimed that anyone who allowed X would be morally wrong, he was not sincere. He is a hypocrite. He had some ulterior motive for making the claim. (2) Although he still disapproves of letting X take place, he was tempted by some attractive nonmoral reason not to interfere with the course of events. He feels guilty. There is a difficult question here about whether such a man is really to be regarded as being psychologically capable of preventing X or not. In that argument I take no sides here. Those who would label all such cases as "psychological impossibility" can ignore this type of explanation. I shall call it "weakness of will." (3) Since he made the claim he has changed his mind. (4) He has a reasonable excuse. By that I mean, while he admits X is a bad thing, he believed that the only means of combating X successfully was via Y, and that would have been even worse. He opted for the lesser of the two evils. Although, other things being equal, to permit X would be morally wrong, it is justified in this instance.

As this concept of a "reasonable excuse" will figure a good deal in what follows, I shall try here and now to deal with two possible objections to the above account.

1. Although this paper purports to be neutral between various moral systems, my description of a reasonable excuse reveals my act-utilitarian bias for all the world to see. It is only plausible if one assumes that on any occasion a man ought to produce as much nonmoral good as possible. In reply to this I will plead guilty to the charge of being pro-utilitiarian but argue that this concept can be expressed in deontological nonutilitarian terms if anyone so desires. To borrow the terminology of W.D. Ross, the prevention of X may be regarded as a prima facie duty. If the agent has no other prima facie duties, then the prevention of X will be an absolute duty. If he has a prima facie duty to prevent Y also, if not-X plus not-Y is impossible, if his duty to prevent Y is more stringent than his duty to prevent X, and if he has no other prima facie duties apart from preventing X and Y, then it is his absolute duty to prevent Y. And he has a "reasonable excuse" for not preventing X.

2. I have talked as though what was to count as a reasonable excuse was a fixed and objective feature of any situation. Subjectivists will point out that what one man considers to be acceptable another will not. From my own relativist standpoint I must see this. "Who is to judge that an excuse is reasonable?" is the important question. Again I accept the basic charge and claim that the concept is convertible into subjectivist-relativist terms. An excuse in this sense is reasonable if it is acceptable in terms of the agent's own moral system. Here at least a man is his own judge.

Now we can apply this to tolerance. There are two necessary conditions for calling A's attitude "tolerant." (1) Another party, B, must behave in a manner which A sincerely regards as wrong, and A must be aware of this. (2) A must be capable of preventing or at least hindering B in this activity. To accept the inevitable may be realistic, but it is not tolerant. This second condition is perhaps oversimplified. We might talk of A only thinking that he could prevent B, or even of knowing that he could not but considering being critical after the event, and so on. However, as such refinements do not touch the central issues, I shall ignore them, concentrating only on the case where A could prevent B and knows it. In this situation, if A makes no effort to prevent B we might call him tolerant, or we might not. Why we might withhold the judgment I hope to make clear later.

The class of tolerant actions then is a subspecies of the more general class of actions where one permits an event to occur which one could have prevented and which one regards as a bad thing. Earlier I listed four types of explanations of this class of action which I considered to be exhaustive. Of these the first three do not apply to tolerance. The tolerant man is not a hypocrite or weak willed, though some apparent cases of tolerance may disguise a genuine weakness of will, and he has not changed his mind. He must therefore have a reasonable excuse. What sort of excuse could this be? We may imagine this kind of situation. B is going to bring about X or let X happen. A regards X as nonmorally undesirable and B's behavior in allowing X or in actively pursuing it as morally wrong. If X were a natural event not connected with any other person, A would not hesitate to prevent it. And yet because B, who regards the bringing about of X as either obligatory or at least permissible, is the instigator of X, A allows X. Why? Setting out A's attitudes, we have this picture. A thinks that, other things being equal, there is a possible state of affairs, Y, which is better than X. But other things are not equal since A knows that B approves of X rather than Y. If A has a reasonable excuse for letting X occur, he must say this: (1) X is worse than Y, but (2) X plus B's approval is better than Y plus B's disapproval. The new factor, B's attitude, is enough to tip the scales in favor of X. Let it be.

I have already conceded that what is to count as a reasonable excuse will vary from person to person, but the above presents some special problems which should be taken into account.

1. Above the level of what to have for lunch, almost all our actions, choices, and decisions will be disliked or disapproved of by someone. If we were to accept the rule "No action without unanimous approval" we would never do anything. And many others would disapprove of that.

2. It is B's favorable attitude to X which makes A decide to allow X to occur. But what about his own unfavorable attitude? That must be weighed in the balance also. What he now says is: (1) X is worse than Y, but (2) X plus B's favorable attitude plus my unfavorable attitude is better than Y plus B's unfavorable attitude plus my favorable attitude. From this it follows that he finds B's attitude as being of more importance than his own. On occasion this might indeed be a correct interpretation of A's thoughts. But one must notice what it implies. It implies that at least on this occasion A thinks B is more knowledgeable or sensitive or morally aware than he, A, is. He thinks the

odds are that B is actually right. But if so, this is not at all an example of tolerance. It is not for A to "tolerate" B's "immorality." At the very least he has agreed to suspend his judgment on B, at the most to be converted.

3. We have talked about A giving way to B in these circumstances. We could equally have talked of B allowing A to overrule him. If the argument in favor of tolerance works for one it should work for the other. They should both try to allow the other to do what they consider to be wrong. One is reminded of two men ushering each other through a doorway. Neither can be so impolite as to go through first. They both starve to death. It is impossible for us all to be morally self-effacing all the time.

It will be claimed with some justice that in the above I have produced a travesty of our normal concept of tolerance. I have rather oversimplified the position and consequently distorted it. That is neither how the world is nor how it ought to be. The root cause of the trouble is this. I have naively assumed that the moral community is a collection of individuals desperately struggling against one another to ensure that their own views prevail—a moral free-for-all with no rules governing members' behavior. Fortunately, in practice this is not so. A society will have a complex system of rules, rights, and obligations laying down not what ought to be done in a given circumstance but who has the legal/moral right to decide what ought to be done. These rules I shall call "decision-assigning rules," or "DA rules" for short. In common coin our unofficial acceptance of some tacit and ill-defined network of DA rules is manifested in the concept of "minding your own business." Without the network of DA rules, that concept could have no meaning. That we also often agree on the content of particular DA rules is witnessed by normal reactions to reading Mills' *On Liberty*. There may be criticism of the soundness of Mill's arguments or the vagueness of his formulation, but his fundamental point that in certain areas a man has a right to make his own mistakes is disputed by no one.

If one accepts DA rules one may regard them as separate from and logically prior to other moral rules. That is, the first question in any moral situation would be "Who has the right to make the choice here?" Only if the answer is "I" or perhaps "I among others" does the central moral question "What ought I to do?" arise at all. The recognition of this logical priority of DA rules would be sufficient to extricate tolerant A from the difficulty in which we left him. He does not need to resort to the incredible excuse of claiming that B's moral beliefs are somehow more important than his own. He simply says B has the right to make this particular choice, and while he, A, totally deplores it he is obliged not to intervene. Tolerance is the acceptance of a DA procedure and of the unpalatable but inevitable truth that others are going to make decisions which we may regard as foolish, disgusting, or wicked, and that we have no right to stop them. It may be added that this leaves relativism still in a strong position. Within the moral community there may be many different perspectives but behind them considerable agreement on the content of the DA rules.

Despite a certain attraction, I find this analysis too neat and tidy to be true. I would now like to introduce a concrete instance of a clash of two moralities which I hope will clarify the part played by DA rules. The case is becoming something of a cliché, but I am unrepentant since I find it so illuminating. Smith is a doctor, and Jones is a Jehovah's Witness. Jones's daughter is badly injured in a car accident, and it is Smith's considered medical opinion that without a blood transfusion she will die. Jones, however, has convictions which prohibit blood transfusions, and Smith is well aware of this. We shall assume that both Smith and Jones can argue their case from well-established moral systems differing in their ultimate moral principles. Smith has time to order and complete the transfusion before Jones arrives. Should he do so?

If my first simplified analysis of moral disputes had been correct, it would be hard to see what excuse Smith could have for holding back. His own moral attitude is at least as well founded as that of Jones, and that there exists a man, Jones, who does not approve of transfusions and who stands in no special moral relation to the girl (without DA rules there are no special relations) cannot be a reason for not saving her life. To withdraw in such circumstances would show a deplorable lack of moral self-confidence.

But we have already rejected the first simplified account. If we apply a DA rule to this situation the scene will change considerably. Smith can say he is not using the excuse "On balance the girl's death and Jones's approval is better than the girl alive and Jones's disapproval." He has asked the questions in the right order. First, "Who is to make the decision?" He accepts the DA rule that below a certain age all the major decisions for children are made by their parents or legally appointed guardians. This is a major decision; Jones is the girl's father and therefore stands in a morally special relation to her. So he is to make the choice. For Smith the question "Should I give this girl a blood transfusion?" does not even arise. It is not that he has been tried and found not guilty. On the contrary, there was never any charge to answer.

The most appropriate among the possible polite replies to this defense would come naturally from a Sartrean as being *mauvaise foi*. The doctor is surely ducking the issue. The de facto decision about the transfusion was his, and given that he takes seriously his responsibility to save life, he cannot claim that this was none of his business. If we look at Smith's case again I think we may find that his excuse rests on two implausible assumptions. (1) Too much weight is being put on the DA procedure. There is an assumption that for every choice which has to be made there is either one person uniquely fitted by the DA procedure to make it or, if this is not so, there is some agreed means of allocating the right to choose to a group of people, for example, a vote of all present. It is possible that one might design a moral system in which this were so, but it is unlikely that such a system would gain wide acceptance. In this case there is some argument that the father is uniquely fitted to make a decision about his daughter's life. As presented it is a relatively simple situation. Suppose we add a complication. Mrs. Jones, improbably perhaps, is not a Witness and is convinced that her child should have a transfusion. Who is now to say which parent stands in the more important moral relation to the girl? Again, one could devise a system where the father always has the right to decide, but in most circumstances to opt for either parent against the other seems purely arbitrary. Nor can other means of settling disputes like this be easily envisaged. The usual means do not work. They cannot take a vote, as it would be an even split; they cannot call on a third party, since no third party would be acceptable to both; and in so serious a matter they cannot draw lots. Nor can they agree to differ, since one must get his or her way.

Smith may deny that he believes there is one unambiguous rational answer to all DA questions but still hold that in some cases, including this one, there will be a generally acceptable verdict. He survives the first objection, but it is more difficult to see how he can resist the second. (2) This objection is to an assumption already mentioned. This is the assumption that the question "What ought I to do? is separate from the question "Who is to make the decision?" and that the latter is logically prior to the former. This assumption is quite mistaken and rests on the belief that "It is Jones who makes the decison in this case" is a statement of fact like "It is Jones who is the father of this child." But it is not. It is in itself a moral position like "This parent has a right to educate his child as he sees fit." Once we see that, we also see that "Who is to make the decision?" is not separate from "What ought I to do?" but part of it. It is as if Dr. Smith is asking himself, "I have the power and the opportunity to make this decision myself; ought I to allow it to pass to someone else?" This is why Smith cannot claim that the child's death would not be his responsibility. He is responsible for holding two moral rules to be binding. *(a)* Parents have the right to make major decisons which concern their children. *(b)* Doctors have the duty to save the lives of their patients. To have a reasonable excuse Smith has to be able to explain to himself why on this occasion he allowed the former to override the latter. Whether he can satisfy his conscience will depend on the circumstances and on his own moral system.

III

So far we have two arguments with opposed conclusions. In Part I it was claimed that anyone who took a relativist view of morality would be committed to tolerance as the one virtue he must accept. In Part II I argued that tolerance had no special place among the virtues, whether or not one was a relativist, and indeed that it raised some awkward conceptual problems of its own. As the latter argument represents the position I actually wish to adopt, I shall have to attempt to expose the weakness of the former.

Before confronting this problem directly, let us fill in some of the relevant background. In any activity it is always logically possible to separate the participants in that pursuit from the observers of it. Or since they may be the same person at different times, it is always possible to separate the role of observer from the role of participant. We can differentiate between doing your job and talking about it, between living your life and writing your memoirs. The feature of the participant is that he acts, talks, and thinks within the conventions of that activity, while the observer is essentially playing by rules which are external to the behavior observed. This is as true of morality as anything else. The participants in this case are the moral agents, making decisions, adopting attitudes, following principles, and so on. But it should be noted that we can also include a second group—the moral critics, propagandists, preachers, etc.—in the class of participants. This may seem odd in that moral criticism, for example, is clearly a second-order activity, dependent on the first-order activity of moral and immoral behavior. Therefore the critic looks like an observer rather than a participant. However, the critic when he denounces or the preacher when he exhorts is still acting within the conventions of morality, and therefore, within the meaning of the act, they are participants. To get the genuine observer role, we need to introduce the psychologist or anthropologist or, in some circumstances, the moral philosopher. I hesitate over the last case in that while what is commonly called "metaethics" would certainly count as external-observer country, I am inclined to think that normative ethics is a form of participation.

Applying this to the argument from relativism to tolerance, I arrive at the following conclusion. Relativism is a metaethical theory, and its truth or falsity is a question for an outside observer. Advocating tolerance or being tolerant are activities which are internal to particular moral systems—the activities of participants. There is nothing that the relativist, qua relativist, can say either for or against tolerance from a moral point of view. The moment he does this he ceases to be an observer of morality and becomes a user of a moral system. And on a relativist analysis of morality, this is exactly what one would expect. If tolerance is to be defended, or, come to that, attacked, it may be from a Christian or Kantian or utilitarian point of view, but it must be from *some* point of view. There is no such thing as a moral judgment made from a morally neutral or "extramoral" position. One may, of course, conceive of morally noncontroversial judgments agreed on by all parties, but that is a different thing altogether.

Much of what is wrong with the first argument can be traced back to the view which I previously expressed in the highly ambiguous remark that "looked at objectively, one moral system is as good as another." As this essentially confused idea is often popularly regarded as the central tenet of relativism, it is necessary to unpack the proposition here and now. The key phrase in the ambiguity is "as good as," which can be taken in either a moral or a nonmoral sense. In the nonmoral sense it is a conclusion which it is quite in order for a relativist to reach, although it is, as a matter of fact, an unlikely one. What he would mean is that, for example, all moral systems were equally consistent and coherent or that all were equally incapable of being deduced from factual premises. While this is legitimate enough, it seems far removed from any argument for tolerance. For example, how do we get from (1) "B's moral system is equally as consistent and coherent as A's moral system" to (2) "A has no right to prevent B doing anything which accords with B's own moral system"? (1) certainly does not entail (2). To do that, we must combine it with the premise (3), "No one has the right to prevent another person from acting in accord with that person's own moral system, where that system is as logically consistent and coherent as his own." One can always adopt any moral principle if one chooses, but I find it difficult to see what reason anyone could have for adopting that one. Apart from (1) entailing (2), what other relation could there be between them? Some might see (1) as a reason for (2) without bringing in strict entailment, but "being a reason for" is such a cloudy notion that it would be an unilluminating reply unless spelled out in some detail. And even then it would require the acceptance of some belief similar to (3).

    If we put a moral interpretation on "as good as," then we would have a reason for being tolerant. For if morality A is as good from a moral point of view as morality B, then there could be no moral reason for preferring either A or B and hence no reason for preventing anyone from acting in accord with either A or B. But we cannot put such an interpretation on "as good as." If we do, it becomes a moral judgment, and as I have already noted, no relativist, being an outside observer, can make a moral judgment. Once he does so he becomes a participant, making his judgment from a particular moral standpoint. And what we may further notice is that this is one moral judgment which no participant could ever actually make. It is true that we could understand a man who said, "All moralities apart from mine are equally good" (this is perhaps more correctly interpreted as "equally *bad*"). But if he said, "All moralities including mine are equally good," we should be at a loss. Could, for example, a Christian who admitted that other religious/moral positions were just as good as Christianity still be regarded as a Christian? I think not, in that adopting a morality will necessarily involve rejecting at least some aspects of any rival doctrine which is not compatible with one's own. One variant on the moral interpretation might be thought to be this. For the relativist's purposes, all moral systems can be treated *as if* they were morally equal. This does not mean that they have all been tested against some moral standard and come out with equal scores, but that no such test is relevant. For the purposes of the Inland Revenue, all men are of equal height. However, while this does fairly represent what a relativist wants to say it does not solve the problem, since it is really only the negative version of the view that "as good as" must be regarded nonmorally, and it reintroduces the difficulties involved in that interpetation. You cannot get from "All moralities may be *treated* as morally equal" to any proposition about appropriate levels of tolerance.

Given that morality can be viewed in these two ways, internally and externally, someone might raise the question "Which is the correct standpoint?" And this might be something of a rhetorical question, carrying with it the suggestion of an obvious reply that, as the outside observer is both impartial and more aware of alternatives, he is the better judge. But anyone who raises this question, whether rhetorically or not, has missed the whole point of the distinction. To ask which is the better position would be like asking which is the better means of transport—a bicycle or an ocean liner. Well, it all depends on where you want to go. The two standpoints do not represent rival positions. If you want to answer moral questions or solve moral problems, then you must be a participant. If you want to answer nonmoral questions or solve nonmoral problems about morality, then you must be an outside observer. The two do not overlap. Only two closely related points of asymmetry may be noted. First, the observer role is logically dependent on the participant role. That is, there can be participants without observers but not observers without participants. Second, while one cannot avoid being a participant—everyone who lives in a society and is sane has some moral point of view—one can easily avoid being an observer. No one is compelled to be a moral philosopher.

Before we leave this point, there is one final objection to my view which deserves a reply. A critic may accept the distinction between acting within morality and studying it from without but still raise the question "May not the discoveries made as an observer dictate or modify the decisions taken as a participant?" Or more specifically, "Why should an acceptance of relativism as a true account of moral reasoning not lead to the acceptance of tolerance as a virtue?" This could possibly be regarded as a factual question, for example, "Do relativists tend to be more liberal or more tolerant than non-relativists?" I must confess that I do not know the answer to that, but it is clearly a question for the psychologists rather than the philosophers. From the philosophical point of view, the question would be "Is a belief in relativism a reason for being tolerant?" If this is the question, then I claim to have already answered it.

IV

In order to clear some possible misunderstandings from the scene, I shall close with three explanatory notes.

1. Despite the contrary appearance of much that has gone before in this paper, I am not in general against tolerance but, rather, in favor of it. All I hoped to show is that it has no necessary connection with relativism. If I were defending tolerance I would do so from a utilitarian point of view, as Mill did in *On Liberty*. While I do not regard Mill's actual arguments as too impressive, his general strategy is quite correct. The real problem in explaining the link between utility and tolerance is that if you hold a moral theory which advocates treating each case on its merits there is a difficulty about laying down general reasons for any style of behavior. Bearing that in mind, I offer the following considerations as points in favor of tolerance.

a) The utilitarian wishes to promote happiness. As people are happier if they can do what they want without outside interference, there is a prima facie utilitarian presumption in favor of tolerance. The onus of proof is always on those who wish to intervene.

b) Many cases are too trivial to warrant intervention. For example, although we may be able to modify someone's behavior for what we consider the better, this benefit may well be outweighed by the ill will our interference would engender. This is a case of the cure being worse than the disease.

c) Many cases will involve (typical utilitarian problem) doubt about the facts. This may occur in two quite distinct ways. We may believe that our solution to a problem is better than another person's and that we could stop him acting in the wrong way but, due to lack of evidence, feel that we are not really entitled to force our answer on him. He may, conceivably, be right. This must be one of the more common reasons for tolerance. The alternative way in which the facts might give us pause would be the case where, although we have enough evidence to convince us we are right, we are not sure that we have the means to alter the other party's behavior—a case of some frustration.

d) The last class of cases is the most interesting and the most difficult. I am thinking of cases of reciprocal arrangements. The utilitarian permits nonutilitarian behavior which he could prevent on the assumption that nonutilitarians will accord him a similar right to follow his own beliefs. This is the basis for any "decision-assigning procedure," and the case of the doctor and the Jehovah's Witness prove how difficult this may be in practice.

2. I have talked as though all cases of tolerance were cases of allowing X to happen although one disapproved of X and could prevent it. Some people may feel this is a somewhat restricted usage and include in the term a rather difficult sort of picture. An individual might be properly called "tolerant" not

if he believed that many of the acts of his neighbors were wrong but refused to interfere, but rather if he realized that others had different ideals from his but that these ideals were not necessarily wrong. In other words, he thinks many different views of life are equally good. I would really prefer to call such a person broad-minded, but I am not really interested in a dispute over correct English usage. All I would point out is that this type of tolerance has little to do with this paper.

3. I said earlier that not all cases of allowing something to happen where one disapproved of it and could prevent it would typically be called tolerant. The reason for this is that in common parlance "tolerance" is a partially evaluative term with a favorable meaning. Just as we would not usually apply 'courage' to a criminal act of daring, or 'freedom' to a situation where everyone followed his immediate desires, we should not be happy about describing behavior of which we disapprove as 'tolerant.' For instance, the policies of the British and French governments toward Nazi Germany before 1939 were not 'tolerant' but 'appeasing'. However, I have tried in this essay to use 'tolerance' in a more neutral and perhaps technical sense in which it does only mean "allowing to happen what you believe to be wrong" without any favorable or unfavorable overtones.

Bibliography

Aron, Raymond. *Introduction to the Philosophy of History*. Boston: Beacon press, 1962. Section 4.

Attfield, Robin. "How Not To Be a Moral Relatvist." *The Monist* 62:4 (1979): 510–21.

Barton, John. "Reflections on Cultural Relativism." *Theology,* March and May 1979

Beard, Charles. "Written History As an Act of Faith." *American Historical Review* 39 (1934).

Becher, Carl. "What Are Historical Facts?" In *Detachment and the Writing of History*. Ithaca: Cornell University Press, 1958.

Bell, Linda. "Does Ethical Relativism Destroy Morality?" *Man and World* 8 (1975): 415–23.

Bidney, David. "The Philosophical Presuppositions of Cultural Relativism and Cultural Absolutism." In *Ethics and the Social Sciences,* edited by Leo Ward. Notre Dame, Indiana: University of Notre Dame Press, 1959.

Black, Max. "Linguistic Relativity: The Views of Benjamin Lee Whorf." In *Models and Metaphors*. Ithaca: Cornell University Press, 1962.

Bloor, David. *Knowledge and Social Imagery*. Boston: Routledge Direct Editions, 1976.

Booth, Wayne. "Knowledge and Opinion" and "The Worst Thing That Can Happen to a Man." In *Now Don't Try To Reason with Me*. Chicago: University of Chicago Press, 1970.

Brandt, Richard B. *Hopi Ethics*. Chicago: University of Chicago Press, 1954.

_____. *Ethical Theory*. Englewood Cliffs, N.J.: Prentic-Hall, 1959. Chapter 11: "Ethical Relativism."

Brenkert, George G. "Marx, Engels, and the Relativity of Morals". *Studies in Soviet Thought* 17 (1977): 201–24.

_____. "Frankena and Metaethical Absolutism." *Philosophical Studies* 34 (1978): 153–68.

Brigge, Morris L. "Why Not Positive Relativism?" *Philosophy of Education: Proceedings* 22 (1966): 269–75.

Briskman, Larry. "Toulmin's Evolutionary Epistemology." *Philosophical Quarterly* 24 (1974).

————. "Historicist Relativism and Bootstrap Rationality." *The Monist* 60 (1977): 509–39.

Brown, Harold I. "For a Modest Historicism." *The Monist* 60 (1977): 540–55.

————. *Perception, Theory, and Commitment.* Chicago: University of Chicago Press, 1979.

Burke, T.E., "The Limits of Relativism." *Philosophical Quarterly* 29 (1979).

Burnyeat, M.F. "Protagoras and Self-Refutation in Later Greek Philosophy." *Philosophical Review* 85 (1976): 44–69.

————. "Protagoras and Self-Refutation in Plato's Theatetus." *Philosophical Review* 85 (1976): 172–95.

Carnap, Rudolf. "Empiricism, Semantics, and Ontology." In *Meaning and Necessity.* Chicago: University of Chicago Press, 1956.

Carr, David. *Phenomenology and the Problem of History.* Evanston: Northwestern University Press, 1974.

Coakley, Sarah. "Theology and Cultural Relativism: What Is the Problem?" *Neue Zeitschrift fur Systematische Theologie und Religionsphilosophie* 21:3 (1979): 223–43.

Coburn, Robert. "Relativism and the Basis of Morality." *Philosohical Review* 85 (1976): 87–93.

Cohen, Brenda. "Three Ethical Fallacies." *Mind* 86 (1977): 78–87.

Collingwood, R.G. *An Essay on Metaphysics.* Oxford: Oxford University Press, 1940.

Cooper, David E. "Moral Relativism." *Midwest Studies in Philosophy* 3 (1978): 97–108.

Copleston, Frederick C. "The History of Philosophy: Relativism and Recurrence." *Heythrop Journal* 14 (1973): 123–35.

Crittenden, Brian S. "Sociology of Knowledge and Ethical Relativism." *Studies in Philosophy and Education* 4 (1966): 411–18.

Cunningham, Frank. *Objectivity in Social Science.* Toronto: University of Toronto Press, 1973.

Cupitt, Don. *The Leap of Reason.* London, 1976.

Danto, Arthur. *Nietzsche As Philosopher.* New York: Macmillan, 1965. Chapter 3.

Darwall, Stephen L. "Harman and Moral Relativism." *The Personalist* 58 (1977): 199–207.

Davidson, Donald. "On the Very Idea of a Conceptual Scheme." *Proceedings of the American Philosophical Association* 47 (1973–74): 5–20.

De Marneffe, J. "Cultural Relativism." *Indian Philosophical Quarterly* 1 (1974): 313–23.

Destler, Chester M. "The Crocean Origin of Becker's Historical Relativism." *History and Theory* 4 (1970): 335–42.

Dewart, Leslie. "Language and Religion." *Philosophic Exchange* 1 (1972): 35–44.

Dilley, Frank. *Metaphysics and Religious Language.* New York: Columbia University Press, 1964. Chapter 1, 5, 8.

Dilthey, Wilhelm. *Gesammelte Schriften.* Volume 8. Pp. 75–118. Translated by William Kluback and Marin Weinbaum as *Dilthey's Philosophy of Existence* (New York: Bookman Associates, 1957): also translated in H.P. Rickman, ed.,

Dilthey: Selected Writings (Cambridge: Cambridge University Press, 1976), 133–54.

Diorio, J.A. "Cognitive Universalism and Cultural Relativity in Moral Education." *Educational Philosophy and Theory* 8 (1976): 33–52.

Doppelt, Gerald. "Kuhn's Epistemological Relativism: An Interpretation and Defense." *Inquiry* 21 (1978): 33–86.

_____. "A Reply to Siegel on Kuhnian Relativism." *Inquiry* 23 (1980): 117–23.

Drange, Theodore M. "A Defense of Metaethical Relativism." *Journal of the West Virginia Philosophical Society* 9 (1975): 20–23.

Dray, William. *Philosophy of History.* Englewood Cliffs, N.J.: Prentice-Hall, 1964. Chapters 3, 4.

Duncker, Karl. "Ethical Relativity." *Mind* 48 (1939): 39–53.

Durka, Gloria. "Relativism in Philosophy." *Aitia* 3 (1975): 20–23.

Edel, Abraham, *Ethical Judgement.* Glencoe, Illinois: Free Press, 1955. Chapter 1.

_____. "On a Certain Value-Dimension in Analyses of Moral Relativism." *Journal of Philosophy* 67 (1970): 584–88.

Esposito, Joseph L. "Science and Conceptual Relativism." *Philosophical Studies* 31 (1977): 269–77.

Evans, J.D.G. "Aristotle on Relativism." *Philosophical Quarterly* 24 (1974): 193–203.

Feyerabend, Paul K. "Problems of Empiricism." In *Beyond the Edge of Certainty,* edited by Robert Colodny. Englewood Cliffs, N.J.: Prentice-Hall, 1965. 145–260.

_____. "Problems of Empiricism, Part II." In *The Nature and Function of Scientific Theories,* edited by Robert Colodny. Pittsburgh: University of Pittsburgh Press, 1970.

_____. *Against Method.* London: New Left Books, 1975.

_____. "Rationalism, Relativism, and Scientific Method." *Philosophy in Context* 6 (1977): 7–19.

_____. "Democracy, Elitism, and Scientific Method." *Inquiry* 23 (1980): 3–18.

Foot, Philippa. "Moral Relativism." The Lindley Lecture, The University of Kansas, 1978.

Foucault, Michel. *The Order of Things.* New York: Pantheon, 1970.

_____. *The Archaeology of Knowledge.* New York: Harper and Row, 1976.

Frankena, William K. *Ethics.* Englewood Cliffs, N.J.: Prentice-Hall, 1973. Pp. 92–94.

Gadamer, Hans-Georg. *Truth and Method.* New York: Seabury Press, 1975.

_____. *Philosophical Hermeneutics.* Berkeley and Los Angeles: University of California Press, 1976.

Gardiner, Patrick. "German Philosophy and the Rise of Relativism." *Monist* 64 (1981): 138–54.

Gindburg, Morris. *On the Diversity of Morals.* New York: Macmillan, 1956.

Glidden, David K. "Protagorean Relativism and Physics." *Phronesis* 20 (1975): 209–27.

_____. "Protagorean Relativism and the Cyrenaics." *American Philosophical Quarterly Monograph No. 9* (1975). Pp. 113–40.

Gombrich, E.H. *Art and Illusion.* Princeton: Princeton University Press, 1960.

Goodman, Nelson. *Ways of Worldmaking.* Indianapolis: Hackett Publishing Co., 1978.

Hanson, N.R. *Patterns of Discovery.* Cambridge: Cambridge University Press, 1965. Chapter 1.

Harman, Gilbert. "Moral Relativism Defended." *Philosophical Review* 84 (1975): 3–22.

———. "Relativistic Ethics: Morality as Politics." *Midwest Studies in Philosophy* 3 (1978): 109–21.

———. "What Is Moral Relativism?" In *Values and Morals: Essays in Honor of William Frankena, Charles Stevenson, and Richard Brandt,* edited by A. Goldman and J. Kim. Dordrecht: Reidel, 1978.

Harrison, Geoffrey. "Relativism and Tolerance." *Ethics* 86 (1976): 122–35.

Hempel, Carl G. "Comments on Goodman's *Ways of Worldmaking.*" *Synthese* 45 (1980): 193–99.

Herskovits, Melville J. *Man and His Works.* New York: Knopf, 1948. Pp. 61–78.

———. *Cultural Relativism.* New York: Random House, 1972.

Higham, John. *History.* New York: Harper Torchbooks, 1973. Part 2, chapter 4.

Hirsch, E.D., Jr. *Validity in Interpretation.* New Haven: Yale University Press, 1967.

———. *The Aims of Interpretation.* Chicago: University of Chicago Press, 1976. Part 1.

Howard, V.A. "Do Anthropologists Become Moral Relativists by Mistake?" *Inquiry* 11 (1968): 175–89.

Hubner, Kurt. "On the Question of Relativism and Progress in Science." *Man and World* 7 (1974): 394–413.

Husserl, Edmund. *Logical Investigations.* London: Routledge and Kegan Paul, 1970. Volume 1 chapters 3–8.

Ingarden, Roman. "Remark Concerning the Relativity of Values." *Journal of the British Society for Phenomenology* 6 (1975): 102–08.

Jacobs, Ruth Harriet. "Karl Mannheim's Search for a Philosophy of Education Consistent with Relativism." *Studies in Philosophy and Education* 7 (1972): 190–209.

James, Gene G. "Was Charles Beard an Historical Relativist?" *Transactions of the Charles S. Peirce Society* 12 (1976): 56–70.

Jensen, Henning. "Gilbert Harman's Defense of Moral Relativism." *Philosophical Studies* 30 (1976): 401–8.

Jones, W.T. "Philosophical Disagreement and World-Views." *Proceedings of the American Philosophical Association* 43 (1969–70).

Jordan, James E. "Protagoras and Relativism: Criticisms Good and Bad." *Southwestern Journal of Philosophy* 2 (1971): 7–29.

Kassiola, Joel. "Cognitive Relativism, Popper, and the Logic of Objectivism." *Philosophical Forum* 6 (1975): 366–79.

Kaufman, Gordan. *Relativism, Knowledge, and Faith.* Chicago: University of Chicago Press, 1960.

Kluckhohn, Clyde. "Ethical Relativity: Sic et Non." *Journal of Philosophy* 52 (1955): 663–77.

Kohlberg, Lawrence. "Indoctrination versus Relativity in Value Education." *Zygon* 6 (1971): 285–310.

Korner, Stephan. *Conceptual Thinking.* New York: Dover, 1959.

———. *Categorial Frameworks.* Oxford: Basil Blackwell, 1974.

Korsmeyer, Carolyn. "Relativism and Hutcheson's Aesthetic Theory." *Journal of the History of Ideas* 36 (1975): 319–30.

———. "Pictures and the Relativity of Perception." *The Personalist* 60 (1979): 290–97.

Krausz, Michael. "The Logic of Absolute Presuppositions." In *Critical Essays on the Philosophy of R.G. Collingwood,* edited by Michael Krausz. Oxford: Clarendon Press, 1972.

———. "Relativism and Rationality." *American Philosophical Quarterly* 10 (1973): 307–12.

Kuhn, Thomas. "Reflections on My Critics." In *Criticism and the Growth of Knowledge,* edited by I. Lakatos and A. Musgrave. New York: Cambridge Univeristy Press, 1970.

———. *The Structure of Scientific Revolutions.* 2nd ed. Chicago: University of Chicago Press, 1970.

———. "Second Thoughts on Paradigms" and "Reply to Shapere." In *The Structure of Scientific Theories,* edited by Fred Suppe. Urbana: University of Illinois Press, 1974.

Ladd, John. *The Structure of a Moral Code.* Cambridge, Mass.: Harvard Univerity Press, 1957.

———. "The Issue of Relativism." *The Monist* 47 (1963): 585–609.

———. ed. *Ethical Relativism.* Belmont, Calif.: Wadsworth, 1973).

Lakatos, I., and Musgrave, A., eds. *Criticism and the Growth of Knowledge.* Cambridge: Cambridge University Press, 1970.

Laudan, Larry. *Progress and Its Problems: Toward a Theory of Scientific Growth.* Berkeley and Los Angeles: University of California Press, 1977.

Lazari-Pawlowska, Ija. "On Cultural Relativism." *Journal of Philosophy* 67 (1970): 577–83.

Linton, Ralph. "Universal Ethical Principles: An Anthropological View." In *Moral Principles of Action,* edited by Ruth Anshen. New York: Harper and Row, 1952.

Lukes, Steven. "On the Social Determination of Truth." In *Modes of Thought: Essays on Thinking in Western and Non-Western Societies,* edited by Robin Horton and Ruth Finnegan. London: Faber, 1973.

———. "Relativism: Cognitive and Moral." *Aristotelian Society Supplementary Volume 48* (1974): 165–89.

Lyons, David. "Ethical Relativism and the Problem of Incoherence." *Ethics* 86 (1976): 107–21.

Machamer, Peter K. "Feyerabend and Galileo." *Studies in the History and Philosophy of Science* 4 (1973): 1–46.

Mandelbaum, Maurice. *The Problem of Historical Knowledge.* New York: Liveright, 1938.

———. "Subjective, Objective, and Conceptual Relativisms." *The Monist* 62 (1979): 403–28.

Mannheim, Karl. *Ideology and Utopia.* New York: Harcourt, Brace, and World, first published in 1936.

Margolis, Joseph. "Robust Relativism." *Journal of Aesthetics and Art Criticism* 35 (1976): 37–46.

McClintock, Thomas L. "The Argument for Ethical Relativism from the Diversity of Morals." *The Monist* 47 (1963): 528–44.

————. "The Definition of Ethical Relativism." *The Personalist* 50 (1969): 435–47.

————. "The Basic Varieties of Ethical Skepticism." *Metaphilosophy* 2 (1971): 29–43.

————. "Relativism and Affective Reaction Theories." *Journal of Value Inquiry* 5 (1971): 90–104.

————. "Skepticism about Basic Moral Principles." *Metaphilosophy* 2 (1971): 150–57.

————. "How To Establish or Refute Ethical Relativism." *The Personalist* 54 (1973): 318–24.

McEvoy, John G. "A 'Revolutionary' Philosophy of Science: Feyerabend and the Degeneration of Critical Rationalism into Sceptical Fallilism." *Philosophy of Science* 42 (1975): 49–66.

Meiland, Jack W. *Scepticism and Historical Knowledge.* New York: Random House, 1965. Part 3.

————. "Cognitive Relativism: Popper and The Argument from Lanugage." *Philosophical Forum* 4 (1973): 406–21.

————. "The Historical Relativism of Charles A. Beard." *History and Theory* 12 (1973): 405–13.

————. "Kuhn, Scheffler, and Objectivity in Science." *Philosophy of Science* 41 (1974): 179–87.

————. "Concepts of Relative Truth." *The Monist* 60 (1977): 568–82.

————. "Is Protagorean Relativism Self-Refuting?" *Grazer Philosophische Studien* 9 (1979): 51–68.

————. "On the Paradox of Cognitive Relativism." *Metaphilosophy* 11 (1980): 115–26.

————. "Relativism, Criteria, and Truth." *Philosophical Quarterly* 30 (1980): 229–31.

Miller, Donald E., and John B. Orr. "Beyond the Relativism Myth." *Change* 12 (1980): 11–15.

Mitchell, Basil. *The Justification of Religious Belief.* London: Macmillan, 1973.

Mouloud, N. "The Doctrine of Language and the Relativity of Truth." *Scientia* 109 (1974): 66–81.

Newman, Jay. "Ethical Relativism." *Laval Theologique et Philosophique* 28 (1972): 63–74.

————. "Metaphysical Relativism." *Southwestern Jouranal of Philosophy* 12 (1974): 435–48.

————. "Popular Pragamatism and Religious Belief." *International Journal of the Philosophy of Religion* 8 (1977): 94–110.

————. "The Idea of Religious Tolerance." *American Philosophical Quarterly* 15 (1978): 187–95.

Nielsen, Kai. "Varieties of Ethical Subjectivism." *Danish Yearbook of Philosophy* 7 (1970): 73–87.

_____. "Anthropology and Ethics." *Journal of Value Inquiry* 5 (1971): 253–66.

_____. "On Locating the Challenge of Relativism." *Second Order* (1972).

_____. "On the Diversity of Moral Beliefs." *Cultural Hermeneutics* 2 (1974): 281–303.

_____. "Principles of Rationality." *Philosophical Papers* 3 (1974).

_____. "Rationality and Relativism." *Philosophy of the Social Sciences* 4 (1974): 313–31.

_____. "The Embeddedness of Conceptual Relativism." *Dialogos* 11 (1977): 85–111.

Nordenbo, Sven Erik. "Pluralism, Relativism, and the Neutral Teacher." *Journal of the Philosophy of Education* 12 (1978): 129–39.

Nowak. Leszek. "Relative Truth, the Correspondence Principle, and Absolute Truth." *Philosophy of Science* 42 (1975): 187–202.

Nowell-Smith, P.H. "Cultural Relativism." *Philosophy of the Social Sciences* 1 (1971): 1–18.

Olen, Jeffrey. "Theories, Interpretations, and Aesthetic Qualities." *Journal of Aesthetics and Art Criticism* 35 (1977): 425–31.

Ortega y Gasset, Jose. *The Modern Theme.* New York: Harper, 1961.

Patterson, Orlando. "On Guilt, Relativism, and Black-White Relations." *The American Scholar* 43 (1973–74): 122–32.

Phillips, D.Z., and Mounce, H.O. *Moral Practices.* New York: Schocken Books, 1970.

Popper, Karl. "Facts, Standards, and Truth: A Further Criticism of Relativism." In *The Open Society and Its Enemies.* 5th ed. rev. New York: Harper, 1966. Addendum 1 to volume 2.

Postow, B.C. "Ethical Relativism and the Ideal Observer." *Philosophy and Phenomenological Research* 39 (1978): 120–21.

_____. "Moral Relativism Avoided." *The Personalist* 60 (1979): 95–100.

Purtill, Richard L. "Kuhn on Scientific Revolutions." *Philosophy of Science* 34 (1967): 53–58.

Putnam, Hilary. "Reflections of Goodman's *Ways of Worldmaking.*" *Journal of Philosophy* 76 (1979): 603–18.

Redfield, Robert, *The Primitive World and Its Transformations.* Ithaca: Cornell University Press, 1953. Chapter 6.

Reid, Charles L. "Popular Subjectivism and Relativism." *Journal of Critical Analysis* 2 (1970): 36–42.

Rorty, Richard. "The World Well Lost." *Journal of Philosophy* 69 (1972): 649–66.

_____. *Philosophy and the Mirror of Nature.* Princeton: Princeton University Press, 1979.

Rotenstreich, Nathan. "On Ethical Relativism." *Journal of Value Inquiry* 11 (1977): 81–103.

Runciman, W.G. "Relativism: Cognitive and Moral." *Aristotelian Society Supplementary Volume 48* (1974): 191–208.

Runzo, Joseph. "Relativism and Absolutism in Bultmann's Demythologizing

Hermeneutic." *Scottish Journal of Theology* 32 (1979): 401–19.

Scheffler, Israel. *Science and Subjectivity.* New York: Bobbs-Merrill, 1967.

———. "Vision and Revolution: A Postscript on Kuhn." *Philosophy of Science* 39 (1972).

———. "The Wonderful Worlds of Goodman." *Synthese* 45 (1980): 201–9.

Shapere, Dudley. "The Structure of Scientific Revolutions." *Philosophical Review* 73 (1964): 383–94.

Siegel, Harvey. "Epistemological Relativism in Its Latest Form." *Inquiry* 23 (1980): 107–17.

Smith, Henry Lee, Jr. "Linguistic Relativity: A Response to Professor Dewart." *Philosophic Exchange* 1 (1972): 47–52.

Stace, W.T. *The Concept of Morals.* New York: Macmillan, 1962. Chapters 1, 2.

Stevenson, Charles L. "Relativism and Non-Relativism in the Theory of Value." In *Facts and Values.* New Haven: Yale University Press, 1963.

Strout, Cushing. *The Pragmatic Revolt in American History: Carl Becker and Charles Beard.* New Haven: Yale University Press, 1958.

Suppe, Fred. "Introduction: Weltanschauung Analyses." In *The Structure of Scientific Theories.* Urbana: University of Illinois Press, 1974. Pp. 125–221.

Taylor, Paul W. "Four Types of Ethical Relativism." *Philosophical Review* 63 (1954).

———. "Social Science and Ethical Relativism." *Journal of Philosophy* 55 (1958): 32–44.

Tillich, Paul. *My Search for Absolutes.* New York: Simon and Schuster, 1967.

Todd, William. "Relativism." *Methodology and Science* 9 (1976): 174–94.

Toulmin, Stephen. "Conceptual Change and the Problem of Relativity." In *Critical Essays on the Philosophy of R.G. Collingwood,* edited by Michael Krausz. Oxford: Clarendon Press, 1972.

———. *Human Understanding.* Volume 1. Princeton: Princeton University Press, 1972.

Trigg, Roger. *Reason and Commitment.* Cambridge: Cambridge University Press, 1973.

Troeltsch, Ernst. *The Absoluteness of Christianity and the History of Religions.* Translated by David Reid. Richmond, Virginia, 1971, and London, 1972.

Walton, Kendall. "Linguistic Relativity." In *Conceptual Change,* edited by G. Pearce and P. Maynard. Dordrecht: D. Reidel, 1973.

Watnick, Morris. "Relativism and Class-Consciousness: Georg Lukacs." In *Revisionism,* edited by Leopold Labedz. London: George Allen & Unwin, 1962.

Wegrzecki, Adam. "On the Absoluteness of Values." *Journal of the British Society for Phenomenology* 6 (1975): 109–15.

Weinstein, Michael A. "The Problem of Relativism: A Reinterpretation." *Human Context* 7 (1975): 422–25.

Wellman, Carl. "The Ethical Implications of Cultural Relativity." *Journal of Philosophy* 60 (1963): 169–84.

———. "Ethical Disagreement and Objective Truth." *American Philosophical Quarterly* 12 (1975): 211–21.

Westermarck, Edward. *Ethical Relativity.* London: Routledge and Kegan Paul, 1932.

Wheelis, Allen. "Relativity of Knowledge." In *The End of the Modern Age.* New York: Basic Books, 1971.

————. *The Moralist.* New York: Basic Books, 1973.

Whorf, Benjamin Lee. *Language, Thought, and Reality.* Cambridge: The MIT Press, 1956.

Wilcox, John. *Truth and Value in Nietzsche.* Ann Arbor: University of Michigan Press, 1974.

Williams, Bernard. "An Inconsistent Form of Relativism." In *Morality: An Introduction to Ethics.* New York: Harper & Row, 1972. Chapter 3, pp. 20–26.

————. "The Truth in Relativism." *Proceedings of the Aristotelian Society* 75 (1974–75): 215–28.

Wilson, Bryan, ed. *Rationality.* New York: Harper, 1971.

Winthrop, Henry. "Ethical Relativism and Its Irrelevancy for the Issues of a Complex Society." *Religious Humanism* 11 (1977): 2–10.

Index